THINKING THROUGH THE ARTS

THINKING THROUGH THE ARTS

edited by

Wendy Schiller

Institute of Early Childhood
Macquarie University, Australia

harwood academic publishers
Australia • Canada • France • Germany • India • Japan • Luxembourg
Malaysia • The Netherlands • Russia • Singapore • Switzerland

Amsteldijk 166
1st Floor
1079 LH Amsterdam
The Netherlands

British Library Cataloguing in Publication Data

A catalogue record for this book is available from the British Library.

ISBN 90-5702-496-9

CONTENTS

Contributors   vii

Chapter 1   Art, Thinking, Young Children?: An Overview   1
Wendy Schiller

Chapter 2   Beads, seeds and emu feathers: Thinking through the issues
surrounding Indigenous art, children and galleries   7
Christine Stevenson

Chapter 3   Growing ideas: Accessible starting points for an integrated drama,
movement and music program with young children   19
Louie Suthers and Veronicah Larkin

Chapter 4   Art goes back to my beginning   28
Ann Veale

Chapter 5   Inheriting dance: Past philosophies for contemporary contexts   38
Diane Wilder

Chapter 6   Seeing beyond marks and forms: Appreciating children's visual   48
thinking
Ursula Kolbe

Chapter 7   Teaching dance to young children   61
David Spurgeon

Chapter 8   Young children telling it like it is: Insights for teachers   68
Jennifer Nicholls

Chapter 9   Nursery Rhymes: Everything old is new again   82
Kathlyn Griffith

Chapter 10   Thinking through puppetry: Developing a quality puppetry
curriculum in early childhood   92
Veronicah Larkin

Chapter 11   Dynamics, images and imagination: Landscapes in cyberspace   107
Margaret White and Kathryn Crawford

Chapter 12   Thinking for the new millennium: The contribution of process drama   118
Kathleen Warren

Chapter 13   Uncovering the potential of rhythm: Education through arts   131
Kathleen Kampa

Chapter 14   Drawing: Making thinking visible   154
              Janet Robertson

Chapter 15   Visual thinking in technology education   163
              Marilyn Fleer

Chapter 16   Early childhood arts environments: Functional and inspirational?   177
              Wendy Shepherd and Jennifer Eaton

Chapter 17   Thinking with the body: Dancing ideas   191
              Wendy Schiller and John Schiller

Chapter 18   Child-initiated curriculum and images of children   204
              Sue Dockett

Chapter 19   Finding the balance: Enhancing piano lessons as learning
              experiences for young children   212
              Emily Ap

Index   243

CONTRIBUTORS

EMILY AP

Emily Ap is a piano teacher in Sydney, a trained Early Childhood teacher and has also taught Secondary classroom music. A member of the Suzuki Piano Committee (NSW), Emily holds a Master of Early Childhood at the Institute of Early Childhood, Macquarie University and is currently a doctoral candidate in music education/psychology at the University of New South Wales.

KATHRYN CRAWFORD

Kathryn Crawford is the director of the Novae Research Group at the University of Sydney and coordinator of the education program at the Australian Technology Park. She is particularly interested in the ways in which creativity and imagination can be fostered by the use of contemporary technologies.

SUE DOCKETT

Sue Dockett is an Associate Professor in the Faculty of Education and Languages at the University of Western Sydney (Macarthur). Her research interests are child development and curriculum and she is the early childhood representative to the NSW Board of Studies.

JENNIFER EATON

Jennifer Eaton is Assistant Director at Mia-Mia Child and Family Study Centre at the Institute of Early Childhood, Macquarie University. She works with the preschool aged children and also teaches part time in the Institute's academic program. Her main areas of interest include the learning environment, children's play, and relaxation with young children.

MARILYN FLEER

Marilyn Fleer is an Associate Professor at Canberra University. Her research interests include early childhood science education, technology education and cross-cultural research.

KATHLYN GRIFFITH

Kathlyn Griffith is an early childhood teacher who lectures in children's literature, literacy and play at the Institute of Early Childhood, Macquarie University. She has worked in a range of early childhood settings in Australia and the United Kingdom. Her current research interests include the study of nursery rhyme illustrations, the changing social and cultural significance of the nursery rhyme and the relationship between play and literature.

KATHLEEN KAMPA

Kathleen Kampa is a dance/music coordinator at Seisen International School, Tokyo, Japan. She specialises in developing arts-based strategies to enhance language development in an international setting.

URSULA KOLBE

Ursula Kolbe has worked in early childhood education for over twenty years as a teacher, lecturer, writer, and producer/writer of films and videos. She now divides her time between working as an exhibiting painter and working part time as artist-teacher with children at Mia-Mia Child and Family Study Centre, Institute of Early Childhood, Macquarie University. She is currently writing a book for parents and teachers on the visual arts and young children.

VERONICAH LARKIN

Veronicah Larkin is an early childhood trained teacher, tertiary educator, researcher and writer. Veronicah is the co-author of a series of early childhood books and is currently undertaking a doctorate investigating early childhood performing arts.

JENNIFER NICHOLLS

Jennifer Nicholls lectures in drama and theatre studies. She also works as a consultant for the New South Wales Department of Education, Board of Studies, NSW Art Galleries, youth arts organisations and children's theatre companies. She is presently co-writing a book, *Theatremaking*, which draws on techniques of the theatre and applies them to a teaching context.

JANET ROBERTSON

Janet Robertson has been a teacher, director and advisor. Her return to teaching was prompted by visits to Reggio Emilia. She now works and researches at the Institute of Early Childhood, Macquarie University, Sydney, specifically at Mia Mia Child and Family Centre, where she teaches the toddler groups.

WENDY SCHILLER

Wendy Schiller is an Associate Professor at Macquarie University. She is an early childhood teacher, author and researcher. She is a consultant to the Australian Broadcasting Authority, the Australian Sports Commission, Australian Gymnastic Federation and Ausdance NSW. She is a tertiary representative on the NSW K-6 Creative Arts Syllabus Committee.

JOHN SCHILLER

John Schiller has been a teacher and principal in South Australia and Canada. He is a Senior Lecturer and teaches postgraduate courses in leadership and management at the University of Newcastle, using flexible delivery approaches to delivery and interaction which blend traditional external techniques with new communication technologies.

WENDY SHEPHERD

Wendy Shepherd is the Director of Mia-Mia Child and Family Study Centre (Mia-Mia is the demonstration centre for the Institute of Early Childhood teacher education program). Early childhood learning environments have been an abiding interest and focus throughout her teaching practice in infants, preschool and long day-care settings.

DAVID SPURGEON

David Spurgeon is a Senior Lecturer in the School of Theatre, Film and Dance at University of New South Wales, Australia. David's interests include drama and dance and he is the author of *Dance Moves* (1991) and a book written specifically for youth *Dance Until You Drop* (1998).

CHRISTINE STEVENSON

Christine Stevenson lectures in visual arts at the Institute of Early Childhood at Macquarie University and chairs the IEC Arts Unit. Current research interests include contemporary images of children in popular culture, children's response to artworks including indigenous works and the contextual issues surrounding children's art. She co-curated an exhibition (with Margaret White) 'Drawings in the Art of Children: An Historical Exhibition of Children's Art in the Twentieth Century' shown in Sydney (1997) and Melbourne (1998).

LOUIE SUTHERS

Louie Suthers is a lecturer in the Institute of Early Childhood, Macquarie University. She has written for children's television and radio, authored books and resources for teachers and is the repertoire consultant for a series of Australian CDs introducing young children to orchestral music. Louie's research focuses on the musical development of children from birth to five years.

ANN VEALE

Ann Veale has recently retired from the position of Head of School of the De Lissa Institute of Early Childhood and Family Studies at the University of South Australia. Ann has been an early childhood teacher, a teacher educator, and author. She has always been an advocate for arts education in early childhood, and is particularly interested in the ways that adults can foster the development of young children's beginnings in art.

KATHLEEN WARREN

Kathleen Warren has taught drama in early childhood in many countries including children and teachers in Australia, New Zealand, England, Ireland, Canada, United States of America, Holland, Portugal and Sweden. Previously a Senior Lecturer at the Institute of Early Childhood, Macquarie University and at the University of Western Sydney, she is currently teaching adjudicating, advising and directing, acting and consulting in drama in New South Wales. Her book *Hooked on Drama: The Theory and Practice of Drama in Early Childhood* has been successful within Australia and internationally.

MARGARET WHITE

Margaret White lectures in arts at the Institute of Early Childhood, and works with a range of arts organisations in developing programs for children and tertiary students. Her current research is focused on the processes of change in arts education in the twentieth century and, in particular, the ways in which visual arts have influenced the practice of art education. She recently co-curated the exhibition 'Drawing on the Art of Children: An Historical Perspective of Children's Art in the Twentieth Century'.

DIANE WILDER

Diane Wilder is currently Director of a large long-day care centre in inner Sydney. She is also a dancer and dance teacher, has worked as an early childhood advisor for the New South Wales Kindergarten Union, lectures at Macquarie University, and is currently completing doctoral studies on dance education/history.

ARTS, THINKING, YOUNG CHILDREN?

An overview

Wendy Schiller

When children's play is discussed it is widely accepted that for a child, play is a serious business: it is a way of thinking through problems presented by particular settings and situations, of exploring options, often of making new connections in trying to make sense of the world. No serious observer or researcher of children's play would suggest that play is a solely physical sensation. Play is recognised as a child's way of learning: it can be problematic, raise new questions, challenge a child, and lead to new understanding of self and others. Play has status and credibility because of its place in a child's world. Why then are the arts not similarly respected for the richness and diversity they bring to children's learning, communication and expression?

Howard Gardner's (1983, 1994) theory of multiple intelligences recognised visual–spatial, logical–mathematical and bodily–kinaesthetic intelligences among others, and has been utilised in classrooms around the world, yet cognition in the arts has enjoyed less popularity and attention than it deserves, particularly in relation to young children's ways of learning. Perhaps this is because in the arts children's voices are heard, and their ideas can be legitimately communicated. Perhaps adults feel inadequate, thinking that special talents and creativity are necessary to stimulate children's interest in the arts. Perhaps the arts are seen as too difficult to assess, too esoteric to teach, too time-consuming in an outcomes-driven agenda. Malaguzzi put this tendency bluntly when he argued that: 'The school and the culture separate the head from the body' (cited in Edwards, Gandini & Forman, 1993: vi.)

The title of this book, *Thinking Through the Arts*, relates directly to its dual purpose, namely to look at ways of *thinking through* the arts with young children, and to promote *thinking*, through arts, with young children. Much is written about the value of the arts in early childhood but does rhetoric match reality? Do arts today fulfil Plato's pedagogic principle of harmony and balance of mind and body through 'gymnastic for the body and music for the soul', or have arts become marginalised in a crowded curriculum (Taylor &

Andrews, 1993). How does engaging in arts activities involve cognition, interpretation and intention to communicate as well as playful exploration for young children? Are there social and cultural benefits for children and adults through participation in the arts? How can we know the answers to some of these questions, and what are the issues involved in conducting studies in the arts with young children?

WHAT CONSTITUTES 'THE ARTS'?

Eisner (1998) claims that the arts predate written history and reflect human effort to tell of experiences, aspirations and fears through visual images, dance, music, poetry, drama and storytelling. Enduring symbols in rock art, for example, have shown the cultural significance and universality of humankind's need to interpret and communicate events and experiences (Cribb, 1992; Hausman, 1980; Schiller & Veale, 1996). That is, we *know* more than we can tell (Polyani, 1967) and we can *show* more than we can tell (Redfern, 1978).

Arts are often associated with imagination, creativity and aesthetic appreciation, but the arts can also portray ethical dilemmas, multiple perspectives, personal interpretation and problems which have no clear solution. So, the arts can show new ways of thinking and working, new combinations of media and method if inquiry is open ended. Eisner expresses this eloquently:

> The arts and humanities have provided a long tradition of ways of describing, interpreting and appraising the world: history, art, literature, dance, drama, poetry and music are among the most important forms through which humans have represented and shaped their experience. These forms have not been significant in educational inquiry for reasons to do with limited and limiting conception of knowledge (1998:2).

Finnish philosopher and educator Irmeli Niemi (1997) and Canadian historian, Alan Cunningham (1978) saw the arts as being as important as life itself. Citing examples such as the poems, stories, and drawings of the children imprisoned at Terezin between 1942 and 1944, who faced sickness, poverty and even death, Cunningham and Niemi observed that despite staggering adversity the impulse to create, communicate and express ideas, emotions and experiences through some medium was so strong that it constituted a 'basic human need'.

Indigenous Australian educator, artist, writer and poet Oodgeroo Noonuccal also saw the vital importance of the arts in culture and society, and in passing traditions on to the young. She set up a special place on Stradbroke Island at which children can learn traditional values through the arts, and she urged educators to 'listen to the children' because children are open and will be the ones to change the world, rather than adults who 'are mentally constipated' (1990:186).

If, as is suggested, engagement with the arts is 'a function of individual need and inclination' and 'a function of social and cultural dynamics' (Hausman, 1980:xiii), then the arts are too important to be left to chance in the lives of the young. They are culturally significant and powerful tools for teaching and learning (Bernard van Leer Foundation, 1999).

However, as Eisner pointed out, 'these forms have not been significant in educational inquiry for reasons to do with limited and limiting conception of knowledge' (1998:2).

Rather the arts have become somewhat isolated in educational approaches intent on competence-based education and training, a push for national curriculum content and functional skills which are 'observable and measurable against an established set of outcomes' (Schiller, 1996:3; Goodlad & Morrison, 1980). The current trend is towards a 'back to the basics' approach in pedagogy, policy and practice in education (Kagan, 1999:2).

Such an approach to education and curriculum , especially for young children, has been deemed unsuitable and ill advised (Taylor & Andrews, 1993; Jackson, 1998). Instead, the back-to-basics movement in early and elementary education has been criticised for its 'subtraction' model of curriculum (Elkind 1992:46). That is, aspects of the program which address human individuality such as the arts have been de-emphasised so that more time can be spent on fundamentals, testing and socialisation skills which are thought to lead to employability (Almy, 1985; Eisner, 1998; Gardner, 1993; Schiller & Veale, 1996; Taylor & Andrews, 1993). As Elkind suggested, a more balanced approach is needed in educational settings:

> Along the way, all of us — parents, teachers and citizens — must assert the value of the arts in schools ... children also work better, learn better and yes, grow better if the time they spend in social adaptation — learning the basics — is alternated with healthy periods devoted to avenues for self-expression. Far from being a luxury, time and money spent on the arts enhance learning and development by reducing the stress of personal adaptation and giving children an aesthetic perspective to balance the workday perspective (1992:75).

This quest for balance and harmonious development in education is ongoing but does not negate the need to step back and reflect on directions, purpose and method influencing arts education. For example, Hargreaves (1989) urged educators not to fall into the trap of categorising science as convergent thinking versus arts as divergent thinking, because children's test performance on creativity had little to offer in relation to children's arts accomplishments in real life (Getzels & Jackson, 1962).

It is also evident that cultural context has a role to play in arts. Many tests and ways of working in the arts used in Australia have been influenced by North American education systems and contexts (Hargreaves, 1989), and may be neglectful of the traditional values of Asian cultures (Jackson, 1998) and of indigenous cultures and experiences (Ball & Pence, 1999; Bernard van Leer Foundation 1996).

This raises the very real situation of program designers having to understand contextual and environmental factors as well as the developmental domains of learning in the arts. Niemi (1997) reminded us that walls can become too tight — that 'educational values can become so clearly defined that they leave little room for artistic expression and creativity', and can lead to the arts becoming institutionalised.

Perhaps, as Wolf suggested, we need to look at the arts as 'conversations or mutual influences among abilities' (1989:23). Indeed, the very nature of the arts is that they invite 'continuing dialogue and reappraisal'(Hausman, 1980: xv), hence effective educators transform curriculum, settings and contexts to acknowledge and facilitate child-initiated choice and responsibility while themselves documenting children's theories, conversations, interactions and projects (Edwards, Gandini & Forman, 1993; Jalongo, 1990; Katz, 1993; Schiller, 1996; Tinworth, 1997).

Various authors in this book have looked at unobtrusive ways of researching children's behaviour while engaged in arts experiences, and recorded what children are saying as they collaboratively construct images or solve arts problems, interpret performances by other artists, and show their interpretations and creations to others (Eisner, 1998; Gardner, 1990; Hargreaves, 1989; Jackson, 1998; Schiller, 1996). What emerges from the various studies is a somewhat 'demystified' study of the arts, identified by observable outcomes and skills as well as socially constructed knowledge. This book then goes beyond a prescriptive 'how to' approach to the arts; instead a 'why to' focus on the arts is presented.

Thinking Through the Arts is written for a wide audience and invites the reader to revisit, research and rethink the role of the child, the adult and the environment in the arts in early childhood. Prominent writers including Gardner (1994), Rinaldi (1993), and Hargreaves (1989) have urged educators to move beyond 'the self' in art, to emphasise both cognition in the arts, and adults and children as co-researchers in the arts, while Eisner (1992, 1998) advocates the use of new technologies in arts media with young children. Hargreaves (1989), Elkind, (1992) and Taylor & Andrews (1993) have emphasised that 'naturalistic investigations are coming into their own as a vital and indispensable part' of research, and that this trend goes beyond the arts to reconcile psychology and educational practice, and to provide the focus for the chapters of this book.

Because issues discussed are interdisciplinary, span the curriculum, and have specific cultural contexts, chapters have not been organised in sections with like art-forms being grouped together. Rather, the arts are recognised as serious areas for study and inquiry and addressed in the same inclusive way as they are in the Australian National Statements and Profiles of the Arts (1992). Although the book places particular emphasis on Australia and Asia, the issues addressed are examples of ways in which various cultures and communities approach the arts, and can therefore serve to stimulate inquiry by educators and researchers in other countries and contexts. Similarly, the multicultural and gender issues discussed reflect an Asia-Pacific context but the principles can be applied more widely.

Most of the studies are based on personal research. Just as children make their thoughts visible to each other as they work, these researchers make visible their thinking through of processes in the arts and encourage the reader to do the same. We see the teacher/ researcher's reflections on process as they reveal different cognitive mindsets, teaching strategies and ways of working in the arts with young children. They describe and analyse children's conversations, co-constructions and critiquing as natural ways of proceeding in the arts, and the emphasis subtly shifts from a child's individual explorations to socially based processes in early childhood settings, with peer and adult interaction as important factors in the development and construction of meaning. In this way, the book delves below the surface of curriculum to explore the complexities and nuances of approaches to the arts with young children.

Kolbe and Robertson outline how very young children in day care settings clarify for themselves and others what they are thinking using graphics as a means of communication. Robertson suggests that map-making emerges through animated drawings and interactions, and builds from individual concepts to shared meaning and jointly held understandings, resulting in joint map-making through drawings. Here, the adult role becomes one of partner and interpreter. Kolbe shows how graphic marks may have a different function. Using interactions with graphic media and clay, Kolbe focuses on very young children's visual thinking, their search for meaning and order, and the role of the adult.

Fleer looks at arts, technology and culture in early childhood curriculum. She discusses the value of teachers' understanding and presenting both 'front-view' and 'plan-view' perspectives, even with very young children, in order to broaden approaches and ways of thinking about problem-solving. Stevenson presents a powerful argument for artists, teachers and galleries to work collaboratively in enhancing learning about indigenous art and culture. White and Crawford focus on imagination, and how interaction with new communication technologies can inform arts experiences for young children.

Warren discusses the importance of thinking through process drama with young children. She presents a comprehensive and compelling account of the benefits for both teachers and children in engaging in decision making and problem solving as partners in imaginary situations which allow the teacher to interact, negotiate and positively use ambiguity while 'in-role', and for children to try out ideas and possible scenarios and view situations from other perspectives as part of process drama. Nicholls looks at how performances by drama companies are received by young children, what constructs children use to make meaning from such performances, and how they communicate their understandings to others.

Veale traces the influence of childhood experiences on several well-known artists and their work, and Wilder looks at how past teachings in dance can inform the present and also renew a sense of purpose and direction in approaches to arts education today. Spurgeon addresses the issue of gender in the arts and the influence of popular culture and imaging on adult and children's expectations. Ap discusses links between cultural perceptions, responses and expectations in an exciting approach to children's piano lessons, and Dockett discusses development, imaging and expectations of children, and the importance of child-initiated curriculum for today's children.

Schiller & Schiller outline a tertiary project to overcome the barrier of geographic isolation and demystify the teaching of dance composition using basic technology and a problem-solving approach, and Griffith shows how nursery rhymes can be constantly reinvented and 'inventive' in dealing with current issues for children. Suthers and Larkin discuss how educators adapt arts ideas for use in the classroom and provide us with evidence that it is the arts which prevent the curriculum from becoming stale. As a teacher who enhances arts experience for very young children in social settings, Kampa presents an international school perspective on science, music and dance experiences for young children and introduces family and community 'informances'.

Shepherd and Eaton provide excellent guidelines for building and evaluating an arts environment for young children. Their work embodies the idea that only by observing a landscape from all angles can we understand the children entrusted to our care and provide inviting and inspiring environments for both children and adults.

This book offers a rare glimpse of teachers as researchers in the arts, sharing with us their thoughts and theories, struggles and strategies, collaborations and findings in early childhood arts, as they listen to, observe and work with, and for, young children. It is hoped that the dialogue will continue, that this book will be a beginning, a stimulus to think through the arts in early childhood and to give children a voice.

References

Almy, M. (1985) Letter, *Young Children*, July 20.
Australian Education Council (1992) National Curriculum Statement in the Arts. (Draft) Canberra: AEC.

Ball, J. & Pence, A.R. (1999) Beyond developmentally appropriate practice: Developing community and culturally appropriate practice. *Young Children,* **54**(2), 46–50.

Bernard van Leer Foundation, (1999) *Early Childhood Matters*, **91**, 20–23.

Cribb, J. (1992) Our heavy rocks the top art form. *The Australian*, January 25.

Cunningham, A. (1978) The children of Terezin. Keynote address. Proceedings of the first Dance & the Child International Conference, University of Alberta, Edmonton, Canada, 58–63.

Edwards, C., Gandini, L., & Forman, G. (1993) *The Hundred Languages of Children*. Norwood: NJ: Ablex.

Eisner, E.W. (1992) The misunderstood role of the arts in human development. *Phi Delta Kappan*. April, 591-595.

Eisner, E.W. (1998) *The Enlightened Eye. Qualitative Inquiry and the Enhancement of Educational Practice*. New Jersey: Merrill/Prentice-Hall.

Elkind, D. (1992) *Images of the Young Child*. Washington: National Association for Education of Young Children.

Gardner, H. (1983) *Frames of the Mind*. New York: Basic Books.

Gardner, H. (1994) *The Arts and Human Development*. New York: Basic Books.

Gardner, H. (1993) *Creating Minds*. New York: Basic Books.

Goodlad, J., & Morrison, J. (1980) The Arts and Education. In *Arts and the Schools*, edited by J. Hausman. New York: McGraw-Hill.

Getzels, J.W. & Jackson, P.W. (1962) *Creativity and Intelligence: Explorations with Gifted Students*. New York: Wiley.

Hargreaves, D. (1989) (ed.) *Children and The Arts*. Milton Keynes: Open University Press.

Hausman, J. (1980) (ed.) *Arts and the Schools*. New York: McGraw-Hill.

Jackson, P. (1998) Child-centred education for Pacific-Rim cultures? *Early Child Development and Care*. **143**, 47–58.

Jalongo, M.R. (1990) The child's right to the expressive arts: Nurturing the imagination as well as the intellect. *Childhood Education*, Summer, 195–201.

Kagan, S. (1999) Going beyond 'Z'. *Young Children*, **54**(2), 2.

Katz, L. (1993) What can we learn from Reggio Emilia? In *The Hundred Languages of Children*, edited by C. Edwards, L. Gandini and G. Forman. Norwood, NJ: Ablex.

Niemi, I. (1997) Schools and dance. Keynote address. 7th Dance and the Child International Conference. Kuopio: Finland. July 28–August 3.

Noonuccal, O. (1990) Writer, poet and educator. In *Aboriginal Voices*, edited by L. Thompson. Sydney: Simon & Schuster.

Polyani, M. (1967) *The Tacit Dimension*. London: Routledge & Kegan Paul

Redfern, B. (1978) Keynote address. Proceedings of the first Dance and the Child International conference,. University of Alberta, Edmonton, Canada, 3–24.

Rinaldi, C. (1993) The emergent curriculum and social constructivism. In *The Hundred Languages of Children,* edited by C. Edwards, L. Gandini and G. Forman. Norwood, NJ: Ablex.

Schiller, W. (1996) (ed.) *Issues in Expressive Arts Curriculum for Early Childhood*, Amsterdam: Gordon & Breach.

Schiller, W. & Veale, A. (1996) The arts: The real business of education. In *Issues in Expressive Arts Curriculum for Early Childhood*, edited by W. Schiller. Amsterdam: Gordon & Breach.

Taylor, R. & Andrews, G. (1993) The arts in the primary school. London: Falmer Press.

Tinworth, S. (1997) Whose good idea was it? Australian child-initiated curriculum. *Australian Journal of Early Childhood*, **22**(3), 24-29.

Wolf, D.P. (1989) Artistic learning as conversation. In *Children and the Arts*, edited by D. Hargreaves. Milton Keynes. Open University Press.

Woodhead, M. (1996) *In Search of the Rainbow: Pathways to Quality in Large-scale Programs for Young Disadvantaged Children*. The Hague: Bernard van Leer Foundation.

CHAPTER 2

BEADS, SEEDS AND EMU FEATHERS

Thinking through the issues surrounding indigenous art, children and galleries

Christine Stevenson

The turn of the century is a crucial time in the history of Australia and other countries facing the enormous challenge of improving the relations between indigenous peoples and their wider communities. In 1994, Pat Dodson, former Chair of the Council for Aboriginal Reconciliation, remarked:

> We need to show that we are capable of resolving the causes of disharmony and injustice that have so often marked this relationship. ... It is imperative that we all look for innovative ways of ... working together (Aboriginal Australians, Minority Rights Group International Report, 1994:10).

ISSUES FOR EDUCATORS

Educators in Australia, cognisant of the significance of their role, have been attempting in diverse ways to contribute to this process of reconciliation. For instance, the artworks of indigenous people have been used as a resource for teaching about indigenous cultures. Some of the activities offered in schools and centres however, do not appear to enhance children's understanding of Aboriginal cultures. Stevenson (1996:41) underlined some of the issues which surfaced in discussions with early childhood personnel in relation to activities designed for children to respond to Aboriginal art. Some of these were:

- the problem of inadvertently reinforcing stereotypes of Aboriginal people (in particular, that Aboriginal people are only good at art or sport);
- the problem of introducing an Aboriginal perspective with limited media, such as paint in earth colours, and encouraging the children to use techniques, such as painting with dots on bark, thus reinforcing the notion of Aboriginal art as being resistant to change;

- the need to use resources which reflect the richness and diversity of contemporary Aboriginal society, which can be difficult as resources in schools and early childhood settings are often limited.

The first issue relating to stereotypes is difficult for educators to address, as the most familiar positive media images of Aboriginal Australians are still of Aboriginal artists and sportspeople. (For example, Cathy Freeman, a champion sprinter and indigenous Australian, was recently named Australian of the Year.) One response to the other two issues has involved the use of specialist indigenous galleries and museums to bring children face to face with authentic contemporary Aboriginal art and artefacts.

In this chapter some of the issues relevant to educators in relation to young children's visits to specialist indigenous art exhibits will be discussed. The Yiribana Gallery at the Art Gallery of New South Wales (NSW), Sydney, is used as the focus for a discussion of the process of learning about indigenous culture which occurs in these settings. Strategies for enhancing children's learning in such settings will be suggested and areas for research will be indicated.

Suina (1994:267) justifies museum experiences for young children on the basis of their 'potential to involve multiple senses ... [and] the fact that learning in a museum invariably involves the culture of a people'. This statement might also apply to indigenous art galleries like the Yiribana Gallery, though it should be emphasised that art galleries are not *only* in the business of education. The Yiribana Gallery has one of the largest permanent exhibitions of Aboriginal and Torres Strait Islander art in Australia, and as such is a drawcard for teachers who have limited resources for enriching multicultural programs in the curriculum.

Changing attitudes to Aboriginal art such as that included in the exhibitions at the Yiribana Gallery are reflected in current art education, philosophy and policy. The right of indigenous people to be consulted has, sadly, not always been the practice in art education in Australia. The 1974 New South Wales Curriculum for Primary Schools in Visual Arts, for instance, did not recommend consultation with *any* cultural groups, let alone minority groups such as the Aboriginal community (Hall, 1992). Consequently, another important feature of the Yiribana Gallery is that Aboriginal people themselves have been responsible for curating the exhibitions, editing the catalogue and having substantial input into the education program .

The principle of involvement by Aboriginal people in the presentation of their culture has recently been advocated in art education journals. Note, for instance, Pearson's claim that 'Indigenous people ... should maintain control over how their culture is presented in ... art education' (1990:57). Henrietta Fourmile, a member of the Yidindji group in the Cairns region of Australia, has consistently argued for the opportunity for Aboriginal communities to interpret their art and their cultures to others (see Fourmile, 1994). These directions are exemplified in the first curator Margot Neale's vision for the Yiribana Gallery: 'We wanted a gallery that functioned as a cultural centre; a place of learning and sharing, a place where stories could be told, perceptions expanded and stereotyping challenged' (1994:12).

Aboriginal art: separation or mainstreaming; traditional or contemporary?

The Yiribana Gallery is physically separate from other sections of Australian art at the Art Gallery of NSW in recognition of its representation of a distinct cultural context. Aboriginal visual arts are able to be more easily integrated with other Aboriginal arts (such as storytelling, dance and music) when they are separated from other examples of Australian art. For young children who draw on many areas of the arts to communicate their own stories this concept has particular relevance. The notion of using many art forms is demonstrated in the current daily performances by Sean Choolburra (see Figure 1.1), a Bwaculum performer who communicates stories through oral dialogue, dance and music to a backdrop of paintings and sculpture in the Yiribana Gallery. Choolburra's performances will be discussed later in this chapter.

Many Australians have clung to the idea of Aboriginal art as being traditional and unchanging. It is not the purpose of this chapter to debate the reasons for this attitude. It is however not surprising that many Australian children are interested in finding out about issues relating more widely to indigenous cultures, such as how Aborigines dressed in the past, or how they cleaned their teeth or washed their hair. Questions which sought answers to these issues to be put to an Aboriginal guide were compiled by eight year olds at a Sydney primary school prior to an Aboriginal field study excursion to Ku-ring-gai National Park in 1995. Where we might take issue with adults' romanticised notions of Aboriginal culture, the questions children ask are often prompted by a genuine curiosity about families perceived to live differently to their own. The fact that children are often surprised to find many similarities in the way many Aboriginal people today dress, eat and shop reveals much about Australian society's attitudes and understanding of contemporary Aboriginal

Figure 1.1 Yiribana performer-in- Residence, Sean Choolburra.
Photograph: Jenny Carter, courtesy of the Art Gallery of New South Wales, Australia.

culture. Two Ngarrindjeri women, Leah and Harriet Rankine, who make feather flowers in the Murray Bridge region, South Australia, are intrigued when children ask where they get the feathers from. Leah comments:

> Do we go into paddocks? and Do we use grass or things like that to dye them with? I don't like to tell them lies, I tell them the truth. I tell them we go into the shop and buy dye and crepe paper and all that (cited in Pring, McLean & McNamee, 1994:17).

At the Yiribana Gallery, young visitors have ample opportunity to reassess their views of Aboriginal culture as being resistant to change. 'Traditional' paintings in ochre on bark, still used by many artists, are found beside paintings using 'contemporary' media such as acrylic on canvas. Conceptualising devices for exhibitions are similar to those employed by curators of non-indigenous art exhibitions. For instance, an exhibition at the Yiribana Gallery used *the snake*, a powerful symbol in Aboriginal art particularly in the guise of the Rainbow Serpent, to unify the exhibition. Works in different media, made at different times, are thus juxtaposed for the opportunities they provide for the exploration of cultural or thematic connections, rather than being presented as a chronological survey of artworks. Exhibitions like this also demonstrate the fact that Aboriginal art is not static but dynamic, as, of course, is the art of all cultures. As Maloon pointed out:

> Traditional does not mean something old and unchanging — a static art form. Nor does 'urban art' mean that artists who work in 'non-traditional' styles have no cultural traditions ... They are both contemporary art practices (1994:8).

This rejection of the 'traditional' versus 'contemporary' categories is consistent with other recent writing on Aboriginal art. Johnson (1993) observed that these awkward categories have been dropped because of their inability to recognise the right of urban artists to address cultural concerns, and the right of 'tribally-oriented' artists to be perceived as making art which is relevant to the present.

Gallery programs for children

Artists-in-residence or 'cultural educators', as they are now called by the Art Gallery of NSW, are perceived to be particularly important for Aboriginal culture, which has strong oral traditions. The employment of an Aboriginal artist to work directly with children has been recommended to teachers as '... a most important and authentic way to implement an Aboriginal perspective' (Toole & Pratt, 1992:191). In the last five years, the artist-in-residence program of the Art Gallery of NSW has included Aboriginal visual artists, storytellers and performers such as Sean Choolburra. The fact that these artists are now referred to as 'cultural educators' emphasises the significance of the role of the educator in indigenous sites.

The programme 'Animal Tracks' (recently renamed 'Circles, Snakes and Songlines') was developed in relation to a 1992 exhibition of Aboriginal art, 'My Story, My Country: Aboriginal Art and the Land' at the Art Gallery of NSW. In the education kit designed for the exhibition, Gibson (1992:14–15) makes some suggestions for pre-visit activities in the classroom. Some of these include: making detailed drawings of an Australian animal to show its organs and skeleton; making markings with a variety of ochres, rocks and charcoal; and discussing the different track and footprints made by people and animals. At the gallery, Gibson suggests that children might, for instance, follow the tracks and trails made by humans and animals through the paintings, find out why they are depicted so frequently in Aboriginal art, explore sights, sounds, smells and impressions in a painting, imagine how animals would move and communicate, and relate these concepts to stories and storytelling in the children's own cultures.

'Circles, Snakes and Songlines' continues to be offered by the Art Gallery of NSW as one of a number of 'art adventures' for children, and is in demand by Sydney school groups. The volunteer children's guides, trained by Aboriginal museum educators, assist children in discovering 'the diversity and scope of Aboriginal art ... and a culture which draws inspiration from its stories, history and land' (publicity handout). Those responsible for training the children's guides speak highly of their efforts. Small bags containing seeds, beads, emu feathers, ochres and clapsticks are provided for the guides to enrich the children's experiences. Children's encounters with the works do appear more meaningful and extensive with the guided tours than without them.

In view of Pearson's (1990) and Fourmile's (1994) recommendations for indigenous control over the representation of their own culture, however, it is significant that none of the children's guides observed by the author in 1995 and 1997 were Aboriginal. The interactions observed at Yiribana Gallery between children and guides therefore raise questions about the kinds of meaning that are constructed in relation to Aboriginal art and culture. The following discussion from an 'Animal Tracks' tour in early June 1995, recorded with a group of young primary school children at the Yiribana Gallery, illustrates the way the children's guides attempt to give children the opportunity to discover for themselves important things about Aboriginal art and culture. This discussion was in relation to Jimmy Njiminjuma's painting *Rainbow Serpent*, then exhibited at the entrance to the Yiribana Gallery.

Guide:	What do you think this is?
Adam:	I think it's a spirit.
Trent:	No, it looks like a snake.
Guide:	You're both right. It's a kind of spirit–snake.
	(Turning to Trent): What made you say it's a snake?
Trent:	The way the tongue comes out like a fork.
Adam:	The body ... it's a long, curvy, wormy snake.
(Laughter)	
Guide:	Yes. It's like a snake but we call him the Rainbow Serpent. He's big and fierce and meant to be frightening. (Pauses) When does a rainbow usually appear? Have a little think about it.
Petra:	After rain?
Guide:	Yes. There are huge monsoon storms in the Northern Territory. The Rainbow Serpent is important to the people there because the people believe he clears away the storms.

In the above encounter the guide has acknowledged the way children gained clues from looking closely at the work and has enriched their understanding of the significance of the Rainbow Serpent to Aboriginal people in the Northern Territory. She has also attempted to relate the work to the children's own experiences of rainbows.

The second extract raises issues about the kinds of meanings constructed about indigenous culture when there is little time for connecting the children's prior experiences with a complex artwork. The extract below refers to an installation, 'Fruit Bats', by Lin Onus of one hundred fibreglass fruit bats suspended from a Hills Hoist clothesline. (The Hills Hoist clothesline was a 1950s invention now often used as a symbol of Australian suburbia.) The ingenuity of the radiating support which enables the fruit bats to move slightly and the puzzle of the 'droppings' on the floor below contributes to its appeal to children of all ages. (For a more detailed description of this work see Neale, 1994:116.)

Guide:	(Asks a group of children [aged between 7 and 9 years] to take a look at the installation, then to turn around and face her.) What do you remember about this work?
Children:	Bats ... hanging, sleeping ... flowers on the ground.
Guide	Yes, they symbolise bat droppings. They're fruit bats. Where do you normally see fruit bats?
Tess:	(slightly puzzled): Normally on trees?
Guide:	Yes, they like to eat the fruit in trees.
Sam:	But that's a clothesline.
Lola:	The bats look like clothes hanging ...
Guide:	Notice the patterns on the bats. The artist has created ... a sort of coat for them.
	Are they moving ... the bats? Look at them closely.
Jack:	Yes, they are ... just a little. (Another boy waves his clipboard to make them move a little faster.)
(Delighted laughter from the group.)	
Guide:	There's a meeting of cultures here ... urban Australian and traditional Aboriginal culture. Let's look at another work now.

There are obvious difficulties with introducing complex artworks to children, particularly children unfamiliar to the guide. The guide's last comment would have made little sense to these children. The knowledge of the artworks that the guide wants to communicate is often not what immediately engages children. The fact that the bats could move fascinated one of the children so much that he quickly figured out how he could make them move faster. Not surprisingly, the children responded more enthusiastically to the fast moving bats than they did to factual information about the installation.

On the same day that this interchange was observed, three girls about eight years old from another school had been given the task of writing about the same work. One girl was observed referring to the wall label and pointing to the circles decorated with the clan designs on the floor. She exclaimed authoritatively in a harsh whisper, 'It's meant to be bat poo.' Her friend replied, 'You're kidding ... they look like flowers'. The third girl asked tentatively, 'So, you just write bat poo?' Yes, replied the first ... 'BAT POO'. In this episode, the task of writing about the work took precedence over any personal enjoyment or understanding of the work.

From these and other observations by the author in the Yiribana Gallery in a series of random visits in 1995 and 1997, it appears that children arrive at certain conclusions about an artwork in question by observation, guesswork, reading labels, listening to others in the group, and by listening and responding to an informed adult. The most significant encounters appeared to be amongst groups where some previous encounter with the material had been made possible.

Prior experiences for children

Discussion of a sequence of experiences at an inner-city Sydney school with a class of eight year olds points the way to some experiences in which children could be involved prior to a visit to the Yiribana Gallery. These children had been investigating aspects of their environment and looking in particular at monuments, landforms and buildings which were of special significance. These included Sydney harbour, the Sydney Harbour Bridge, the local town hall and the roundabouts linking major roads in their suburb.

The teacher introduced to the children an example of a contemporary Western Desert painting by Clifford Possum Tjapaltjarri from the Yiribana catalogue. She showed some acrylic paints of the kind that may have been used in the painting. This sparked a discussion about art materials and why these materials in particular were used. The children gathered and assembled leaves, sticks, seeds, grass and ground clay on the floor to approximate the way ground paintings might have been done before acrylics were used for painting. A range of other contemporary Aboriginal artworks, including examples of silk batik and incised carvings of animals, stimulated further appreciation of the ways in which many contemporary Aboriginal artists attend art schools in cities and use art materials common to many artists.

The following week the same painting was viewed in order to identify how the artist had represented his people's land. The children were able to identify symbols that were common to their own culture — human footprints and arrows. The circles were more puzzling but the teacher explained that they represent the place where the snake men gave ceremonial dances to instruct the people in the area. One of the children, Keiran, pronounced it 'a bird's eye view' which gave some children ideas about looking at places from different perspectives .

The children were inspired to use symbols to make 'place' drawings about their own area in felt pen or coils of clay, as if 'drawing' with clay. Some of the grasses, seeds, pebbles and sticks that the children had previously collected were incorporated in some of the clay drawings. When these drawings were dry the children arranged them on a window ledge to form a collaborative 'mosaic' of the community. This provided opportunities for discussion about family networks, including those of the children's families and those of Aboriginal families.

Laura, one of the first to remove her clay drawing from the coloured paper sheet the children had used to work on, exclaimed that she had made a 'ghost map'. The shrinking clay had dried out the pigment of the paper leaving a white line drawing where the clay had been. This discovery was one of those delightful unplanned outcomes, as it seemed as if the spirit of the drawing had remained behind. The purpose of art as making something live again seemed magically to be present in the 'absent coil' drawings. This reinforced the significance of repetition in Aboriginal art in the form of storytelling, songs and drawings, and the idea that by drawing things or telling things over and over Aboriginal artists believe they can keep it alive.

Another child, Raoul, spontaneously built up from his clay drawing to make Sydney Tower, and others followed suit. The teacher capitalised on the children's interest in the three-dimensional potential of clay by introducing the children to a poster of a pot made by an Aboriginal artist, Thancoupie, who had gained permission from a Queensland group to use some of their Dreaming stories on her pots. The idea of getting permission to use designs was considered an important concept for the children to know in order for children to develop respect for Aboriginal art and culture.

The children had by this stage gained some awareness of the significance of art to Aboriginal people and to the continuation of Aboriginal culture. They had learnt something about the importance of the land through their own work with symbols in drawing. It seemed an opportune time to visit the Yiribana Gallery. Three works were chosen for examination: a pot by Thancoupie, a desert painting by Clifford Possum Tjapaltjarri, and *Rainbow Serpent* by Jimmy Njiminjuma. Some of the children were surprised by the size of the works, especially the desert painting which was displayed in the gallery as a ground painting. The children walked around it and pointed out what they thought the symbols stood for. Joel decided he'd like to be in the corner of the painting because 'it is a long way from the snakes'. Further questions to encourage the children to use all their senses included, 'If you could touch, smell, hear this place, what would it be like?'. In this way, the teacher was able to link the children's previous learning to the art in the gallery in a way which fully engaged the children.

Teachers, children and museum and gallery visits

One reason why the above encounter with Aboriginal artworks at the Yiribana Gallery was successful may have been that the children were not overwhelmed with a multiplicity of unfamiliar objects. Jensen offers some guidelines regarding museum programs in general; these suggestions could also be applied to art gallery programmes.

> Museum programmes for children should focus on only a few objects of interest to them and present ideas about those objects that are graspable and relevant. Otherwise the artefacts in museums will be for children like so many other things in their lives — simply there, without explanation and outside their control. A selected and limited focus will foster in children a sense of mastery and command in a potentially strange and overwhelming setting and will increase the chances of their really understanding the ideas behind the words and objects to which they are introduced (1994b:270).

A common approach to children's excursions to museums and galleries is the 'handover' approach, in which the teacher's main responsibility is to ensure the children's safety during the journey from the school or centre to the museum or gallery. On arrival at the museum or gallery the children are 'handed over' to museum guides who are perceived as having expertise in a particular area to be 'passed on' to the children. The teacher's role becomes a passive one, at best as a learner alongside the children willing to absorb information from the guide, at worst as a disciplinarian ensuring the children do not run about or create a poor impression of their school.

In general, the teachers who accompanied the children on the guided tours at the Yiribana Gallery did not make any comments or ask any questions of the children. This appears to be the children's guides preferred way of working with the children. However, it is the teachers who know the children in their care — their likes and dislikes, their differing learning styles, their differing ways of communicating. There is a potential for teachers to be more actively involved in these 'art adventures'.

It may be useful at this point to look at the results of a 1993 study conducted by Bank Street College in New York of nine- and ten-year-old children's memories of museum visits. The study concluded that when a combination of three factors was present at a museum, the children had specific, vivid and detailed memories. These factors were: high personal involvement for an individual child (as opposed to the whole class); links with the curriculum (when the teacher embellished the unit with many varied classroom activities); and multiple visits (Jensen 1994a:302.) By contrast, focused museum visits in which children had to fill out worksheets, draw pictures and take notes to bring back to the classroom were described as 'boring'. This is exemplified in the episode above with the eight-year-old girls and their encounter with 'Fruit Bats'.

How then can teachers make the best possible use of specialist, indigenous galleries and museums? At the very least, teachers need to consider the following questions before arranging an excursion to a gallery or museum specialising in indigenous art and culture.

• When is the best time to visit a gallery or museum: at the beginning, embedded within, or at the end of an investigation of indigenous art and culture?

This is a key question and needs to be carefully considered. The teacher at the inner-city school referred to above embedded the visit in the program when the children's interest (investigating their own environment) was at a high level. This is not always possible in schools and centres where notification of excursions must be given several weeks prior to a gallery visit.

• Which works in particular provide the best opportunities for children in different age ranges and different settings to construct knowledge and build from their own experiences?

This involves a prior visit to the gallery by the teacher and a careful consideration of teaching kits. Teaching kits also need to be revised regularly by the gallery to incorporate new perspectives, approaches and information. (The Art Gallery of NSW regularly revises teaching kits for the Yiribana Gallery.)

• How can I work with a museum or gallery guide to ensure that the children's prior experiences are acknowledged?

Supplying the guide with copies of some of the drawings or other work children have done prior to the gallery visit may give the guide a starting point for consideration.

• How can the knowledge learnt at a gallery or museum be reinforced in the classroom or centre after the visit?

At this stage, it is crucial to follow up the clues children give as to some of the interests they wish to investigate further. For instance, if the children show a particular interest in the snakes in a painting, this could provide an area for further exploration through many areas of the curriculum including creative and expressive arts.

• Should I consider a number of short visits rather than one long visit, so that the children do not suffer from 'overload'?

Yes, this is preferred to keep children's interest high. For example, in the sequence of experiences described at the inner-city school, the teacher decided to take the children back to the gallery several weeks later to see a performance by cultural educator Sean Choolburra. Some children were also keen to revisit some of the works they had seen on the first visit.

The value of performance

Performances by Sean Choolburra at the Yiribana Gallery, observed in the winter of 1995 and the spring of 1997, were cleverly designed to engage the children at a personal level. When Choolburra showed children how to rub the ochre to a powder and add water to make a paste, he invited them to 'Put your finger in there ... paint your friend, paint your schoolteacher!'. The attention of each child was intently focused on Choolburra's ritual of painting his arms, legs and torso. The 'high personal involvement' referred to in the Bank Street study is characteristic of this artist's intuitive way of working with children. When Choolburra showed the children the emu feathers around his waist, inviting them to feel the 'human hair belt' on his waist and joking that he had to 'scalp his mate to get his dreadlocks', he had the children spellbound. One of the main strengths of Choolburra's performance was his ability to demonstrate the relevance of a traditional genre (storytelling) to contemporary subject matter. Through manipulating the range of sounds of the didgeridoo, he dramatised subjects of interest to children (such as, a hitchhiker sweating on a busy road who gets a lift on a semi-trailer).

CONCLUSION

Specialist indigenous museums such as the Yiribana Gallery at the Art Gallery of NSW are exciting resources for teachers who are planning to develop an indigenous perspective. They provide opportunities for teachers and children to explore new ways of understanding indigenous art and culture. Cultural educators like Sean Choolburra involve children in highly personal experiences which assist in their understanding of the way the arts are integrated in indigenous cultures. This is consistent with the notion of art expressed in the words of Aboriginal artist Wandjuk Marika:

> There is no real distinction for us between art and life; art is the expression of our beliefs, it upholds the laws by which we live and is an important element in the way in which we relate to the physical world around us. It is an integral part of our lives, not separate as it is so often in the life of Western man, but an important function in our ritual and of prime importance in our learning process (cited in Fourmile, 1994:77).

The experiences recounted above suggest there is a need for teachers to take a more active role in the process involving children's encounters with indigenous artworks. In view of their knowledge of the children, their interests and abilities, they should be more mindful of 'catching the children's ball and throwing it back' (Edwards, 1993:153). As Houck (1997:33) observed in relation to the approach taken at the Reggio Emilia preschools of Italy, teachers often operate on several levels simultaneously:

- as a partner with the child in the learning process;
- as the facilitator of a constructivist curriculum;
- as a provocateur who challenges children to solve problems;
- as the 'memory' for the group as documenter of their discussions and activities;
- as a nurturer and validator of a child's sense of purpose and belonging;
- as a mediator who encourages children to settle their own disputes; and
- as a learner and researcher, who shares observations and reflections with colleagues on a frequent and regular basis.

In a visit to a gallery or museum, the first five roles are particularly important for the teacher. Sensitivity to the guide is also emphasised as she/he is often attempting to establish some kind of authority with the group for the first time. In an ideal world, Houck's final suggestion of sharing observations and reflections is a worthwhile goal for a good relationship between teacher and gallery guide. Research in collaborative learning approaches (in which meanings are shared and built upon together) among children, teachers, guides and cultural educators in museums and galleries is urgently needed.

The influence of galleries and museums such as the Yiribana Gallery on children's perceptions of indigenous people and culture is a potential area for further research. Such a focus could conceivably enhance our understanding of the ways in which attitudinal change towards indigenous people can be encouraged. Visits to indigenous galleries and museums may indeed have the potential to influence the pace of attitudinal change necessary to bring about reconciliation between indigenous and non-indigenous peoples of the world.

Acknowledgement

The author wishes to thank Angela Martin, Co-ordinator of Aboriginal Programs, Public Programs, Art Gallery of NSW, Sydney for her invaluable advice on Aboriginal art and cultural issues.

References

Edwards, C. (1993) Partner, nurturer and guide: The roles of the Reggio teacher in action. In *The Hundred Languages of Childhood: The Reggio Emilia Approach to Early Childhood Education*, edited by C. Edwards, L. Gandini and G. Forman. New Jersey, USA: Ablex.

Fourmile, H. (1994) Aboriginal arts in relation to multiculturalism. In *Culture, Difference and the Arts,* edited by S. Gunew & F. Rizvi, pp. 69–85. Sydney: Allen and Unwin.

Gibson, E. (1992) Educational kit to accompany exhibition, 'My Story, My Country: Aboriginal Art and the Land'. Art Gallery of NSW, 8 July –16 August 1992.

Hall, L. (1992) Visual arts education (K- 6): An Aboriginal perspective. *Aboriginal Studies Association Journal,* 2(1), 27–46.

Houck, P. (1997) Lessons from an exhibition: reflections of an art educator. In *First Steps towards Teaching the Reggio Way*, edited by J. Hendrick, pp. 26–39. New Jersey: Prentice Hall.

Jensen, N. (1994a) Children's perceptions of their museum experiences: A contextual perspective. *Children's Environments*, **11** (4), 300–324.

Jensen, N. (1994b) Children, teenagers and adults in museums. In *The Educational Role of the Museum*, edited by E. Hooper-Greenhill, pp. 268–274. London: Routledge.

Johnson, V. (1993) The Aboriginal art movement. *Art and Australia*, **31** (2), 180–181.

Maloon, T. (1994) How we see Aboriginal art. In *Yiribana: An Introduction to the Aboriginal and Torres Strait Island Collection Sydney*, edited by M. Neale, p.7. Sydney: Art Gallery of New South Wales.

Neale, M. (ed) (1994) Introduction. In *Yiribana: An Introduction to the Aboriginal and Torres Strait Islander Collection*, pp. 6–11. Sydney: Art Gallery of New South Wales.

Pearson, P. (1990) Taha Maori and art education: Hegemony trimmings for beginners. *Australian Art Education*, **14** (2), 7–11.

Pring, A., McLean, G. & McNamee, H. (1994) *Aboriginal art and the Dreaming: Teaching about Aboriginal art, craft and design*. Adelaide: Department for Education and Children's Services, South Australia.

Stevenson, C. (1996) The arts curriculum and indigenous art: Hands off or on? - A personal view. In *Issues in Expressive Arts: Curriculum for Early Childhood,* edited by W. Schiller, pp. 31–46. Amsterdam: Gordon & Breach Publishers.

Suina, J.H. (1994) Museum multicultural education for young learners. In *The Educational Role of the Museum*, edited by E. Hooper-Greenhill, pp. 263–267. London: Routledge.

Toole, R. & Pratt, L. (1992) Teaching about Aboriginal art as a non- Aboriginal. In *A national priority* (vol. **1**), *Conference Proceedings of the Second Annual Conference of Aboriginal Studies Association,* edited by D. Coghlan, R. Craven & N. Parbury, University of New South Wales, September.

CHAPTER 3

GROWING IDEAS

Accessible starting points for an integrated drama, movement and music program with young children

Louie Suthers and Veronicah Larkin

The value of facilitating a quality drama, movement and music program in the early childhood years is widely affirmed in both the Australian and international literature (see, for example, Birlenshaw-Fleming, 1997; Chenfeld, 1995; Feierabend, 1996; Forrai, 1997; Jalongo & Stamp, 1997; Larkin & Suthers, 1995, 1997; Schiller & Veale, 1989; Suthers & Larkin, 1996; Taunton & Colbert, 1984; Wright, 1991).

Many early childhood educators wish to make their performing arts programs more responsive to the particular needs of their children and more suited to their own teaching strengths and interests. Many believe that simply drawing upon material from published resource books does not enable them to adequately address the issue of creating a unique and personalised drama, movement and music program. Such teachers and caregivers recognise the merit in looking upon published resource material as a starting point only, and demonstrate high levels of competency in modifying that material to more fully address the specific learning needs and current interests of their children as well as their own teaching style.

As the researchers considered this issue the following questions emerged:

- How are new ideas generated from a basic starting point such as a rhyme, song or rap?
- How do early childhood teachers and caregivers approach the task of creating performing arts experiences from these basic starting points?
- In what ways might these learning experiences develop and change over time?
- What level of experimentation is evidenced by early childhood teachers and caregivers in the ways in which they plan and present performing arts experiences to children?
- In what ways might the children themselves influence the manner in which performing arts materials are adapted or modified?

THE STUDY

A pilot study was undertaken during 1997 in a community-based long day-care centre located in the Sydney metropolitan area. The following staff members agreed to participate in the study: Edna, a trained teacher's assistant working in the baby room, with eighteen years' child-care experience, Jake, an early childhood trained teacher working in the toddler room, with seven years' child-care experience, and Harriet, an early childhood trained teacher working in the four-year-olds room, with four years' child-care experience. (Pseudonyms have been used for the names of all adults and children participating in this study.)

The researchers selected both the research site and the three subjects on the basis that neither the institution nor the personnel expressed any particular specialist knowledge, skill or aptitude for the performing arts. It was the objective of the researchers to examine how non-specialists devised, implemented and reflected upon their use of performing arts curriculum material.

The researchers devised an original rhyme, *Wishy Washy* (Figure 2.1A), an original song, *Running Feet* (Figure 2.1B) and an original rap *Happy Rap* (Figure 2.1C), specifically written for each age group under investigation in the study. Edna, Jake and Harriet were provided with their respective rhyme, song and rap, with no suggestions supplied by the researchers

A   **Wishy Washy**
     (for children aged 0–2 years)

     Wishy washy
     Swishy swashy
     Scrub-a-dub-a-doo
     Wishy washy
     Swishy swashy
     Clean as new.

B   **Running Feet**
     (for children aged 2–3 years)

     I am running quickly
     Running on the street
     I am running quickly
     With my running feet.

C   **Happy Rap**
     (for children aged 3–5 years)

     I'm rapping on the door ha ha ha
     I'm rapping on the wall ha ha ha
     I'm rapping on the floor ha ha ha
     Come along now
     Let's do some more
     one, two, three, four
     Do the happy rap ha ha ha ha
     Yes the happy rap ha ha ha ha
     Do the happy, snappy, tappy, yappy,
     zappy, happy rap
     No more !

Figure 2.1 Rhyme (A), song (B), with music, and rap (C) devised for the study

as to how each might create performing arts experiences from this material.

Each staff member participating in the study was invited to use this material in whatever way they chose on at least six occasions over a six-week period. They were asked to record their reflections on the implementation of these experiences in a diary. Whilst the formatting of this diary was left up to each staff member, the researchers provided them with the outline in Figure 2.2 as a guide only.

At the conclusion of the six-week period, the researchers undertook a semi-structured interview with each staff member and these interviews were audiotaped and later fully transcribed. The interviews sought to elicit from the staff members their reflections on the process of creating performing arts experiences, and the outcomes of these experiences for themselves and their children. Data gathered through these interviews and through analysis of the diaries provided the researchers with an insight into how these staff members approached the task of creating performing arts experiences. A summary of each staff member's reflections appears below.

RESULTS

Wishy Washy

Edna found that *Wishy Washy* worked well during everyday caregiving routines such as changing and dressing children. She did not report any changes to the words, but rather described a variety of different contexts in which the rhyme was used.

REFLECTIONS ON THE EXPERIENCE

Date _____

Number of times previously presented _____

Duration of experience _____

Location of experience _____

Number of children participating _____

Number of adults participating _____

Brief description of the experience _____

_____

_____

_____

Figure 2.2 Guide provided for diary entries

All the staff in Baby Room liked *Wishy Washy* straight away. It was a simple little rhyme, easy to remember and not too long. We used it with individual children in spontaneous ways during indoor and outdoor play time.

Sometimes I put Lissie (6 mths) on my lap and I would say it as I tickled her tummy, face, arms and legs. We have a lot of very ticklish babies so it was a great success with them.

I also used it with Archibald (10 mths) as a kind of galloping horsie game. I know the words aren't about horses but they fitted in very well to a sort of galloping rhythm and Archie enjoyed it every time I did it with him. Georgie (4 mths) is starting to show that she doesn't like it when we put a singlet or jumper over her head. I have been using rhymes, including *Wishy Washy* with her as I dress and undress her because I think she feels a little more secure if she can still hear my voice even if she can't see me for a moment.

Laya (1 yr 9 mths) particularly loved this rhyme and we did it with her often at nappy changing time as she often gets restless and doesn't like to be changed. I found that if I said 'wishy washy swishy swashy' as I cleaned her she would smile with delight and it made the whole process much easier and happier for both of us. Just the other day a staff member was cleaning out our fish tank and as she was wiping the insides of the tank in a circular motion Laya distinctly said 'shishy shoshy shishy shoshy' so she has remembered some of the words. We have two children Raul (1 yr 4 mths) and Stella (1 yr 2 mths) who love any kind of water play and this rhyme was just perfect to use as they sloshed the water about. It's quite a good rhyme for any messy kind of experience.

Generally I didn't make any changes to the words, although I sometimes just said the 'wishy washy, swishy, swashy' part. I feel this rhyme doesn't need to have any changes as it works well the way it is.

Running Feet

Jake enthusiastically described to the researchers some of the different ways in which he utilised *Running Feet* in his toddler program.

Initially I shared the song with individual children in spontaneous ways throughout the first week and I found myself quite adept at changing the lyrics to suit the occasion. Whilst Katisha (2 yr 8 mths) was confidently using the jumping-board I held her hands and the song became 'I am jumping quickly ...' Later I gently coaxed Alladin (2 yr 3 mths) onto the jumping-board as he is just beginning to gain confidence in this experience. Here the new lyrics became 'I am jumping slowly...'. The following day Tarah (2 yr 4 mths) and Hamish (2 yr 6 mths) were kneeling down on the jumping-board bouncing together and naturally the lyrics became 'We are bouncing ... with our bouncing knees.'

The use of the word 'quickly' in the song was a consideration. There were times when I changed the word to 'slowly' however there were other occasions when I didn't really wish to dictate speed to the children. In other words I was happy for the children to move at whatever pace they chose. I experimented with different substitutions including 'okay', 'my way' and 'yeah yeah' until I stumbled upon the most flexible and easy to remember solution which was to simply repeat the verb, for example 'I am running running ...'.

During the rainy spell I found that the children really needed to stretch their legs so Lucy (my assistant) and I took the children out onto the covered verandah. I noticed that Lucy had placed herself up one end so I took a position down the other end. Without any 'game plan' in mind I started to sing *Running Feet*. The children independently devised a game where they ran up to Lucy and touched her hand and then turned and ran back to me to touch my hand. The children repeated this sequence more than six times. Lucy and I repeated the song, substituting different actions such as jumping, marching, leaping and stamping. Despite our use of different action words the children essentially ran back and forth along the verandah. I suppose after a few days spent indoors most toddlers just want to run.

Any short action song with simple words can be used very well with two year olds and I'm sure I'll use this one often, especially with changed words to suit the moment.

Happy Rap

Harriet reflected on the implementation and development of ideas arising from the brand new experience of using a rap with her children.

I had never shared a rap with the children. To be honest I didn't even know there was such a thing as raps written specially for young children and I wasn't completely sure they would take to it. Despite my initial scepticism I presented *Happy Rap* as a whole group experience and the children absolutely loved it from the start. In fact, in no time at all they were rapping better than me. The children seemed to just enjoy doing it and I didn't think there was much point in messing around with it. I guess I tend to change songs and poems and games when they aren't all that suitable for me or for the children. At first I couldn't think of any particular ways to add to it, however after about a week of using it every day at group time some ideas began to slowly appear.

I encouraged the children to help me think of other things we could 'rap on' and we came up with 'I'm rapping on my head, ... tum, ... foot' and 'I'm rapping going up, ... down, ... round'. Indira (4 yr 8 mths) suggested 'I'm rapping on the girls,... boys, ... everyone.' Whilst Indira's suggestion didn't fit exactly into the rhythm we found we could easily adapt the way we said the line so that we could squash in 'everyone'. Franco (4 yr 2 mths) offered 'I'm rapping on my gun, ... gun, ... gun' and this encouraged Quentin (4 yr 5 mths) to announce to the group 'I'm rapping on my bullets and guns and killing baddies and rapping on dead people because I killed them.' I thanked both boys for their contribution however I didn't use them with the group. When you ask children to make their own suggestions you sometimes get responses that are hard to incorporate.

We did *Happy Rap* as a question-answer game where I said the words and the children responded with the 'ha' section and we all said the 'no more' at the end. We also did it as an echo game where I said each line and the children repeated it. By about the end of the second week I introduced the tapping sticks and the children rapped and tapped with great enjoyment. A few days after I added the tapping sticks I divided the children into two groups and distributed the tapping sticks to one group and the shakers to the other. The tapping sticks group rapped and tapped the words and the shakers group shook their instruments and said the 'ha' section, with everyone joining in together on the 'No more.'

During outdoor play Clara (4 yr 9 mths) and Yvetta (4 yr 10 mths) joined forces and carefully planned a *Happy Rap* performance which they later shared with the children at afternoon group time. The girls devised hand actions for each line of the rap, twirled around on the spot on the 'one, two, three, four' line and then joined hands and bobbed down at the 'No more' line. Clara and Yvetta spent around forty minutes creating and rehearsing this performance and later Yvetta told my assistant that she and Clara were planning to do 'a lot of other dancing' for the group because 'we do better dancing than all the other children.'

I'm very interested in finding out if there are other raps I can do with the children. Thinking up ways to make games out of them isn't so difficult now that I have seen how much the children enjoyed it.

DISCUSSION

An examination of the reflections of each of the participating staff members in this study suggested some commonality and some diversity in the way each approached the task.

Differences in the way the rhyme, song or rap were used naturally arose based on the ages, developmental levels and interests of the particular children. Additionally the individual teaching styles and approaches of each staff member influenced both the implementation of the experiences and their thoughts and reflections upon them.

Edna, in her work with children under two years of age, demonstrated that her performing arts program was readily integrated into daily caregiving routines such as nappy changing, washing and dressing as well as in planned play experiences. *Wishy Washy* became a lap game, a tickling game, a galloping game, a nappy changing/washing/dressing accompaniment and a rhyme to share during water play experiences. Edna's occasional use of the first two lines only of the rhyme was an example of modification to suit a particular nappy changing situation. Similarly Edna utilised the rhythmic elements of the rhyme to respond to a child's current interest in galloping games. It may be seen that *Wishy Washy* was used in a variety of different contexts, adapted to the differing needs of the children in Edna's care.

Running Feet was seen to be a particularly variable and flexible song, with Jake reporting a range of applications both with individual children and small groups. It was used as a spontaneous accompaniment to jumping-board experiences where the lyrics were changed to accommodate the varying motoric responses and competency levels of the children. The substitution of 'I' for 'we' enabled the song to be used by both individuals and groups.

Jake commented that the use of the adverb 'quickly' did not always suit the situation. It is noteworthy that Jake thought about and tried out new lyrics, showing a willingness to experiment with different versions until he arrived at one he deemed more appropriate for particular situations. Jake also observed that the children independently devised their own game to accompany *Running Feet* while playing on the verandah. Although attempts by Jake and his assistant to extend the children's thinking by introducing new action words to encourage different responses were unsuccessful, Jake acknowledged the children's mood and the weather conditions as a possible influence here. The fact that the children continued to run, despite other action words being substituted is perhaps an indication that the lyrics did not strongly influence the children's motoric responses.

For some teachers the introduction of a new performing arts experience can be a challenge, and Harriet freely expressed her initial hesitancy in using a rap with her four year olds. Harriet's observation of her children's obvious enjoyment of this new experience encouraged her to gradually devise a range of useful activities as the study progressed. *Happy Rap* became a question–answer game; an echo game; a tapping sticks game and a game where both sticks and shakers were used.

The planning, rehearsal and performance of the *Happy Rap* dance by Clara and Yvetta showed how valuable child-initiated dance performance can be. Here was a personal and highly creative dance interpretation of the rap by these two children who undertook this process without seeking adult intervention or assistance. Harriet's support and recognition of this endeavour, allowing the girls to share their work with the group, indicated her affirmation of the children's current interest in dance and performance.

It is common for teachers of three- to five-year-olds to invite the children to suggest new sounds, actions, words and scenarios in performing arts experiences. The suggestions provided by Franco and Quentin of guns, bullets and killing baddies demonstrated that in some situations the responses provided by children may afford a teacher a greater insight into individual children's thinking processes, stimulate a forum for more fully exploring particular subjects and, as many arts experiences do, occasionally challenge attitudes and values.

While this project was a small study, it does highlight several key aspects of planning and implementing arts experiences for young children. These implications may be useful for early childhood teachers and caregivers in their own planning and programming.

Implications for practitioners

- Be open to new ideas.

  Harriet had never tried a rap with her children before and she expressed some initial hesitancy about the new experience. However, she quickly responded to the children's positive reactions and concluded that the introduction of *Happy Rap* had been a great success. If teachers and caregivers working with young children are open to new ideas, innovative arts experiences can be positive for adults and children alike. Rather than avoiding new arts activities, teachers who think of them as exciting challenges to be tried and reflected upon may find that innovative arts experiences have the potential to revitalise the setting's programme. In practice, new arts activities can quickly become the children's 'old favourites'.

- Arts experiences can be successfully altered to suit changed circumstances.

  Some teachers might assume that a rhyme, song or rap must always be used in its original form, the way that it appears in print or on a recording. This study demonstrates the value of thinking in flexible ways about arts materials. Altering the lyrics or adding additional experiences (as Edna and Jake did), inviting children's contributions and affirming the children's own interpretations through child-initiated performance (as Harriet did) are examples of performing arts stimuli which may evolve in response to the thoughts and responses of children and teachers. A simple starting point such as a rhyme, song or rap can be developed and expanded in many ways to contribute to a diverse range of arts experiences.

- Arts experiences can evolve and grow over time.

  Harriet initially expressed some reservations about modifying the original form of *Happy Rap*. However, after observing and critically reflecting on the children's responses, Harriet readily found a range of useful and highly productive variants which served her children well. This happened because Harriet allowed herself time to consider the children's responses and to analyse how *Happy Rap* could be modified to suit their needs and the current objectives of her programme. Teachers and caregivers need to keep in mind that changing an arts experience does not always happen immediately and that changes may be instigated by an adult or, more frequently, by children. Many arts experiences evolve slowly over time as a result of the group's growing familiarity with the activity and growing confidence in expressing their ideas.

- Arts experiences do not require lots of equipment.

  The arts experiences in this study required either no equipment or everyday items, such as tapping sticks and shakers, found in most early childhood settings. Practitioners working in services experiencing budgetary constraints need not feel ill-equipped to plan and implement wonderful arts experiences. Imagination and enthusiasm, not expensive trimmings, are the keys to a successful early childhood arts program.

• Arts experiences can be effective in many locations.

In this study the staff had success with arts experiences in a variety of locations: in the playroom, in the change room, on the verandah and outside in the playground area. A familiar arts experience can assume new dimensions and encourage different responses simply by changing the environment in which it occurs.

• Observation is a crucial component of arts experiences.

Throughout this study Edna, Jake and Harriet were engaged in ongoing, systematic and careful observation of the children in their playrooms. These observations, together with the staff members' critical reflection upon what they observed, enabled all three to effectively modify the arts experiences to better meet the children's needs, extend and challenge the children further, and adapt the experiences to changing circumstances. Observation and reflection allow teachers and caregivers to record the responses of individuals, reinforce and nurture imaginative self-expression, plan and scaffold appropriate future experiences, and adapt and extend familiar experiences to meet the changing needs of the children in the group.

Arts experiences also provide unique opportunites and challenges to adults' and children's thinking about the arts, drama, movement and music, about the world and about themselves.

Thinking through performing arts-based experiences

• Adults' thinking.

The three staff members in the study reflected upon their existing arts programme (prior to the study) and thought through how they might use the arts stimulus material they were given. In doing this the staff members thought about the their own abilities, strengths and interests, and they considered the current needs and interests of their children. At the end of the project they discussed their thoughts on implementing the arts experiences, the strategies they had used, and the outcomes for the children. The staff members expressed their thoughts about the arts experiences both verbally (in the interviews) and in writing (their implementation diary).

The adults in the study thought both analytically and creatively in response to the arts stimuli and arts experiences, and they had the opportunity to express their thoughts in different ways.

• Children's thinking.

The children in the study were encouraged to think in a variety of ways by the arts experiences provided by their teacher and caregiver.

When Harriet invited the children to suggest alternative lyrics for the rap, they had to *think through* the arts experience. They had to *remember* different action words they knew and the names of different body parts. They then had to *solve the problem* of how to put these alternative words into the existing structure of the rap. Yvetta and Clara were *thinking through* performance: they needed to plan the structure and steps of their dance. Their thinking involved the processes of trying out ideas, discussing and refining these, rehearsing their dance and then performing it. *Negotiation* and *problem solving* are important thinking skills which are inherent in many arts experiences.

CONCLUSION

This study reinforces the importance of drama, movement and music experiences in programmes for young children. It highlights that for young children such experiences are often integrated, involving activities which include aspects of two or three performing arts — movement, music and drama. Further, integrated arts experiences can be developmentally appropriate and meet a range of diverse needs of individuals and groups of children aged from birth to five years.

One of the most exciting aspects of providing performing arts-based experiences for young children is the way in which a rhyme, song or rap can grow and evolve over time. With encouragement and support from adults, children's own individualised responses can be nurtured, incorporated into group experiences and given a variety of outlets.

While for many teachers the performing arts may be an area in which they feel uncertain or lack confidence, most young children feel no such reservations. Given opportunities young children will sing, play, move, enact and create their own stories, dances, drama and music. Teachers who work with young children are urged to put aside their reluctance, as Edna, Jake and Harriet did, and to try a song, a rap or a rhyme as a stimulus with their group. Furthermore, it is important to be open to children's responses and ideas, and to focus on the processes of the experience rather than anticipating a polished performance at its conclusion. Careful observation of the responses and reactions of individual children is also vital. And afterwards, it is essential to take time to reflect upon the experience and its outcomes for the children who participated. Then, as the staff in this study found, it will be possible to discover the rich variety of ways in which the performing arts can enrich programs in early childhood playrooms. Singly, or in combination, drama, movement and music offer young children unique opportunities to express their feelings and ideas, to react to significant events in their lives and to create new realities of their own.

References

Birkenshaw-Fleming, L. (1997) Music for young children: Teaching for the fullest development of every child. *Early Childhood Connections*, **4** (2), 6–13.

Chenfeld, M.B. (1995) *Creative Experiences for Young Children* (2nd edn). Fort Worth: Harcourt Brace.

Feierabend, J.M. (1996) Music and movement for infants and toddlers: Naturally wonder-full. *Early Childhood Connections*, **2**(4), 19–26.

Forrai, K. (1997) The influence of music on the development of young children: Music research with children between 6 and 40 months. *Early Childhood Connections*, **3**(1), 14–18.

Jalongo, M.R. & Stamp, L.N. (1997) *The Arts in Children's Lives.* Boston: Allyn and Bacon.

Larkin, V. & Suthers, L. (1995) *What Will We Play Today? Drama, Movement and Music Arts Games for Children aged 0–5 Years.* Sydney: Pademelon.

Larkin, V. & Suthers, L. (1997) *What Will We Play Today? Drama, Movement and Music Arts Games for Children aged 0–5 Years,* vol. 2. Sydney:Pademelon.

Schiller, W. & Veale, A. (1989) *An Integrated Expressive Arts Program.* Canberra: Australian Early Childhood Association (AECA).

Suthers L. & Larkin, V. (1996) Arts games for young children. *Journal for Australian Research in Early Childhood Education*, **1**, 146–154.

Taunton, M. & Colbert, C. (1984) Artistic and aesthetic development: Considerations for early childhood educators. *Childhood Education*, **61**(1), 55–61.

Wright, S. (ed.) (1991) *The Arts in Early Childhood.* Sydney: Prentice Hall.

ART GOES BACK
TO MY BEGINNING

Ann Veale

The title of this chaper is a quote from Australian artist and author Sally Morgan (cited in Milroy, 1996:9). Using this concept, this chapter addresses early influences of home, parents, and culture upon adult artists.

Whether artists are born or made, or whether there is artistry in all of us waiting to evolve is a question that may have no answer. Nor is it easy to say who is an artist. The focus for this chapter is the emergence and awareness of art in people who became artists, and looking at ways that art was nurtured. Often this happens in the family setting. Often the family follows the child's lead, rather than leading the child. Morgan recalls:

> I was obsessed with drawing. When I couldn't find paper and pencils, I would fish small pieces of charcoal from the fire, and tear strips off the paperbark tree in our yard, and draw on that. I drew in the sand, on the footpath, (on) the road, even on the walls when Mum wasn't looking. One day a neighbour gave me a batch of oil paints left over from a stint in prison. I felt like a real artist (Milroy, 1996:4).

For Sally the urge to draw was irresistible. She needed materials and opportunities. There is every reason to provide art teaching along with other forms of literacy for all children in a civilised society. With the very young, one cannot predict which children will be the most likely to profit from this teaching.

Most people would like to consider themselves as having pride and mastery of materials in some particular practical way, whether it be with tools, food, home decorating, computers, sport, catching fish or drawing up a plan. Each of these personal skills has an aesthetic component which gives special salience to our lives. When we pass on these artistries to our children, they are imbued with not only the meaning of what we say, but also with a sense of personal significance that these experiences have, as part of the process. In these subtle yet powerful ways, artistic messages are transmitted from older generations to younger ones. The teaching may arise from a nurturing instinct rather than from a conscious desire to instruct. Thus children may be introduced to art or craft as a natural part of daily activity, especially if the family has strong cultural traditions in which art is important. In this sense, Rush's comment 'Parents are their first teachers' (1977:6) is both valid and important.

Some artists are not necessarily born to art, but need nurture and experience for their talent to flourish. Cox found that '... many eminent people were stimulated by availability of cultural stimuli and materials related to their field of eminence, and also by teachers, parents, and other adults' (cited in Stariha & Walberg, 1995:270). Studying precursors for artistic eminence, Stariha and Walberg found that '...the early traits, stimulation, and other conditions that help girls to become significant artists are similar to those that help women in other fields, in so far as the present research suggests' (1995:270). In her review of arts policy, Rush expresses the same view from another perspective:

> There is no evidence that children left to their own devices develop into artists or people who appreciate art … they need a person who understands their quest. Many art educators now suspect that a school environment without adult guidance cannot adequately nurture children's artistic abilities (1997:7).

Thus the salience of earlier experiences in the home is highlighted. Parents are not normally thought of as 'teaching art', but perhaps some children 'catch art' in their home environment. This chapter explores how significant adults in the family have successfully nurtured children in art. One of the ways to determine whether this theory has any validity is to explore artists' recollections of the 'when and where' of their earliest experiences in art.

PARENTS AND CHILDREN IN ART

In an earlier study of 'art as development' (Veale, 1999), three artists were asked to talk about their earliest experiences in art. In each case, a parent was involved in the child's early play experiences, influencing their early development as an artist. Formal study of the discipline of art followed much later. Take the example of Lucy, a professional potter. Her mother recalled that when the children were young, they lived in a regional Australian town where they were able to play outdoors with abundant natural materials. They played with red mud, sand and water, and left moulded objects in the sun to dry. It seemed a natural progression when, as a young adult, Lucy was drawn to another natural material as her chosen medium of expression; she began to work with clay. A course of study and success with her pottery wheel helped make ceramics an engrossing pastime. Many years later, now a professional ceramicist, Lucy weaves themes from her early life into the shapes and written messages on her pots. There is a fusion for her between substance, form and symbolism that ties in with her life experience and gives meaning to her work.

Lucy's start with red mud, sand and water finds a parallel in the experience of sculptor Augusta Christine Savage. Savage is reported to have had 'from an early age … an interest in modelling the local red clay into figures' (cited in Stariha & Walberg, 1995:279). This early interest was not appreciated by her father, who thought her models were 'graven images' prohibited in the Bible and he punished her whenever he found these figures. She persisted however, and he eventually came to accept her works. It is clear that in Savage's case, her drive to use sculpture as a form of expression was a compelling instinct which withstood her father's initial disapproval. Stariha and Walberg reported that Savage, having herself suffered the impediments developed by racism and poverty '…aided in the development of talent even in those who could not pay. Her own deprivation and suffering led her to help others and left not only her own works of art but those of students that she helped achieve recognition' (1995:280).

Ingrid, a collage artist, remembers seeing her mother draw. She implored her mother to 'draw for me' and was given drawing materials so she too could draw. Colour became an important dimension for her, and she added squares of coloured paper to her drawings. As a mature artist, collage has become her preferred medium for expression. Perhaps her early experience with the squares of coloured paper became a starting point for the discovery of her own way of making meaning through art. Ingrid also drew upon, and was influenced by illustrations that she found in children's books, particularly those written by Enid Blyton. Her favourite drawings were those by an artist called Eileen A. Soper, whose name she remembers complete with initial. She recalls in particular being very interested in the techniques by which Soper made fabrics look like satin and hair appear shiny. From such early fragmentary experiences, we can begin to discern the personal starting points for the development of artistic vision, as well as its orientation and translation into different forms.

A fourth artist invited to discuss her early life in art was the daughter of an established landscape artist. She lived among artists throughout her developing years and had always drawn herself, using a wide range of pastels, coloured pencils and pens. She now creates an aesthetic environment in her classroom in which young children are provided with multiple drawing and painting materials and a range of objects to arouse visual interest. The children are encouraged to make symbols in a variety of pictorial forms using various media. The insights gained from her own artistic heritage, are now being offered to another generation of children through her teaching.

Another source of understanding early influences on artistic development is by means of studying published biographies of artists. For example, in her autobiography, South Australian artist Nora Heyson, daughter of renowned South Australian artist Hans Heysen, reminisced about her early development in art. She was one of the fortunate people born to parents who were artists and who lived in a picturesque rural environment, the setting for her father's landscape paintings. She learned (literally) at her mothers knee, and by her father's side. Nora Heysen spoke of the children 'lying on their tummies and drawing' (Klepac, 1989:9). In later years, already showing artistic promise, she was privileged to cycle with her father on his sketching trips outdoors where she started her drawings of gum trees in the style of her father.

Josie, the daughter of another landscape artist, told of how she came to regard gum trees as the province of *her* father. 'Dad's gum trees' was her way of describing the trees that were the subject of his paintings (Veale, 1999). This synergy between the children of artists and the icons of their fathers' work reveals the kinds of learning that are possible given a positive relationship between parent and child. In terms of the theory of the aesthetic education movement, the concept of 'knowing of' is considered to be the essence of the 'treatment of the roles of form, content and feeling within aesthetic knowing' (Reimer, 1992:98). When a child learns these meanings via a beloved parent, knowing becomes both a taken-for-granted element of their everyday life and, at the same time, an experience which has a heightened sensitivity for them.

THE INFLUENCE OF THREE GENERATIONS

Examples of parent-to-child influences in early art development have been given, but family influences can extend to another generation. In her biography, blind writer Barbara Blackman, wife of a renowned artist, friend, model, and mentor of many other artists, uses words rather than brush strokes for her images. She writes of the influence of her grandmother and enjoyment of her grandmother's collections of treasured objects in developing her aesthetic sensibilities (Blackman, 1997), both of which suggest that when children are learning they absorb experiences through many media and from a variety of people in their lives. These images become those which they recall later when expressing their personal meaning through art. Thus, artefacts of personal history may acquire symbolic significance. Parents, grandparents and extended family may all contribute to the tapestry of influences that impinge on a child.

Milroy notes that artist Sally Morgan's 'interests and attitudes were shaped in her childhood by her grandmother. Sally's grandmother taught her a respect for wild things, for watching, for listening, for seeing each creature as special with its own contribution to make to the world around us' (Milroy, 1996:8). Morgan was aware of her place in history, as a storyteller and as a woman artist. Art had strong cultural affiliations, significance and respect as a way of communicating. Morgan said:

> ... what I paint doesn't really change. I have a sense of coming from a long line of artists, of people who drew to tell stories. A line of women? I feel that I am the culmination of this inheritance. I am part of a great family circle that comes out of and goes into the land. I am tied to those before and after me. I am the one who has been recognised, but my mother and my daughter also paint and write and teach. Art goes back to my beginning ... when I am drawing on a wet canvas with a pointed palette knife I am again a child drawing on wet sand with a pointed stick (cited in Milroy, 1996:9).

Art academic Polly came to art as a high school student inspired by the influence of a teacher. As the eldest of nine children, there was no money to spread around for art resources, although her father drew. Yet at seventeen years old she remembers saving up for her first book on art. It seemed a natural sequence of events that, after completing a teacher education course, she found herself adopting art as a teaching approach. Art became pivotal in her personal life, as well as a means of teaching. She subsequently extended her vision with a formal scholarship in art and by study at university.

It was as a young mother that Polly's interest turned to a formal study of children's art. With her own young children's developing art unfolding in front of her eyes, her home was a rich vein of study. Her kitchen was full of drawing materials for the children to use, and housed a gallery of artworks fastened on the wall with their 'stories' written underneath. In contrast to Polly's experience, her children, a boy and girl, both went to art classes for seven or eight years. As a mother, she was also able to observe the art classes while her children were there. This provided a chance to reflect, to blend theory and observation, thus crystallising her own theoretical ideas. Polly also acted on her belief that art is important, by inviting her children to paint the wall of the oil tank at their family home.

Polly's children, now young adults, are both artistic. They are discerning about their visual environment and are equipped with a foundation of skills learned from their art classes, to which they can return. It is more than likely that if they become parents themselves they will provide the same opportunities for art tuition for their children.

ARTISTS' VIEWS OF THEIR BEGINNINGS

The major influences on art considered so far have been significant people in the immediate home environment. Yet there are many other secondary influences that seem capable of triggering artistic development. Children's literature brings significant pictorial images in close focus for children (James, 1990:140). The intimate setting for story reading brings adult and child together in shared enjoyment. As mentioned above, Ingrid told of her memories of the illustrations in a book by Enid Blyton. She remembers striving to emulate the drawing techniques used by the artist to make hair look shiny. Her words endorsed the influence of the illustrated children's books on her childhood. A well-designed picture story book has the double impact of language and illustration to enhance the reading experience for children. When the book is shared and close proximity to a well-loved person is recalled, the experience is heightened yet again.

International artist Sam Gilliam said of his family 'Almost all of my family members used their hands to create. My father was a carpenter; my mother was a member of a sewing group; my brother made a Model T Ford run; and my sister made paper dolls. In this atmosphere of construction, I too began to flourish' (Sizemore et al., 1996:113). Rush stated that 'the opportunity for inventive activity through art — not facts about art — is what aesthetic literacy offers all children' (1997:3). Such a range of inventive activities serves as a reminder of the breadth of dimensions of the artistic process.

Aesthetic literacy, however, is not just about appreciating pretty pictures — it is much more than this. John Kenneth Galbraith brought the importance of art and aesthetics into perspective with the observation that 'Artistic perception is as necessary to the modern manufacturer of consumer goods as engineering skill' (Galbraith, 1971). Art is diverse and a part of everyday life.

While Sam Gilliam's family were 'makers', Robert Kuschner's mother was an exhibiting artist. This meant that he often accompanied her to exhibitions. He writes, 'I often went with her but found much of the advanced work that was of interest to her too hard to understand ... But just being in the museums and seeing beautiful things was an important part of my childhood. I would often come home and try to copy what I had seen' (cited in Sizemore et al., 1996:111). All children should be able to experience exhibitions or visits to museums as a part of their general education, not as a privilege but as a right.

Artist Nancy Haynes defined that for her it was 'the experience of place' that brought her to painting, but hers was a different kind of place from Robert Kuschner's experience. She said:

> We travelled a lot, and, more than museums, we visited archaeological sites, religious places. It was inside mosques particularly that my senses were overwhelmed ... In place of a religious epiphany, I had an aesthetic one (cited in Sizemore et al., 1996:112).

When Cox described the psychological traits and environments of eminent women artists, he found that most had been 'stimulated by the availability of cultural stimuli and materials related to their fields of eminence' (Stariha & Walberg, 1995:270). By way of contrast, however, artist Alexis Smith had a playful fascination with 'making' things. 'I just made things when I was a kid — I always just made things out of whatever I could scrounge up, but I didn't think they were anything' (cited in Sizemore et al., 1996:110). For Alexis Smith this was not art, perhaps because the media that he used were not conventional ones involving paints or line drawing. He recalled:

> I made collages out of words and magazines and found objects, but it wasn't until college when a friend sort of forced me into taking art classes that I realised that what I was making already had the possibility of being something (cited in Sizemore et al, 1996:110).

For artist Roger Brown a trip with his family to Atlanta when he was five was a turning point. He recalled:

> We drove to the Atlanta zoo and the cyclorama. I could see what turned out to be American bison roaming along a hill top. That was my first surreal experience. In later years I painted a life-size bison as a commissioned on-site public work of art for the Illinois State building' (cited in Sizemore et al., 1996:112).

Brown's story illustrates the powerful effect of sensory experience — in this case the visual experience of a bison on the cyclorama. It also shows the persistence that such images can have from childhood into adult life for some people. Life experiences all have the possibility of contributing to the bank of childhood images upon which an artist can draw. There is also some evidence that early play materials can have a memorable effect on artists and designers, as the above mentioned artists, Roger Brown, Lucy, Ingrid and Sally Morgan, have shown. Many artistic adults identify colour, form, media used and other experiences within the family or community group as being catalysts from early childhood which profoundly influenced their later creative work. In each case cited the memories are vivid and meaningful for the artist even as an adult.

THE INFLUENCE OF PROGRAMMES BASED ON PLAY

During the late nineteenth century, a kindergarten system devised by Friedrich Froebel flourished in Europe. At the heart of this educational system was a set of materials called 'gifts' and occupations. These comprised 'exercises involving sticks, coloured paper, mosaic tiles and sewing cards as well as building blocks and drawing equipment' (Brosterman, 1997). In Froebel's programs children had 'short sessions of directed play, where the geometric gifts were used to create structures or pictures that fit loosely into three fundamental categories — forms of nature, … forms of knowledge, … and forms of beauty' (Brosterman, 1997). The kindergarten movement that Froebel founded subsequently spread to many countries after Froebel his death. Many pre-World-War-I children experienced Froebel's program in its pure form as a part of their early kindergarten experience. Influential architect Frank Lloyd Wright was one such person influenced as a child by Froebel's theories. Wright commented:

> Mother learned that Frederich Froebel taught that children should not be allowed to draw from casual appearances of nature until they had first mastered the basic forms lying hidden behind appearances … I soon became susceptible to constructive pattern evolving in every thing I

saw. I learned to "see", this way and when I did, I did not draw casual incidentals of Nature. I wanted to design (1957:19–20).

As Brosterman wrote, 'If Wright were the only important 20th century respondent to kindergarten pedagogy, we would still owe a large debt to Froebel's persistent dream' (1997:60). However there were several artists influenced by Froebel as children, including Vassily Kandinsky, Johannes Itten, Piet Mondrian and the architect C.E.J. Le Corbusier. All experienced Froebelian models of schooling which utilised this form of play.

By pegging play with the Gifts to an abstract mode of expression, those who shaped the early kindergartens in effect created an enormous international program ... that taught abstract thinking, and in its repetitive use of geometric form it taught a new way of seeing (Wright, 1957:60).

CONTEMPORARY PROGRAMMES FOR YOUNG CHILDREN

In the 1990s, new education programmes for young children have attracted international interest and attention. Reggio Emilia in Italy has emerged as sponsoring centres of excellence for young children. Art produced by the children in these centres seems to achieve heights beyond those predicted as the outcomes of normal development. The children's achievements became known through an international exhibition of children's art, and a video film called *The Lion* which drew many visitors to Italy to study the programme which achieved such unique results.

In the Reggio centres, the organisation of space in the rooms is one of the first structural elements that is apparent. The preschool environments of this progamme were planned around natural light sources and spaces for art. The founder, Loris Malaguzzi explained:

In addition to the classrooms we have established the *atelier*, the school studio and laboratory, as a place for manipulating or experimenting with separate or combined visual languages, either in isolation or in combination with the verbal ones. We also have *mini ateliers* next to the classroom, which allow for extended project work (cited in Edwards, Gandini & Forman, 1994:56–57).

The *ateliers* provide the context for art creation and embody the idea that the process of art needs continuity in time and space for extended projects of work to take place. The art in progress does not have to be packed away to make way for other routines.

Beyond the spaces and the provision, the roles of the teachers in this process are worthy of study. All the teachers are constant students in their research about the children. As Reggio teacher Fillippini explained:

The teacher sometimes works 'inside' the group of children and sometimes 'just around' them. The teacher studies the children, provides occasions, intervenes at critical moments, and shares the children's heightened emotion (cited in Edwards et al., 1994:152).

Filippini also used the metaphor of ball play to outline the teacher's role: 'We must be able to catch the ball that the children throw us, and toss it back to them in a way that makes the children want to continue the game with us, developing, perhaps, other games as we go along.' (cited in Edwards et al., 1994:153). The process that Filippini described has strong parallels with a Vygotskian process whereby adults 'scaffold' children's learning into the 'zone of proximal development' (Berk, 1999). The Reggio teacher's ability to scaffold children's learning is underpinned by meticulous processes of documentation and attention to aesthetic presentation of children's work in displays throughout the centres. The *atelierista* and staff select and prepare working displays.

> Most of the time these displays include, next to the children's work, photographs that tell about the process, plus a description of the various steps and evolution of the activity or project. These descriptions are made more meaningful with the transcription of the children's own remarks and conversation that went along with their particular experience (which is often tape recorded). Therefore, the displays, besides being well designed and contributing to the general pleasantness of the space, provide documentation about specific activities, the educational approach, and the steps of the process (Edwards et al., 1994:146).

The Reggio approach would seem to provide successful scaffolding of children's development in art. It may also provide the kind of structure that some children are able to find in their own family. In this case, history, culture of the region and the 'climate' of the children's programme provide a social setting that encourages artistry in children. It may yet be found that the Reggio approach has also taught children a new way of thinking and seeing, thus having had an even more extensive impact. The programme itself has proven to be a stimulus to replicate these learning principles in other settings internationally.

The principles of the Reggio program, shown to be so effective, can also be seen in the experiences that Polly provided for her own children. In her story the children had ample drawing materials in their family kitchen, as they do in an *atelier*. They were close to their mother who was there to annotate their drawings and to scaffold their developing experience as artists. It could be that an artistic parent, who is also a skilled teacher, can provide a rich grounding for their children's development in art, as does the teacher in the *atelier* in Reggio centres.

Ursula Kolbe (1996) wrote about new ways of viewing the role of a teacher; her concept of the adult as 'co-player and co-artist' has implicit links with the Reggio philosophy and is an effective way of helping teachers to conceptualise their roles in a care program. The notion of co-player and co-artist also shifts the concept of adult intervention to suggest instead a scaffolding of children's development in a framework that is consistent with the prevailing theoretical perspectives in child development (Kolbe, 1996).

THEORETICAL BASES FOR ART AT HOME AND IN GROUP CARE

Some evidence suggests that even where children have an artistic role model combined with opportunities, it may still not be enough. It seems 'that once most children have worked out how to express themselves representationally, then some assistance with how better to express themselves artistically should be available' (Speck, 1989:8). From the sample of case studies cited, it is clear that some homes can provide assistance for children's artistic development. Home for some is where the earliest artistic opportunities arise; home may also be enriched by the presence of extended family who contribute to the sphere of influence of a child. Whether the presence of an artist parent is the precursor for art, or merely the receptive audience who recognises the first stirrings of interest in a child, this is evidently an important role. Clearly there needs to be mutual recognition by a significant person in a child's life, who can scaffold development and provide the necessary steps for art experimentation and experience.

Many children in Australia do not spend all their time in the years before school at home with their parents; many children's early childhood years include time spent with other adults in early childhood programmes. The staff of these programmes therefore share responsibility for the development of art in children in the early formative stages.

However, while art has traditionally been a part of early childhood programmes, there have been many differences in approach. Lacking sophisticated knowledge about children's growth in art, teachers often provided early art experiences characterised by a changing array of developmentally appropriate experiences with little adult intervention, favouring novelty but lacking depth. With adults stepping back from influencing development opportunities were lost. There is now ample evidence from theories in developmental psychology following Vygotsky and his theory of the 'zone of proximal development', that adults play a central role in supporting children's progress. There is also evidence from art theory to show that effective teaching is necessary to move children beyond their current level of skills into further stages of artistic development. The Reggio program has demonstrated these theories in action very effectively.

In our glimpses of parents as teachers, there is evidence that children who grow up in households where art has a natural place, experience an initiation into the artistic processes. Home provides a crucible of influences, but when a child moves out from home, interaction with other people brings new experiences. Staff in children's centres do this by providing a teaching environment where depth and variety can be added, to complement home experiences. To emphasise the significance of home is not to deny other sources of children's experience. Where the 'beginning' occurs will be different for each child, even within the same family, but it would be an advantage if more children could say 'art goes back to my beginning'. What teachers can provide is a beginning for children who have not yet started. To foster these beginnings, we can take directions from the Reggio approach, from Kolbe's (1996) theory of the teacher as co-artist and co-player, and from Speck's ideas for a 'depth art curriculum'. Using all means at our disposal, we can put art on the agenda for all children and encourage their thinking through the arts.

References

Berk, L. (ed.) (1999) *Landscapes of Development*. California: Wadsworth.

Blackman, B. (1997) *Glass after Glass. Autobiographical Reflections*. Ringwood: Viking.

Brosterman, N. (1997) Child's play. *Art in America*, **85**(4), 108–13.

Di Blasio, M.K. (1997) Harvesting the cognitive revolution: Reflections on the arts, education and aesthetic knowing. *Journal of Aesthetic Education*, **31**, 95–110.

Edwards, C., Gandini, L. & Forman, G. (eds) (1994) *The Hundred Languages of Children*. Norwood, New Jersey: Ablex Publishing.

Galbraith, J.K. (1971) The further dimensions. *The New Industrial State* (2nd edn). Boston: Houghton Mifflin.

James, B. (1990) *Grace Cossington Smith*. Roseville, NSW: Craftsman House.

Klepac, L. (1989) *Nora Heysen*. Sydney: Beagle Press.

Kolbe, U. (1991) Planning a visual arts program for children under 5 years. In *The Arts in Early Childhood*, edited by S. Wright. Sydney: Prentice Hall.

Kolbe, U. (1996) Co-player and co-artist: New roles for the adult in children's visual arts experiences. In *Issues in Expressive Arts: Curriculum for Early Childhood*, edited by W. Schiller. Amsterdam: Gordon and Breach Publishers.

Milroy, J. (1996) *The Art of Sally Morgan*. Ringwood, Victoria: Viking, Penguin Books.

Reimer, B. & Smith, R.A. (eds) (1992) *The Arts, Education, and Aesthetic Knowing*. 1st Yearbook of the National Society for the Study of Education, Part II. Chicago, Illinois: The University of Chicago Press.

Rush, J.C. (1997) The arts and education reform: Where is the model of teaching for 'the arts'? *Arts Education Policy Review*, **98**(3), January/February, 2–9.

Russ, S.W. (1996) Development of creative processes in children. Creativity from childhood through adulthood: The developmental issues. In *New Directions for Child Development*, edited by M.A. Runco, **72** (summer), pp. 31–41. San Francisco: Jossey-Bass.

Schiller, W. (ed.) (1996) *Issues in Expressive Arts Curriculum for Early Childhood*. Amsterdam: Gordon and Breach Publishers.

Schiller, W. & Veale, A. (1996) The arts: The real business of education. In *Issues in Expressive Arts: Curriculum for Early Childhood,* edited by W. Schiller, pp. 5–13. Amsterdam: Gordon and Breach.

Sizemore, G., Smith, A., Kuschner, R., Otterness, T., Amenoff, G., Andre, C., Hazlitt, D., Benglis, L., Weiner, L., Haynes, N., Brown, Gilliam S., Lewitt, S., Moore, F. (1996) Mothers mentors, and mischief (initial interest in art). *ARTnews*, Jan. **95**(1), 110–114.

Speck, C. (1989) A depth art curriculum for the primary school. *Australian Art Education*, **13**(3), December, 6–19.

Speck, C. (1995) Gender differences in children's drawing. *Australian Art Education*, **18** (2), 41–51.

Stariha, W.E. and Walberg, H.J. (1995) Childhood precursors of women's artistic eminence. *Journal of Creative Behaviour,* **29** (4),269–282.

Smith, R.A. (1996) Leadership as aesthetic process. *Journal of Aesthetic Education,* **30**(4), 39–52.

Veale, A. (1999) Art as development. In *Landscapes of Development*, edited by L. Berk. California: Wadsworth .

Wright, F.L. (1957) *A Testament*. New York: Horizon Press.

CHAPTER 5

INHERITING DANCE

Past philosophies for contemporary contexts

Diane Wilder

In 1957 when Australian dance educator and poet Coralie Hinkley left Australia on a Fulbright Scholarship to study dance in New York, she could never have imagined the profound effect that this experience was to have on her future understandings and visions of dance within education (Hinkley, 1980). Similarly, when Johanna Exiner learned of Laban's approach to movement education and left Australia in 1961 to study at the Laban Institute in London, she possessed a limited knowledge of how significant Laban's work would become to her developing definitions of the dance experience for the child (Wilder, 1997).

Exiner and Hinkley had already gained extensive theory and practice in dance education, both having previously studied and worked with Gertrud Bodenwieser[1] (Wilder, 1997). Both implicitly understood the changing nature of the dance process, and hence sought to have their movement and dance questions challenged by others, including their contemporaries within dance education and the modern dance world. Interested in pursuing dance as a *thinking* and *doing* process that contained integrity and purpose, Exiner and Hinkley both committed themselves to *re-vision* and *re-articulation* of dance, as is evident in the following comments:

> I became totally committed to not teaching steps, but teaching children to experience the principles of motion and in making use of the principles ... or how they wanted to communicate and experience dance (Exiner cited in Wilder, 1997:45–46).

> Dance is expressive and creative, and of a compassionate nature. It not only arouses our emotional consciousness but improves the intellectual faculties as our mind learns, receives impressions, selects, manipulates and solves dance problems (Hinkley, 1980:6).

---

1. Gertrud Bodenwieser, former Professor of Dance and Music at the Vienna State Academy from 1924–1938, emigrated to Australia in 1939 and began a modern dance studio in Sydney in the same year (Hinkley, 1980).

Some of the common principles upon which dance education is based today have firm connections with past knowledge. For example, the mind and body knowledge, the development of the whole child, and quality and meaning within dance were the foundations upon which Exiner and Hinkley built, eventually determining their own foci and philosophies about dance within education. Always open to new thoughts and experiences to enhance dance, Exiner and Hinkley further refined their ideas and understandings over time, maintaining their commitment to *thinking and re-thinking* the dance process.

CONNECTIONS OF ART AND SCIENCE IN DANCE

In establishing a connection between the art and science of dance, contemporary educators writing about dance education articulate the concept that learning through dance should not be isolated into components, but rather implemented as an integrated whole that combines mental imagery, physical action and a relationship between the child's multiple worlds (Gardner, 1984; Haselbach, 1994; Hunt, 1994; Schiller & Veale, 1989).

An important aim of dance education for Exiner and Hinkley was to 'draw out' the child's creation of movement, skill in moving and response to movement. Exiner stated that her aim was to 'draw out of the child what (was) valuable' (Exiner in Wilder, 1997:49). Hinkley aimed to 'draw out, to pull out, to stretch out' (Hinkley cited in Wilder, 1997:49) the child's imagination.

Such concepts have important implications for the way in which dance educators view children's everyday movement patterns. Exiner articulated clearly that scientific analysis of movement was required to draw out qualitative dance responses from the child. She examined the connection between dance and a child's play movements as the scientific basis for her understanding of the principles of motion. This was valuable because the child could, for example, visualise being fast, hearing what speed sounds like, and feeling muscles moving fast, thus, truly experiencing speed. 'We have to have the experience of speed before we understand what speed really is' (Exiner cited in Wilder, 1997:95). For Exiner, scientific analysis was equally applicable to all other principles of motion, and extended into expression and characterisation in dance.

Similarly, Russell (1975) made reference to the importance of everyday movement, citing frequent patterns such as running as being an essential component of an inclusive dance program for the child. Relationships, he argued, existed between dance and play that gave a naturalness to the movement expression of an idea. According to Murray (1953), dance had form and compositional arrangement derived from spontaneous dancing that the child experienced through a developing relationship between art and play.

Exiner and Hinkley were acutely aware of the possibilities of integrating the creative mind with the science of the body, having experienced both technical skill and artistry in their early movement training. Their purpose was to more fully understand the movement process and to articulate dance as possessing a psychology, an aesthetic and an informed intellectual function that related directly to the child's way of learning. With this understanding, Exiner and Hinkley advanced their dance education pedagogy drawing upon past knowledge to inform their practice. Francios Delsarte's[2] work provided one such link.

---

2. Francios Delsarte was a French teacher and singer who combined artistic expression with a scientific approach to develop a system of gesture. Exercises for freedom and relaxation of parts of the body served to educate each part in expression of ideas and emotions (Chujoy, 1949).

Delsarte viewed the human being as possessing intellectual, physical and emotional zones which could be restricted or enhanced through the use of natural law phenomena such as time, weight and space (Chujoy, 1949). Exiner built upon Delsarte's original theory of movement gesture by challenging the child to take risks in experimenting with natural science laws in their dance movement. Exiner was always optimistic that a movement problem could be solved simply by thinking about whether all avenues had been explored using the mind and the body. For example, the child needed to move beyond pure imitation or mimicry of another's movement dialogue, to an inner scientific exploration of discovering their body through the principles of motion. In this way, the child became a *'flutterer'* and not just a *'butterfly'* (Exiner cited in Wilder, 1997:57). For Exiner, the child could define and articulate *lightness* as an element of weight, *variations in fluttering* as an element of time, and *varying speeds and accents* as dynamic elements within this one experience. Therefore, the child's observation and exploration of the elements of movement from a scientific base were crucial to the child's 'identification with motion' (Exiner cited in Wilder, 1997:50).

Believing that sensing movement of muscle, cartilage and bone through physical action were crucial to body awareness, Hinkley embraced the idea of a thinking body, and highlighted that technique in dance should serve only 'as a means to an end' (1980:140), because technical skill and proficiency alone would not ensure that dance could be sustained as a valid artform — a concept derived from Margaret H'Doubler[3]. It was the interpretation and execution of an idea that supported dance as a learning medium combining art and science.

Exiner experienced a constant battle between teaching skills in dance and encouraging the child's emerging creativity in dance. Her belief was that creativity and skill were intrinsically connected and therefore a balance had to be established to maintain the artistry and expression of dance. Exiner viewed skill as a way of enhancing creativity which assisted the child to develop aesthetic and kinaesthetic responses in dance. It was important for the child to 'imagine it in the body' (Exiner in Wilder, 1997:96), thereby learning *what* dance consisted of. Exiner went on to describe this developing awareness as becoming acquainted with movement itself, suggesting that freedom of expression in dance was attained through understanding how the body moved, as a skill base, combined with quality and expression in movement. A developing body awareness thus served to liberalise and promote movement potential (Exiner & Lloyd, 1973).

At the time such views were shared by others. Driver (1963) viewed body technique as a way of developing a strong body in which rhythm was carried out with ease and economy. Movement strengthened the body and served to develop the body as an effective instrument which could more readily articulate the beauty of movement itself. Furthermore, this was achieved through the use of natural law phenomena such as rhythm (Driver, 1963). Carroll and Lofthouse (1969:11) stressed that 'movement images ... in dance, (were) formulated in an artistic way that heightens and controls the initial raw experience', indicating a combination of skill and creativity. Russell (1975:9) stated that a major aim of dance education was to 'educate the body as a medium of expression', again drawing upon the use of creativity and skill as parallels in dance education. Murray (1953) emphasised

---

3. Margaret H'Doubler was an American dance educator who began studies in dance education in 1917. Establishing her approach to dance on well founded dance principles, H'Doubler is known for implementing a higher level of freedom and creativity in the dance process than previously experienced in physical education curricula. By 1940, H'Doubler was contributing to the philosophical debate about dance through the production of her most notable work *Dance: A Creative Art Experience*.

increasing co-ordination through exercises that enhanced strength, flexibility, balance and precision. Indeed, Hinkley began every dance experience with a well-defined warming up of the body to generate a level of skill and understanding of what the body needed to function smoothly, effectively and efficiently in dance.

Coe (1994:46) elaborated on the concept of skill in movement by suggesting that a 'teacher-directed technique' could further develop the child's 'movement vocabulary' providing a base from which to interpret and refine ideas. Gallahue (1990) also suggested that learning about body functions through extensive experience in the everyday environment as well as through planned physical instruction periods, served to develop the child's level of body awareness. However, Asker (1994) reminded dance educators of the dilemmas that Exiner and Hinkley faced by reiterating that there is dual tension between the development of the child's creative expression and the emphasis on the attainment of movement skills. Without balance and an understanding of the relationships that exist between the child's learning, expression and technique, the dance process has the potential to lose meaning and quality.

Rudolf von Laban[4] used the elements of movement and Delsarte's theories to develop the concept of a kinaesthetic sense in which the body moved in harmony but with coordinated skill (Preston, 1963). Gardner (1984) described this as kinaesthetic intelligence, in which the child draws upon present knowledge to think and move through an idea thus creating new knowledge. For Exiner and Hinkley, possessing a kinaesthetic sense meant incorporating the elements of movement as a means of understanding *how* and *where* the body moved from a physical, scientific perspective, with *why* and *when* the body moved from an aesthetic, artistic perspective.

Exiner developed her re-interpretation of the kinaesthetic sense by explaining that dance was about 'body movement with quality' (Exiner cited in Wilder, 1997:50). Certainly Hinkley's interpretation of the kinaesthetic sense was to train the mind and the body in unison. In this way, the child utilised both cognitive and physiological functions: a theory derived from H'Doubler (1940:59–60) who maintained that the science of dance rested with the 'systemised knowledge that (told) us how to go to work — how to adjust our efforts to attain the desired ends'.

IMPROVISATION: THE IMAGINATIVE EXPERIENCE

According to Hinkley, the attainment of the kinaesthetic sense was also about developing sensitivity and an openness of mind to the possibility of creation and invention (Hinkley, 1980). The child could combine the skill of technique with the quality of an idea or emotion, thus evoking insight whether as a creator, spectator or performer (Hinkley, 1980). This interactive concept, which uses the elements of improvisation, was discussed by Smith-Autard (1994) in the *Dance as Art* model. Inherent within this approach was the creation, performance and appreciation of dance as an artistic, aesthetic and cultural experience.

---

4. Rudolf von Laban developed a framework for the analysis of movement in 1928 (Chujoy, 1949). His movement elements of time, space, weight, dynamics and force formed the basis upon which dance curriculum for children in Europe, United Kingdom and United States was developed during the early 1900s. In Australia, the Laban framework began to be implemented in schools from the early 1970s even though Hinkley, and particularly Exiner, had been developing the Laban principles in their usage and study of dance from the 1960s.

Indeed, Exiner and Hinkley valued the level of interchange between these areas by allowing the child to improvise movement outcomes and refine movement dialogue, which in turn provided opportunities for the child to develop an overall appreciation and respect for dance as a transmitter of values, beliefs and functions within society. In this way, Exiner and Hinkley supported the aspects of teaching attributed to indigenous dance in which story, music, movement and dance weave a web of life experience for the creator, spectator and performer.

Laban (1963) described improvisation as a means of discovering dance through open-ended exploration, a view supported by the approaches used by Exiner and Hinkley. Lofthouse (1970:4) described dance as 'thinking and feeling and doing': an element attributed to the improvisational component of dance. Using improvisation within dance enabled a 'unity of experience' (Lofthouse, 1970:4) to emerge which assisted in defining the strength of dance as a combination of three areas of concentrated learning in one experience: the intellectual, the sensory and the physical domains.

Contemporary dance educators have formed similar views. Gallahue (1990) and Asker (1994) suggest that through participation in improvisation, the child empowers their mind and body, achieving a heightened sense of awareness, creativity and positive self-identity . Spurgeon (1991) draws upon improvisation as a method that exposes students to differing dance patterns, styles and contexts, and as a basis for developing dance compositions. Again, this kind of experience contributes to the valuable interchange of ideas and expressions so necessary for the development of an informed dance dialogue. These concepts were articulated by Exiner and Hinkley many years earlier.

Exiner was aware of the increased knowledge about the body and mind that an improvisation context could bring to the child. Exiner drew upon the theories of Piaget and Bruner to consolidate a body awareness concept by making the elements of dance more concrete for the child through repetition and experience — a fundamental aim of improvisation. Exiner discovered that 'child development theory supported the concept of developing the whole child "using" experiential methods as a basis for learning (Exiner cited in Wilder, 1997:60). Both Exiner and Hinkley subscribed to this viewpoint by utilising experiential learning through improvisation, to assist the child's understanding about the body and mind.

Exiner used improvisation to develop body awareness by allowing the child time to define movement patterns, thus developing a richer dance vocabulary (Exiner & Lloyd, 1973). Similarly, Hinkley drew upon improvisation to express the ideas of the mind, and to enable the child to be 'fulfilled by the imaginative experience' (Hinkley cited in Wilder, 1997:107) and used word landscapes and word pictures as a means of extending the child's qualitative movement (Hinkley, 1980).

Valuing the spontaneous movement of the child was important to Hinkley because it could develop into satisfying dance expression. It was an essential criterion for the child to delight in moving the body, and was the premise upon which Hinkley based her understanding that movement speaks truth.

According to Exiner and Hinkley, improvisation created meaning within dance. Through dance, the child could interpret experience and draw upon the teachings of others to evaluate meaning and understanding of a problem or concept. In this way, Exiner and Hinkley believed that the child would *re-assess* ideas and *re-construct* meaning by listening, observing and responding within the dance process. Dance was not only about moving and thinking but also about looking and *re-looking* at a problem. The use of improvisation leads to a level of dance quality and interpretation of feeling that renders meaning to the process (Spurgeon, 1991; Smith-Autard, 1994).

INTEGRATING LEARNING THROUGH DANCE

Exiner was concerned with the process involved in dance and its influence on the child as a *moving* and *feeling* being, a concept later explored by Gallahue (1990) and Smith-Autard (1994). Gaining meaningful experiences through dance was important to Exiner because these processes helped to develop the child as an informed mover with an extended dance dialogue. This concept is translated by Gallahue (1990), who suggests that children *move to learn* and in doing so, *learn to move*.

With this concept in mind, Exiner and Hinkley articulated that it was important to demystify dance so that the child could experience the body moving, play with movement and gain confidence and knowledge about the body through this process. Their strategy was to assist the child in developing a physical understanding about the body which could be translated into expression. This occurred through experimentation with the elements of dance: time, space, weight and dynamics.

Boorman (1969) suggested that the child's dance began through experimentation with locomotion: an idea that Exiner and Hinkley supported. Lofthouse (1970) agreed that through experiencing the elements of movement, dance became a *thinking* and *doing* experience. The child could understand the physical and intellectual interdependence that each body part had on another through the dance process.

Learning through dance should not be isolated into components, but rather, implemented as an integrated whole that combines mental imagery, physical action and a relationship between the child's multiple worlds (Schiller & Veale, 1989; Williams, 1992; Haselbach, 1994; Hunt, 1994). Indeed, Gardner (1984) reiterated that the child learns across dimensions in his theory of multiple intelligences. The child would thus benefit from understanding connections between learning domains.

Exiner and Hinkley had earlier explored and articulated this concept. Exiner affirmed that true understanding emerges when the child internalised interconnections between subjects. 'Maths, languages and drawing are all related because everything we do is a form of human behaviour' (Exiner cited in Wilder, 1997:97). She believed that by learning basic movement principles such as time, space, weight and dynamics within dance, the child would internalise that these principles could be experienced within the realm of everyday living. The child's dance encounter was not only physical but involved a combination of learning domains which made dance a multi-disciplinary experience: a view certainly shared by Exiner's contemporaries (Laban, 1963; Boorman, 1969; Lofthouse, 1970; Exiner & Lloyd, 1973; Russell, 1975; Hinkley, 1980).

Indeed today, an interdisciplinary approach to the teaching of dance is discussed by Haselbach (1994) linking dance education to human development using a multi-disciplinary pedagogy. Haselbach suggests that teaching is not about division but about using the child's multiple perceptions to create and articulate across the subject boundaries, assisting the child to *think through* a problem in various ways. Exiner articulated the concept by working on 'multi-dimensional pieces' (Exiner cited in Wilder, 1997:96) in which music, drama, visual art and other subject areas were explored simultaneously.

Hinkley intentionally crossed the boundaries into other subject areas, such as literature, science, visual arts and music (including indigenous art and music), to enhance the dance process for the child because she knew that the 'concepts, insights, expression of feeling and experience [within dance were] consistent with the aims of education' (Hinkley, 1980:143). For Hinkley, education further developed a child's individual perception, personality, communication skills, self-discipline and questioning mind. Dance was viewed as a means of addressing these areas within a differing but supplementary context. Therefore, dance created a space for the child to move through a problem and to articulate this problem using a different but equally meaningful language, namely thinking through problems by using the body and mind. Hinkley also articulated the human dimension of the dance experience for the child, stressing that movement education should never be compartmentalised because its *wholeness* as an experience communicated truth, depth and an intensity of meaning that was related to the development of the child as a *being*. Dance for Hinkley contained a psychological base.

OPENING UP DANCE: PSYCHOLOGICAL ASPECTS

Dance is human observation involving the psychological, the physiological, the aesthetic, and layers of meaning that contribute to the overall qualitative dance base. Exiner and Hinkley supported and expanded Emile Jaques-Dalcroze's[5] concept that the level and sophistication of the interpretation of an idea, which for Dalcroze was a musical idea, was highly dependent upon the quality of the movement. Murray (1953:10) examined quality in dance when stating that dance acted as a 'province of expressive and aesthetic action'. Furthermore, Murray (1953:7-8) determined that 'it is when the ultimate concern is with the meaning of movement that the term *dancing* is accurately applied'.

H'Doubler (1940:135) advocated that dance consisted of 'spontaneous impulses' that were shaped and fashioned by an informed mind to create a sense of unity. The psychological and physiological balance so necessary in dance as articulated by Exiner and Hinkley, had been previously described by H'Doubler (1940:70) as a fundamental aim of dance education whereby the child could feel the 'tones of physical origin', thus training the mind to understand the body, and for the body to express the psychological nature of the mind.

The internalisation of emotions and varying levels of intensity through dance, was also described by Murray (1953) as adding new meaning to previous experiences giving the child an avenue to fulfil needs. Russell (1975) supported the view that dance expression was intrinsically connected to the child's inner world, and that interpersonal communication was enhanced through the dance process. Certainly, he argued, that if the dance experience outcomes developed a *whole* personality, then the worthiness of a dance program was inherent. Smith-Autard (1994) has described the use of expression in dance as not only being that of the child's inner emotions, but rather an interpretation of the emotion that arises from the child's imagination. Indeed, Exiner subscribed to the view that through dance the child could 'perceive the world in motion' (Exiner cited in Wilder, 1997:64), taking in ideas and thoughts and interpreting these through a developing dance dialogue.

---

5. Emile Jaques Dalcroze developed the music and movement system known as eurhythmics. Using this system, students could translate sounds into physical movements rendering a more complete understanding of the musical composition (Chujoy, 1949).

However, the connections that dance had to the development of a child's self-identity were not overlooked by Exiner and Hinkley, who believed that to render the dance experience as being totally objective was to deny a certain level of spirituality, soul and individual expression that enabled the child to truly identify their dance as their own. Smith-Autard (1994:273) agreed that the dance outcome always contained a certain 'self-expressive identity', no matter how objectively the experience was conducted. However, for Exiner and Hinkley, the psychological connections within dance served other purposes in helping the child to more fully understand their ideas in the context of a wider world and to accept and act upon constructive criticism from peers that would ultimately advance their own dance dialogue. Exiner and Hinkley believed that dance was somewhat subjective because it was performed by *thinking* and *feeling* human beings.

For Hinkley, part of the psychological aspect of dance was about re-invention of oneself and the environment thus developing quality and creativity in dance. Hunt (1994) discusses the dance experience as being transformative: dance has the capacity to alter a child's perception and open new dimensions of experience — to act as a liberating force. According to Hunt a child could be transported to new levels of meaning and existence through the dance process, thus *re-inventing, re-visiting* and *re-interpreting* an idea.

For Hinkley, transformation of the mind and body through dance was both necessary and desirable because of the introspective and cerebral nature of dance. She suggested that dance enriched and created the child's being, sharpening perceptions and sensitising the child to the natural and physical environment (Hinkley, 1980).

THE ROLE OF THE TEACHER

Exiner and Hinkley agreed that the method used to teach dance was responsible for the kind of transformation experienced by the child, a concept supported by Asker (1994) and Hunt (1994). The feeling of whole totality as described by Hinkley, which was gained through muscle control, co-ordination and an inherent delight in moving the body, was made possible, according to Exiner, through the kind of language the teacher used. Exiner stated that 'movement-content does not change: there is merely a choice of vehicles for presenting it' (Exiner cited in Wilder, 1997:65).

One of the most important aims for Exiner within the teaching process was to understand the role of teacher judgement in relation to a child's dance. Exiner refused to allow her personal taste to interfere with the child's individual creation of an idea in dance. For Exiner it was essential for the teacher to think about the values of dance and to promote an environment where thinking through movement problems was the norm.

The reciprocal relationship between teacher and child was an essential criterion for Hinkley in creating an openness that could generate and re-generate ideas for the *doing* of dance, allowing thinking to take some precedence (Hinkley, 1980). Russell (1975) suggested that the role of the teacher was critical in providing experiences that supported the child's developing mind. The teacher needed to understand the process of movement, from the functional to the expressive. Murray (1953) also agreed that the attitude of the teacher had a profound influence on the child's dance outcomes, citing that teacher-directed experiences should give way to problem-centred experiences. This concept is shared by Dyer and Schiller (1996) who discuss the need for teachers to utilise problem-finding and problem-solving approaches in teaching dance to young children.

According to Hunt (1994), the very psychology of the dance experience suggested a level of spiritual and emotional investment by the child which could be hampered by a teacher negating a child's individual contribution. Asker (1994) further suggested that it was essential for the teacher to move away from popularist and fashionable images of the body, rather that dance should be available and acceptable for all children regardless of size, shape, race and culture. Exiner believed that a teacher should always be genuine and unadulterated: her view that a teacher should suspend judgement communicates this clearly.

The approach of the teacher to the dance experience has the potential to disengage the child's developing unity of mind and body, rendering an external and somewhat superficial view if product is the only goal. Asker (1994) also discussed approaches to dance as being culturally and socially bound, making the task of teaching dance more challenging for the teacher. Exiner and Hinkley supported the expansion of a child's dance dialogue through collaboration between child, teacher and peers, and the provision of an environment that embraced social equality. Boorman (1969) supported this concept by explaining that the teacher needed to use questioning techniques in order to understand the child's current level of comprehension within the dance experience. Exiner and Hinkley maintained that the teacher was also a learner in such an environment suggesting that the child had much to contribute to the ongoing education of the teacher within the dance process. The values transmitted by the teacher also gave credence to the child's ideas and solutions, and learning was therefore reciprocal.

For Exiner, simplicity in teaching was the key to releasing a child's limitations and assisting them to identify with motion. According to Exiner, the level of meaningful experience was dependent upon the teacher's understanding of dance, and their valuing of the child's rhythm, timing and spatial and bodily awareness, which culminated in a productive, individualised interpretation of the child's dance.

CONCLUSION

It is clear that Exiner and Hinkley not only admired and respected their dance education predecessors but established a pedagogy based also on the teachings and dance education ideas of their contemporaries, including Russell, Boorman, Murray and Driver. Through their training and emerging philosophies on dance education, Exiner and Hinkley developed a reverence and respect for dance as a truly transformative and enlightening experience for a child. Both were open to and actively sought new ideas, because these ideas often directly challenged their thinking about the dance process. Exiner relished challenges and instilled a belief within her students that all problems could be assessed and evaluated through dance. Hinkley challenged her students to incorporate vision and meaning in dance as a process that could open up new possibilities. Exiner and Hinkley were able to constantly evaluate their own pedagogy, to change and refine their perceptions and writings. This remains a fundamental aim of dance education programmes in Australia today where dance is valued as a means of *thinking* through, *acting* upon, and *re-thinking*.

References

Asker, D. (1994) Inscriptions on the body. In *Kindle the fire: Proceedings of the Sixth Triennial daCi Conference on Dance and the Child International,* edited by W. Schiller & D. Spurgeon, pp. 5–4. Sydney: Macquarie University.

Boorman, J. (1969) *Creative Dance in the First Three Grades.* Ontario: Longman Canada Limited.

Carroll, J. & Lofthouse, P. (1969) *Creative Dance for Boys.* London: MacDonald & Evans Ltd.

Chujoy, A. (1949) *The Dance Encyclopaedia.* New York: Barnes & Co.

Coe, D. (1994) Why learning needs courage. In *Kindle the fire: Proceedings of the sixth triennial daCi conference on dance and the Child international*, edited by W. Schiller & D.Spurgeon, pp. 43–50. Sydney: Macquarie University.

Driver, A. (1963) *Music and Movement* (10th edn). London: Oxford University Press.

Dyer, S.M. & Schiller, W. (1996) 'Not wilting flowers again!': Problem-finding and problem solving in movement and performance. In *Issues in Expressive Arts: Curriculum for Early Childhood.*, edited by W.Schiller, pp. 47–54. Amsterdam: Gordon & Breach Publishers.

Exiner, J. & Lloyd, P. (1973) *Teaching Creative Movement.* Sydney: Angus & Robertson.

Gallahue, D. (1990) Moving and learning: Linkages that last. In *Moving and Learning for the Young Child*, edited by W.J. Stinson, pp. 233–239. Washington DC: AAHPERD.

Gardner, H. (1984) The seven frames of mind. *Psychology Today,* June, 20–26.

Haselbach, B. (1994) Dance and the fine arts: An interdisciplinary approach to dance education. In *Kindle the Fire: Proceedings of the Sixth Triennial daCi Conference on Dance and the Child International*, edited by W.Schiller & D.Spurgeon, pp. 151–158. Sydney: Macquarie University.

H'Doubler, M.H. (1940) *Dance: A Creative Art Experience.* New York: FS Crofts & Co.

Hinkley, C. (1980) *Creativity in Dance.* Sydney: Alternative Publishing Co.

Hunt, P. (1994) Dance as a transformative activity for the child: Problems and possibilities. In *Kindle the Fire: Proceedings of the Sixth Triennial daCi Conference on Dance and the Child International*, edited by W.Schiller & D.Spurgeon, pp. 181–187. Sydney: Macquarie University.

Laban, R. (1963) *Modern Educational Dance* (2nd edn). London: MacDonald & Evans Ltd.

Lofthouse, P. (1970) *Dance* (2nd edn). London: Heinemann Educational Books.

Murray, R.L. (1953) *Dance in Elementary Education: A Program for Boys and Girls.* New York: Harper & Row.

Preston, V. (1963) *A Handbook for Modern Educational Dance.* London: MacDonald & Evans Ltd.

Russell, J. (1975) *Creative Dance in the Primary School* (2nd edn). London: MacDonald & Evans Ltd.

Schiller, W. (ed.) (1996) *Issues in Expressive Arts: Curriculum for Early Childhood.* Amsterdam: Gordon and Breach Publishers.

Schiller, W. & Spurgeon, D. (eds) (1994) *Kindle the Fire: Proceedings of the Sixth Triennial daCi Conference on Dance and the Child International.* Sydney: Macquarie University.

Schiller, W. & Veale, A. (1989) *An Integrated Expressive Arts Program.* Australian Early Childhood Resource Booklets, No. 4. Canberra: AECA.

Smith-Autard, J. (1994) Expression and form in the art of dance in education. In *Kindle the Fire: Proceedings of the Sixth Triennial daCi Conference on Dance and the Child International,* edited by W.Schiller & D.Spurgeon, pp. 268–283. Sydney: Macquarie University.

Spurgeon, D. (1991) *Dance Moves: From Improvisation to Dance.* Sydney: Harcourt Brace Jovanovich.

Stinson, W.J. (ed.) (1990) *Moving and Learning for the Young Child.* Washington, DC: AAHPERD.

Wilder, D.L. (1997) *Perceiving the world in motion: Two Australian dance educators 1960–1975.* MA thesis, Macquarie University, Sydney.

Williams, G.M. (1992) Developing communication through movement and dance. *Early Childhood Development and Care,* **81,** 109–115.

CHAPTER

SEEING BEYOND MARKS AND FORMS

Appreciating children's visual thinking

Ursula Kolbe

Learning to see what young children actually do with graphic and three-dimensional media is not a simple matter. Do culturally determined understandings of visual representation limit our abilities to see and appreciate what children achieve? Do we over-emphasise visual depiction and undervalue other forms of visual presentation and representation?

Children's graphic work has been the subject of formal research for at least one hundred years. By analysing children's completed drawings and, in recent decades, by studying how the graphic process affects and determines the emerging product, researchers have gleaned much about young children's development of representation and symbolisation. There are, however, still some considerable gaps in knowledge and understanding of children's visual presentation and representation — gaps which early childhood practitioners can be in an ideal position to assist in narrowing.

The purpose of this chapter is twofold: firstly, to consider questions relating to observation and to discuss barriers that appear to affect understanding of children's processes; secondly, to make suggestions for ways of looking at children's graphic and three-dimensional work. Examples are discussed in reference to the 'gaps' from my perspective as artist and teacher at a demonstration early childhood day-care centre.

Teachers' action-based research is increasingly being seen as critical to the development of their understanding of children's learning, and to curriculum decision making (David, 1996). Forman (1996) sees teachers' documentation of children's actions and products as a vital tool in developing an understanding of how children make meaning. Given that practitioners have the advantage of knowing children intimately and seeing them almost daily, they have the potential to observe aspects of children's spontaneous interactions with graphic and three-dimensional media, particularly with respect to toddlers, that may elude other researchers.

What, then, are some of these gaps in our knowledge and understanding of children's visual representation? As pointed out by Matthews (1988, 1994) and Tarr (1991), relatively little attention has been given to the work of under-three year olds. Consequently, early childhood textbooks still tend to reflect a relatively negative view of toddlers' graphic work as being meaningless and serving essentially a kinaesthetic function. Another gap relates to the area of three-dimensional representation. Apart from studies by Golomb (1974,1989), and the work by the Reggio Emilia educators (Vecchi, 1996), three-dimensional work still tends to receive little attention. Links between children's graphic work and their three-dimensional representations — whether made from dough, clay or blocks — has also not been widely studied. A further gap concerns the narrative dimension in children's graphic work which, although commonplace, has been largely ignored in the psychological literature (Duncum, 1993). Yet another gap concerns the social context in which children's work with visual media occurs. Again, as Matthews (1994) observes with respect to the child–adult relationship, and Kindler (1993) with respect to peer relationships, this aspect has received insufficient attention. Studies have tended to focus on the individual child's work done in isolation. The influence of peer interaction (as well as that of the adult observer) on children's work needs much more investigation. The role of graphic and claywork as a form of communication amongst peers is another aspect that merits attention. Finally, another perceived gap in understanding relates to the lack of recognition of the decorative or aesthetic aspects in children's work. Viewers' attention to pictures in general tends to be drawn to representational aspects, while compositional factors and decorative elements are often ignored (Van Sommers, 1991), so it is not surprising that these qualities in children's work frequently go unnoticed.

The above list of 'gaps' is, of course, selective, and undoubtedly reflects a personal perspective and philosophy. In a way, the gaps are not entirely unrelated in that they all point to a need for greater understanding, on the part of researchers, of the complexity of artistic processes. They are also identified here because all seem peculiarly suitable for the practitioner to investigate through observation and documentation.

Because the psychological literature has largely focused on the development of one aspect of visual representation, namely visual depiction of static objects as seen from a single viewpoint, practitioners have not always found it easy to relate theory to practice. Often what we actually see in children's spontaneous interactions with media encompasses aspects that are qualitatively different from those described in the literature.

Observing and documenting very young children's interactions with media is a challenging process. Analysis of children's drawing, painting and claywork can be influenced by various factors. Problems sometimes stem from the fact that children's work with visual media is commonly labelled and compartmentalised as 'art'. Popular notions about 'art' may give rise to certain expectations, and together with teachers' frequent perceptions of themselves as 'unartistic', can create barriers to understanding and so limit the ability to see what children actually do. Without an insight into children's graphic strategies and, importantly, without awareness of their communicative intentions and differing purposes for drawing, it can be difficult to observe their actions with empathy. As a result, we may miss much of children's thinking and their efforts to make meaning.

FACTORS INFLUENCING OBSERVATION

The complexities of the art of observation are many, but the following brief points may serve, at least as an introduction to further consideration of this issue.

It is of course well known that by virtue of observing, we influence what we observe. As every practitioner knows, the mere act of sitting down and watching a child engaged in an activity often sustains and extends the child's engagement (or discourages it completely). By magnifying a situation in this way, do we perhaps distort what we purport to study? While as teachers we can, of course, justify our position, nevertheless this is a question that as teacher–researchers we should be prepared to ask.

It is also widely acknowledged that observation can never be wholly objective or neutral. We do not see with an 'innocent eye' (Gombrich,1959:11). In other words, we interpret as we see. For example, the viewer who perceives children as makers of meaning will see and record their graphic processes differently from one who uses a frame of reference that focuses on a 'deficit model', in which viewers with little experience of children's graphic artwork often find it easier to perceive what children omit or do not do, rather than what they do achieve graphically. So, we have to ask by which criteria, or against which yardsticks, do viewers perceive (and judge) children's work?

Notions About 'Art'

Preconceptions about 'art' set up expectations in viewers' minds which may influence observation. It is interesting to note that in the Reggio Emilia approach to early childhood education (an approach in which children's graphic and three-dimensional work is regarded as central to children's construction and co-construction of meaning), the educators prefer not to label or classify this work as 'art' or 'artwork' (New, 1990). Instead, terms such as 'symbolic representation' are used which place an emphasis on the meaning-making purpose of such work and acknowledge its centrality both to children's lives and to the curriculum. Avoiding the use of the word 'art', with its various connotations, avoids the trap of viewing children's actions with art media as being separate, and necessarily different in essence from what they may do in, for example, the sandpit, home corner or block area.

In Western culture, the word 'art', when applied to the visual arts, has commonly been associated with visual representation. More specifically, it has been associated with representation of a particular kind: realistic depiction. Although this association of 'art' with realism has changed in some quarters since the rise of modernism, it nevertheless continues to prevail and to influence current research, as Golomb (1994) points out. The more realistic or 'lifelike' the artwork, the more highly it is often regarded; the attainment of realism is considered by some to be the endpoint of artistic development.

Realistic depiction depends on objects being depicted in three-dimensional space from a single viewpoint, according to the rules of perspective. This is a pictorial tradition that has developed in the West since the Renaissance. It is not, however, the only way of representing a scene; traditional Chinese art, for example, uses a different convention as do many other cultures and artistic traditions. Moreover, the depiction of scenes, whatever the tradition, is far from being the only form through which humans express, represent and communicate ideas and feelings visually, or explore visual aesthetic concerns. The visual arts embrace far more than simply picture making. However, a narrow view equating 'art' with visual representation, and visual representation necessarily with realistic depiction, continues to influence many viewers, including researchers.

Many studies of children's work have been made on the assumption that children aim at realistic depiction or imitation. It has been assumed that the information a child includes in, say, a depiction of a human figure, represents the extent of the child's knowledge, and that deviations and omissions are errors. However, children know far more than their graphic abilities allow them to convey. As Arnheim (1974) pointed out, they invent 'structural equivalents' that 'stand for' the objects named. Gradually these shapes become more differentiated and include more details which correspond to certain attributes of the drawn objects, but at no time do children's drawings represent the full extent of their knowledge. However, the stress on realism that is part of our cultural heritage has led to realism being regarded as the endpoint of a hierarchical sequence of 'stages' of development. In a critical review, Golomb (1994) found that such a view has limited researchers' understanding of children's work. It is suggested that documentation of how children's drawings entail a self-invented system of equivalences following its own rules (Willats, 1997) could be a valuable way in which practitioners can assist in furthering understanding of how children make meaning.

The focus on pictorial 'realism' has not only, as already mentioned, contributed to the commonplace disregard for children's 'scribbles', but also to the disregard for other factors in children's work. These factors include organizational characteristics and attention to visual order and pattern making which also merit consideration. Studies of children's search for order and balance in their graphic work (Kellogg, 1969), and of children's pattern making (Booth, 1979) have drawn attention to the non-representational aspects of children's work. However, these aspects are still largely neglected by researchers. Although many practitioners value children's pattern making and 'designs', these works tend to be appreciated as aesthetically pleasing objects, rather than as examples of children's thinking worthy of investigation. Van Sommers (1991) notes that it is very difficult for people to see past representational material, to notice compositional factors, and to discern how representational aspects compete with decorative aspects. Reflecting on the contemporary Western bias against the decorative aesthetic aspects of art, Van Sommers believes that it is time for us to 'resurrect or get decorative aesthetics back to the domain of discussion' (op cit: 66). Early childhood educators might find this a surprising statement since a concern for aesthetic development is well entrenched in early childhood educational theory and practice. However, early childhood texts generally do not focus on children's spontaneous pattern making and search for visual order, nor do they seek to question why the interest in pattern making and decorative aesthetics observed in some children's work is so little studied. According to Jaudon and Kozloff (cited in Chave, 1996:23), 'the prejudice against the decorative has a long history and is based on hierarchies: fine arts above decorative arts, Western art above non-Western, men's art above women's'. It is beyond the scope of this chapter to examine this issue further, but the above points serve to highlight the proposition that notions about art — derived from various sources quite beyond early childhood education — nevertheless exert a powerful influence on how we look at children's work.

How then can we learn to broaden our ways of looking at children's work? How may we teach ourselves to notice features previously overlooked? In his book on the psychology of decorative art, *The Sense of Order* (1979), the art historian E.H. Gombrich observes a fundamental point which, I believe relates also to children's work. According to Gombrich, there are two categories of perception which are common to all the visual arts: the perception of meaning and the perception of order. (Of course these categories are interrelated and in some works one category may predominate while in others a balance may be achieved.) But both categories, it is suggested, are often undervalued in children's, and particularly toddlers', work. If we have both these categories clearly in mind as we look at children's work, we have a sound basis from which to start.

PERCEPTION OF MEANING IN EARLY MARKMAKING

Viewed in the context of pictorial realism, toddlers' markmaking has commonly been seen as meaningless, and done primarily for the fun of making movements. The possibility that toddlers may take an interest in, and are affected by, the visual results of their actions has not received much attention. 'Scribble' and 'disordered scribbling' have been terms commonly used to label toddlers' marks — terms which deny the possibility of meaning-making. Researchers, conditioned into looking for the depiction of objects, have largely not considered the possibility that children's marks may represent other phenomena, such as movement and action, as demonstrated in examples by very young children provided by Matthews (1988, 1994).

By attending to the child's movements, actions, sounds and words, as well as the marks, Matthews finds that marks which appear simply to be scribbles, represent both the shape of objects and their movements in a moment in time and space — for example, the movement of the flight path of an aeroplane, synchronised with vocal sounds and dialogue. Matthews describes this type of drawing, which is not depiction of things so much as representation of events, as 'action representation'.

Consider for example a drawing by J (3 yrs), which he urgently wanted to talk about. (He was not observed making it.) It shows a mass of wavy and looping lines, with three lines forming enclosed circular shapes. A torrent of words, difficult to interpret, accompanied his gesturing to various parts of the drawing. I discerned the words 'daddy', and 'round.' A little probing revealed that a circular shape stood for 'Daddy going around', which J demonstrated by turning himself around. In this light, J's circular shape makes perfect sense as a representation of a circular movement by a body in space. This is not to suggest that J set out intentionally to depict daddy going around — young children frequently see meaning in the marks as they emerge. The act of perceiving emerging marks is a creative one in which children construct meaning as they move hand and arm and watch marks appear.

J's drawing also raises another aspect, namely, the narrative element which seems to be an inseparable part of the drawing. As already mentioned, Duncum (1993) argues that the narrative element deserves much greater attention if we are to learn more about children's drawing and thinking.

As children mature, early drawing strategies are not simply abandoned, as frequently assumed, but become imbedded in the child's repertoire (Matthews, 1988; Matthews & Jessel, 1993). The topic of movement representation in the context of older children's work will be discussed later in this chapter.

PERCEPTION OF MEANING AND ORDER

A series of marks by M (1 yr 10 mths) made on five sheets of paper appear to reveal both meaning and order. Pointing to a horizontal wavy line in the lower third of her first sheet filled with lines in various directions and dots, M stated clearly, 'That's writing.' She definitely wanted it appreciated that this line was different from the others. Possibly its appearance, which clearly resembled adult writing, suggested this idea to her. Here it seems we have an example of a child 'reading in' meaning in her marks, as well as, possibly, awareness that 'writing' is somehow different from other kinds of markmaking, or at least, awareness that marks can have different functions. This is not entirely surprising; toddlers often watch with interest an adult's actions in writing their names on their work. Name-writing appears to assume a significance for young children very early.

M requested a second piece of paper, and announced she wanted to write her name. The second sheet of paper was half the size of the first sheet. Perhaps the change in size temporarily distracted her, for she made no mention of writing her name. After making some dots, lines, and circular movements without comment, she requested a third sheet. This time she made a few marks and then stopped. With great effort and concentration, she made a tiny circular mark, no bigger than the circumference of a pencil, in the top right-hand corner. It was barely visible because she did not have sufficient strength to apply enough pressure to the marker in making such a shape. She paused to look at the mark and possibly also at its position in the very point of the corner. Then slowly her gaze moved to the left-hand corner and very deliberately, she made a similar mark in this corner, and then in the two remaining corners. Although she struggled hard, she was not able to achieve the perfection of her first mark, but the marks were good approximations of the original. She requested a fourth sheet. She made some linear marks near the centre of the sheet, but clearly her interest was now focused on a new goal: again she struggled to make a tiny circular mark in each corner. She then requested a fifth sheet. This time she first made a similar mark in each corner, again at the extreme edge of the sheet with great difficulty. After this she made some lines and dots nearer the centre. She then handed the sheet to me and pointing to the corner markings, said, 'This the number A.'

It would seem that 'the number A' had such significance for M that it demanded special treatment. With every effort that she could muster she had tried to make a kind of mark that was as different as possible from all her other marks, not only different in shape but also different in placement. Despite the effort involved, she persisted with a task which, as often occurs with toddlers, was almost beyond her physical capabilities.

Forman (1996:240) writes of the need for teachers to have a 'third ear' in order to go beyond merely listening to a child's words and 'to hear the implied meanings of children's words'. He describes how teachers might record a child's exact words while at the same time hearing the child's struggle in finding the right words. Perhaps the above is an example of the necessity of having also a 'third eye' to appreciate children's struggles and intentions with visual media.

M's use of the corners deserves comment. Perhaps her attention to the corners was triggered by the change in size of paper — the corners of a small sheet being easier to see in a single glance than those of a large sheet over which the eye has to roam. However, her attention seems in itself noteworthy. Her subsequent use of all corners in each sheet seems to suggest an interest in visual order, perhaps for its own sake (although I would be inclined to see this order not as separate from the meaning, but as integral to it).

The purpose of this anecdote has been to illustrate the search for meaning and the search for order that may be apparent in even the faintest of marks of a very young child. This example also seems to demonstrate 'visual thinking', a term used by Arnheim (1969) to emphasise the proposition that the act of looking is not separate from thinking processes.

VISUAL THINKING

Arnheim (1996:113) insisted that educators should pay more attention to the 'interdependence of thinking and the senses, especially the sense of vision'. To explain his use of the term 'visual thinking', Arnheim described a child with a plaything as follows:

> The handling ... is controlled by the inseparable union of watching, handling and thinking. And what is true for the child holds equally for the way the brains and eyes and hands of great scientists operate. (op cit:114).

Arnheim believed that education is:

> burdened by a tradition that separates perceiving and thinking, as though they were entirely different activities. Many ... believe that we have to feed the sense of sight in one way and train reasoning in quite another (op cit:114).

Experiences which encourage visual thinking in young children clearly include those which involve self-directed explorations with media of good quality which they can control. The following excerpts from observations of a child made over several months highlight the interdependence of watching and thinking.

Figure 6.1 Bird (vertical) by C (3 yrs 1mth)

Observations of a child

The bird in Figure 5.1 was significant because it was (to our knowledge) C's first painted version of a bird in a recognisable form. (The topic of birds was an interest among several children at the time.) It started out as an outlined rectangle in brown. Making rectangles — out of whatever media was at hand, such as drawing media, blocks or clay — had been an abiding interest of C's over several months. He had made many versions of rectangles, even within a single painting. For example, he explored making rectangles that were outlined, double-outlined, filled in, sub-divided, halved, quartered, and so on. On this occasion, he filled in the rectangle with red, almost losing the shape. As he swirled his brush, he seemed to notice something in particular which prompted him to say 'eye', and then quickly make an adjacent mark, saying 'eyes'. He stood looking at this new shape: a departure from his previous rectangles. The eyes then prompted the formation of the beak which he painted, saying to himself 'beak'. He then swiftly added the legs, and turned to me briefly, saying, 'bird legs are not like people legs', before turning again to stare, enraptured, at this bird, almost half his size. I nodded, not wishing to interrupt his train of thought. He unclipped the sheet, and started the following painting.

For Figure 5.2, C began with a square-ish shape. He then turned to me and said, 'It's not a bird yet'. Now we know from the psychological literature that when children first say anything while drawing, their words usually simply correspond to the parts being drawn — as occurred during the first painting. As children mature, they begin to comment on their

Figure 6.2 Bird (horizontal) by C

own processes, however C's remark (made for my benefit or for us both?) is possibly even more than a comment about process. He seems to be saying in essence, this shape is still a shape, not a symbol, but it will become a symbol.

Forman (1996) argues that one of the fundamental purposes of documentation is not simply to record children's interests (for example, birds) but to study the reasons behind these interests, and to study children's ways of talking about how they represent what they know. This sequence seems to provide us with an insight into a child's awareness of his own image-making processes.

Following his remark, C painted a beak and then wings, commenting, 'He's flying.' Then he added, 'You can't see the legs. They underneath'. Here is a good example of how children often use language to explain the absence of parts. However this may only be a partial explanation: C may not yet have invented a system for attaching legs to a horizontal body. The painting is also a good example of how children capture different types of information in their work, arriving at multiple views of objects (Matthews, 1994). One type of information concerns the main characteristics of objects irrespective of any fixed viewpoint (for example, the positioning of the wings). Another type of information concerns the shape of an object seen from a particular view point (for example, the beak). The beak is represented in profile view probably because this is the simplest and least ambiguous way of conveying a beak.

Let us briefly backtrack to the same child, a few months earlier at the claytable with peers. Again we see, as illustrated in Figure 5.3, a rectangle in formation. Swimming pools were a topic of current interest, and the suggestion to make a swimming pool — perhaps prompted by the presence of coils on the table — was made by another child. This was a sufficient trigger for C (then 2 yrs 10 mths) to make the first two right angles, with G (2 yrs 11 mths) making the third. A shared understanding of rectangle-ness, possibly guided by the table shape, seemed to influence this work. The photograph shows a point at which C noticed that G's outline needed an extension.

At the completion of the swimming pool, the other children left and C proceeded to construct the piece illustrated in Figure 5.4 with left-over coils. In its symmetry and feeling for pattern — shown in the repetition of elements — it seems to reflect a sense of order. The repetition, however, is more complex than might first appear. Within the constraints that he has established for himself, C is not simply repeating elements but also creating variations. Why? Is this to make the configuration more interesting visually and therefore more engaging perceptually and intellectually? When we consider that pattern is known to invite in some adults a kind of '... "concentration and letting go" akin to meditative states' (Chave, 1996:42), it seems legitimate to ask what the contemplation of patterns does for a child's mind. Or, to ask a question on another plane, are we seeing here an aesthetic sense that derives satisfaction from seeing a symmetrical arrangement? As yet we have no answers, but this should not deter us from documenting such instances of visual thinking, and, importantly, from asking ourselves whether we provide children with sufficient opportunities to reveal such interests to us. It is also worth noting in this example that non-representational work may occur concurrently with representational work.

COLLABORATIVE DRAWING

An example of 'action narrative' or 'action presentation', complete with synchrony of onomatopoeic sounds, was observed in a series of spontaneous drawings by three boys aged 4 years 8 months, 4 years 11 months and 5 years 1 month respectively. Interestingly, the children were all capable of making pictorial representations of objects with graphic media and clay, however, in this series of drawings, which extended over a period of three to four weeks, visual depiction (in terms of making a pictorial scene) was not of primary interest. The series was inspired by *Star Wars* videos, and while drawing the children frequently exchanged information about *Star Wars* events and verbally constructed versions of the narrative.

By the time the children were first observed making their *Star Wars* drawings, they had already developed a particular graphic vocabulary to suit their purposes. Drawn exclusively with black markers (although there was a choice of colours) on separate as well as shared long sheets, a major part of their drawings, apart from very few recognisable

Figure 6.3 Swimming pool, clay by a two year old

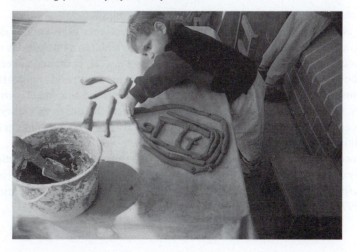

Figure 6.4 Claywork by C (2 yrs 10 mths)

rocket ships, consisted of a series of slow, deliberate and methodically placed parallel broken lines, which occasionally traversed each other, and at intervals were punctuated by small circles. Whenever a circle was drawn, the drawer would make explosive vocal sounds, synchronised with the mark making. If compared with conventional pictures, these drawings would seem deficient. However when we analyse the content based on the children's explanations it becomes clear that the children had no reason to employ their usual pictorial conventions. In this series they were not interested in using visual forms to depict things, but wished to map events — events occurring at great speed and sound in a space–time continuum. Some of the broken lines represented the trajectory of bullets towards moving targets and future explosions. As M explained in the midst of drawing, 'This one hasn't happened yet. These others have happened, but this one isn't exploded yet.' The progress of the series proved interesting to document because it revealed how children may use graphic marks as a form of co-invented, highly ordered and convention-bound communication which they can 'read' but for which adults need explanations. It also seemed to be a sophisticated version of the kind of movement representation discussed earlier. Their achievement can perhaps be appreciated if we reflect on the lack of visual models for this kind of representation. In the history of art, aside from conventions developed in recent times in comic books, a system for visual representation of movement, that is, visual form for things in flux, has scarcely been developed (Kepes, 1995). Interestingly, the *Star Wars* drawings used conventions similar to those used in a child's drawing recorded in Georg Kerchensteiner's 1905 book, *The Development of the Gift of Drawing* (cited in Fineberg, 1995), which shows trajectories of pelted snowballs.

The point of these examples has been to highlight aspects relating to the 'gaps' identified earlier, and to provide a glimpse into the range that it is possible to observe when graphic and three-dimensional work is not compartmentalised as 'art', but is seen instead as being central to the curriculum and a fundamental form through which children construct and co-construct meaning.

TOWARDS DEVELOPING AN INFORMED EYE

How then can we learn to see what we may otherwise miss?

Clearly, observation will be influenced by the observer's sensitivity to the demands of the medium and knowledge of the processes involved. In children's interactions with media there is a constant 'give and take'— a reciprocity — between child and materials which needs to be recognised. Each medium has inherent constraints and affordances (potentialities) which influence children's thinking, processes and outcomes (Forman, 1994).

Empathy with children's processes depends in part on the observer's awareness that artistic processes involve thinking within the medium. By this is meant thinking in terms of visual qualities and their relationships, not in words.

Non-drawers rarely appreciate the fact that graphic representation and depiction involve exceedingly complex processes (Van Sommers, 1995; Willats, 1997). In addition it is often not recognised that drawings can serve various purposes and functions (Matthews, 1994; Willats, 1997). We need to understand the maker's purpose.

CONCLUSION

Teachers' action-based research into children's interactions with graphic and three-dimensional media has the potential to enhance understanding of children's thinking. The philosophical tradition of examining observed phenomena in order to consider 'the "Why?" which looks for reason, and the "Why?" which looks for meaning' (Scruton 1996:25) may provide an appropriate basis for observing and documenting children's work. By focusing on children's visual thinking in their search for meaning and order, rather than on their 'art', it is suggested that the viewer may perceive more clearly children's processes and achievements.

Above all, as Matthews (1994:130) has written, close observation that enables child and adult to 'participate in a web of shared understandings and anticipations about what is unfolding on the paper's surface' is crucial. In the context of observing children's interactions with media, words by the philosopher Bachelard (1964:158) seem peculiarly relevant: 'To use a magnifying glass is to pay attention, but isn't paying attention already having a magnifying glass? Attention by itself is an enlarging glass'.

References

Arnheim, R. (1974) *Art and Visual Perception: A Psychology of the Creative Eye* (2nd edn). Berkeley, Calif: University of California Press.

Arnheim, R. (1969) *Visual Thinking*. Berkeley, CA: University of California Press.

Arnheim, R. (1996) *The Split and the Structure: Twenty eight essays*. Berkeley, CA: University of California Press.

Bachelard, G. (1964) *The Poetics of Space*. Boston: Beacon Press.

Booth, D. (1979) The young child's spontaneous pattern-painting. In *Creativity across the Curriculum*, edited by M. Poole. Sydney: Allen & Unwin.

Chave, A. C. (1996) Disorderly order: The art of Valerie Jaudon. In *Valerie Jaudon,* edited by R.P. Barilleaux. Jackson, Miss.: Mississippi Museum of Art.

David, T. (1996) Developing the early years curriculum: Collaborative learning through research and evaluation, Keynote Address. In Conference Proceedings, *Weaving webs, collaborative teaching and learning in the early years curriculum.* Melbourne: University of Melbourne.

Duncum, P. (1993) Ten types of narrative drawing among children's spontaneous picture-making. *Visual Arts Research,* **19**(1), 20–29.

Fineberg, J. (1995) The innocent eye. *ARTnews,* April, 118–125.

Forman, G. (1996) Design, documentation and discourse, Keynote address. In *Weaving webs, collaborative teaching and learning in the early years curriculum* (conference proceedings). Melbourne: University of Melbourne.

Forman, G. (1994) Different media, different languages. In *Reflections on the Reggio Emilia Approach*, edited by L. Katz & B. Cesarone. Urbana, IL: University of Illinois.

Golomb, C. (1974) *Young children's sculpture and drawing: A study in representational development.* Cambridge, Mass.: Harvard University Press.

Golomb, C. (1989) Sculpture: The development of representational concepts in a three-dimensional medium. In *Children and the Arts*, edited by D.H. Hargreaves. Milton Keynes: Open University Press.

Golomb, C. (1994) Drawing as representation: The child's acquisition of a meaningful graphic language. *Visual Arts Research,* **20**(2), 14–28.

Gombrich, E.H. (1959) *Art and Illusion: A Study in the psychology of pictorial representation.* London: Phaidon.

Gombrich, E.H. (1979) *The Sense of Order: A study in the psychology of decorative art.* London: Phaidon.

Kellogg, R. (1969) *Analyzing Children's Art.* Palo Alto, CA: Mayfield Press.

Kepes, G. (1995) *Language of Vision.* New York: Dover Publications.

Kindler, A.M. (1993) Research in developmental psychology: Implications for early childhood art education practice. *Visual Arts Research*, **19**(1), 16–19.

Matthews, J. (1988) The young child's early representation and drawing. In *Early Childhood Education: A Developmental Curriculum*, edited by G. M. Blenkin & A.V. Kelly. London: Paul Chapman.

Matthews. J. (1994) *Helping Children to Draw and Paint in Early Childhood: Children and Visual Representation.* London: Hodder & Stoughton.

Matthews, J. and Jessel, J. (1993) Very young children use electronic paint: A study of the beginnings of drawing with traditional media and computer paintbox. *Visual Arts Research*, **19**(37), 47–62.

New, R. (1990) Excellent early education. A city in Italy has it. *Young Children*, **45**(6), 4–10.

Scruton, R. (1996) *An Intelligent Person's Guide to Philosophy.* London: Duckworth.

Smith, N. R. (1982) The visual arts in early childhood education: development and the creation of meaning. In *Handbook of Research in Early Childhood Education*, edited by B. Spodek. New York: Free Press.

Tarr, P. (1991) More than movement: Scribbling reassessed. In *Early Childhood Creative Arts: Proceedings of the International Early Childhood Creative Conference*, edited by L. Overby. Reston, Virginia: American Alliance for Health, Physical Education, Recreation and Dance.

Van Sommers, P. (1991) Beauty, cognition and aesthetics. In *Theoretical Perspectives: Research in Children's Cognition and Knowledge in the Visual Arts*, edited by P. Mckeon, G. Sullivan, D. Walker, A. Wheate. Sydney: University of New South Wales, College of Fine Arts.

Van Sommers, P. (1995) Observational, experimental and neuropsychological studies of drawing. In *Drawing and looking: Theoretical approaches to Pictorial Representation in Children*, edited by C. Lange-Kuttner & G. V. Thomas. New York: Harvester Wheatsheaf.

Vecchi, V. (1996) Stability of chairs and bridges: Equilibrium and stability. In *The Hundred Languages of Children: Catalogue of the Exhibit.* Reggio Emilia: The Municipality of Reggio Emilia Infant Toddler Centres and Preschools.

Willats, J. (1997) *Art and Representation: New Principles in the Analysis of Pictures.* Princeton, N J: Princeton University Press.

TEACHING DANCE
TO YOUNG CHILDREN

David Spurgeon

The fundamental concern of this chapter is the proposition that many teachers of dance to primary and preschool children perpetuate and reinforce stereotypic gender expectations, so that by the time a group of children has reached puberty the boys have quit the dance class leaving behind a group of passive, anxious girls. The 'wayward warriors' have abandoned what they see as boring or irrelevant for other, more manly, pursuits, leaving behind the 'docile dollies' (Spurgeon, 1997) to do what they do best — being told how to move and harbouring concerns about how they look. It is beyond the scope of this chapter to detail the causes of, and reasons for this situation; instead the concern expressed above is addressed by a list of suggestions and recommendations designed to assist the teacher of young children to implement a dance program that is attractive and affirmative for all.

There are three important assumptions that underpin and inform what is to follow. Firstly, it is assumed that the case for absent boys and anxious girls in dance classes has been comprehensively documented over the last two decades. The whole issue of dance and gender is now receiving deserved and detailed attention (see, for example, Adair, 1992; Burt, 1995; Connell, 1995; Dempster & Gardner, 1993; Hanna, 1988; Morris, 1996). Secondly, the assumption is made that dance does not exist in some kind of rarefied isolation but that it reflects its culture, and it gives information about its society (Thomas, 1993; Foster, 1995; Desmond, 1997). Thus, most problems associated with dance can reasonably be assumed to have their origin in the culture and wider society in which they operate. Thirdly, it is taken as axiomatic that teachers — particularly teachers of young children — can, and do, make a difference. They are an integral part of the child's culture and society. They impart values and attitudes as well as skills and knowledge. As Ignatius Loyola pointed out many hundreds of years ago, 'give me the child before seven and I will give you the man'. Thus, this chapter commences from the point of view that:

> Dance education is not immune to gender problems that exist in society; symptoms like a scarcity of male students, dancers' body and self-esteem issues and student choreographies that echo media stereotypes should convince us of this (Meglin, 1994:26).

How then should teachers of young children teach dance? What should they do to try to remedy the situation of vanishing men and uncertain women? In what way can those who teach dance be 'responsible for identifying gender messages and making the classroom a place where sex-role stereotyped behaviour can be questioned and transformed' (Meglin, 1994:26)?

'TEACHER, CAN WE BE BULLDOZERS NOW?'

The first recommendation is that *all* children, boys and girls, should receive the same, comprehensive range of dance opportunities. The problem is that 'dance is traditionally a female-populated field which society still tends to view as feminine' (Crawford, 1994:4). Thus, even at an early age, children will begin to expect certain kinds of movements according to their gender. Boys may enjoy jumps, leaps and locomotor activities that use the whole body. They will probably choose strong vigorous movements that use speed and dominate space. Girls may prefer gestures and shape and the more detailed exploration of how to use the body expressively. They may well enjoy slow, gentle movements that accommodate space. As Plummer pointed out:

> The limitations placed on boys in dance technique and performance in terms of mastering 'manly' movement confirm Modern Dance as a female gendered form. Females are free to pursue *any* dance dynamic or vocabulary through the technique, choreography and performance of Modern Dance. Males however are still restricted in dance by the concept of 'manly' versus female coded movements (1995:36–37).

Dance educators may unwittingly perpetuate the situation by fitting content to gender, or by using images with very young children that suggest or condone butterflies and bulldozers, according to gender. In this way a sexist status quo is simply confirmed. Dance educators need to actively promote all aspects of dance for all children. There are several strategies that can assist with this. Visiting dance-in-education companies with male and female dancers, together with a careful selection of dance on video, can promote the idea of dance as an activity which is non-gender specific. Many other cultures view dance as either masculine or non-gender specific, so the encouragement of sharing dance practices with children from other cultures can be helpful and enlightening. Perhaps the most powerful influence is the planning and expectation of the teacher. A class of excited five year olds experiencing dance with a teacher that they like, will tend to assume that what the teacher says, suggests and gives is 'normal'. If the teacher invites the whole class to experiment with soft, gentle movements and to try forming shapes that are strong, weak, sharp, smooth, like an arrow, like a saucepan and so on, and to enjoy pushing quickly through space, then such activities are implicitly legitimised by the group.

It is important to consider, at this point, the issue of 'boys-only' dance groups. The author holds the view that separating boys and girls for dance and giving them discrete activities is best thought of as 'damage control'. That is, when a teacher is faced with an older group of boys who are unwilling to dance, then specific classes perceived by them to be 'manly' may well be a useful short-term solution. However, as Lehikoinen (1997:197) points out in his critique of teaching dance using the sex role theory, using 'a manly way of moving' to teach boys dance does nothing to resolve the fears and conflicts inherent in the boy's view of what it is to be male. At best, giving content-specific dance to 'boys-only' groups provides a temporary reassurance to a fragile masculinity. At worst, it merely perpetuates the expectation that boys and girls dance to a different drummer.

'WHEN ARE WE GOING TO DO SOME WORK?'

A ten-year-old student asked 'when are we going to do some work?' after being taken for what she acknowledged to be an exciting hour of drama, dance and discovery outside — all done with eyes closed. (The class was investigating sight and how it felt to be blind.) What the questioner wanted was for the children to get back to the classroom, sit at a desk and write about what had been experienced. To the student, writing was 'work', dance and drama were 'play', hence implicitly educationally inferior. Thus the second recommendation is that young children be given plenty of opportunity to play with movement, to improvise, to make dances of their own in order to reinforce the value of play as a purposeful, intelligent and legitimate mode of learning. The issue here is the balance between skill acquisition (dance technique, developing a choreographable body) and the 'playing with movement' inherent in dance improvisation and so essential to the choreographic art. 'It takes a lot of time to make art, that is, to ponder, to experiment with half baked ideas' said innovative choreographer Meryl Tankard (1996:14). She went on to make a plea for time to play, to deal with new thoughts. She cautioned that unless this was so 'we will be making dances but they will all be the same dance. It is not that they won't be properly finished, in fact they won't be at all commenced' (Tankard, 1996:14).

Far too much time may be being spent in early childhood and primary dance classes on acquiring and refining technique and on preparing for performance in school, regional or state dance festivals. The proliferation of festivals, shows, spectaculars and eisteddfods in recent times could attest to this. Such events allow the school to show the results of good technique; students can dance on stage and it can look impressive. It can also fulfil the political and economic demands that seek to raise a school's public profile. A neglect of play, improvisation and experimental dance-making can be seen in the difficulty many teachers have in teaching improvisation and composition; in the awkwardness and timidity experienced by mature dance students during improvisation classes in contrast to the focus and commitment of the typical *drama* student in the same classes; in the tendency of older dance students (when pushed to make dances) to rearrange previously acquired movements rather than to evolve something new and different, and in the relief with which secondary and tertiary dance students 'dance the same dance' in preference to pushing themselves beyond their comfort zone.

As the NSW K-12 Dance in Education statement (1982) and the draft NSW K-6 Creative Arts Syllabus (1998) make clear, the young child's initial dance experiences should be centred on the exploration and discovery of what their body can do alone and with others, and on the discovery of dynamics and space. Many dance in education texts contain suggestions that the young child should 'discover ... explore ... create ... experiment with' (Gough, 1993; Harrison, 1993; Lowden 1989; Spurgeon; 1991; Stinson, 1988). Of course, as the child enters upper primary and secondary school this playful exploration is complemented by the acquisition of skills and technique, so that after an ideal dance education a technically competent body is motivated by a playful, positive mind, eager to explore and experiment, and equally confident of being able to demonstrate newly discovered movements.

Strategies for implementing this second recommendation include the continued encouragement of the young child's inherently playful, exploratory nature at the same time as giving the child plenty of dance ideas and materials to play *with*, the gradual introduction of carefully selected dance technique as the child becomes older and the careful consideration of the appropriateness of young children performing dance for an audience. It is possible for a group of five year olds to perform a dance with skill and confidence, a dance that *they* have made, to music that *they* have chosen, at a time that *they* deem appropriate. It is unfortunately all too common to see a stage full of five year olds dressed as insects trying to remember what they have been told to do as their family and friends watch and applaud.

BOYS WILL BE BOYS BUT GIRLS WILL BE WOMEN

The current slogan 'boys will be boys but girls will be women' attests to one of the unfortunate results of a gender-specific education: the proposition that the sexist male adult has never reached emotional maturity, has never really grown up. Biddulph (1995:4) lists the basic, underlying problems of being male as 'loneliness, compulsive competition and lifelong emotional timidity'. This timidity is such that it could be seriously argued that some men may be emotional cripples, with that caring, feeling, nurturing part of their brains forever stunted. It is no wonder that these 'macho men' shun the dance class — an arena where feelings and caring should play an important part.

Most girls will be women but some dancing women try desperately to remain girls: permanently suspended in a prepubescent asceticism.

> Some dancers will walk away from their years of training with no more than a life-long neurosis about food and their bodies — invisible but disquieting emblematic victims of the ways in which eating disorders and unrealistic body images ruin women's lives (van Ulzen, 1994:10).

Many adverse effects of sexism have been well documented especially during the last few decades. This chapter argues that misguided expectations about what it is to be a man or a women, and specious assumptions about what women and men should do, be and look like, lie at the heart of dance education's problem of absent boys and anxious girls. The third recommendation is that teachers should do their utmost to counter sexism, to eschew gender-stereotypic behaviour and expectations and to provide young children with a supportive learning atmosphere in which *all* children are given stimuli and opportunities across the broad spectrum of curricula. The following strategies should assist with this recommendation.

Firstly, and most importantly, teachers of young children need to reassess their own gender expectations and assumptions. Sexism is so prevalent, and in some cases so deeply entrenched, that many dance educators remain unaware of their own behaviours and the hidden curriculum so unwittingly taught. Requests that the girls wash the paintbrushes while the boys carry the tape recorder, reminders that 'big boys don't cry' and that 'playing in the sand will dirty your clothes': praise for Ben's skilful dodging and Jenny's beautiful poise, and derogatory use of words such as 'tomboy' 'sissy' 'gossip' and 'wimp' all convey a clear unmistakable message: that boys should be one thing, girls another. Resources such as the Gender Equity Network (from the Department of Education, Employment, Training and Youth Affairs) can be of real assistance in guiding teachers towards a more equitable education.

Secondly, dance educators are urged to monitor and evaluate their own pedagogy. It is unfortunately all too common to witness primary children being spoken to as if they were permanently four years old (Spurgeon, 1988). This chapter argues that the typical nine-year-old boy and his independently minded female associates will be given a powerful disincentive to dance if they are given dance stimuli which they perceive to be inappropriate or demeaning, for example, to 'be gentle butterflies' or to 'make unhappy shapes'.

Thirdly, teachers are urged to ensure that their classroom (and if possible their school) has a realistic and positive fitness and sport program. At a time when an increasing number of children in industrialised Western societies are unfit or obese, mass sport (sports activities which are highly publicised, highly competitive, spectator oriented and commercially infrastructured) has assisted 'parents and teachers (in playing) a pretty mindless role in harping upon sporting enthusiasm as the only true badge of character' (Conway, 1992). Mass sport fits very neatly into the sociocultural landscape of Western sexism, with its emphasis on winning at all costs, on tacitly acknowledged violence and on acting like a 'real man', like 'one of the blokes' (McKay, 1992:25). An intelligently planned fitness program should 'develop and promote physical development and competence' across a 'broad and balanced syllabus'. It should also 'develop artistic and aesthetic understanding and help establish self esteem' (The Department of Education and Science, 1991:5). In early childhood and primary years there is no reason why a group of young girls and boys should not move effortlessly from learning a new gymnastic skill to practising their newly composed dance. From enjoying a swimming lesson it should be natural to want to explore and play with gravity via falls and jumps. Sport, gymnastics, dance, games should be fun, beneficial and accessible for *all* young children.

Perhaps the most difficult challenge is countering the sexist expectations and images propounded by some teachers, parents and media. It may be necessary for the teacher of young children to positively discriminate in order to counter parent-induced passion for competitive sport and suspicion of the arts. Media images can be so alluring and seemingly commonsensical that the aware teacher needs to counter with alternative, more balanced media inputs.

Sexism, and its effect on young children, is a complex topic. The brevity of this section is not meant to imply a simplistic approach; absent boys and anxious girls are symptoms of a much wider social disease, and a carefully planned, non-sexist, dance class will have little impact if the child's other school and home experiences are profoundly gender-stereotypic.

'I'VE FINISHED PAINTING THAT SONG: CAN I MAKE A DANCE ABOUT THUNDER?'

Teachers of dance to young children are usually in the enviable position of being with their children for most of the day. Unlike their colleagues in secondary and tertiary institutions, they can curtail or extend activities and, more importantly, they can integrate subjects in a very real way. Integration can take several forms and each has the potential to 'normalise' dance — to situate it among other subjects as a usual and legitimate way of learning about oneself and the world. Integration in this paper does not refer to the concept of the 'related arts', that hybrid so beloved of education systems seeking to cut costs. It refers to the following suggested ways in which a teacher can help the child see relationships, understand contexts, construct gestalts and place dance in a wider context.

A teacher can take a topic, idea or experience and encourage children to express and communicate their skills, knowledge and attitudes in a variety of ways. Provided that the child has been receiving the appropriate subject-specific input, even an activity such as a visit to the beach can provoke drawings, stories, pictures, dances, songs, equations and scientific experiments.

The varied meanings of a specific concept can be explored. For example 'directions' is an important topic in mathematics, geography, games, dance and ethics.

Another approach as suggested by the title of this section, involves using one particular art form or science phenomenon as a stimulus for another. For many children, painting 'speed' and moving 'blue' can be equally productive and satisfying. Children, more so than adults, are likely to respond to the vocabulary of one art form as a trigger to images in another.

Dance is not only a body of knowledge in its own right, but may also be used as a means to a better understanding of other subject areas. The reader is invited to consult Exiner and Lloyd (1987) and Spurgeon (1991) for examples of the many ways in which dance and movement can foster understanding across the curriculum.

Many other cultures do not categorise subject areas in the way that Western societies do. They already practise what we might call integration. For example, for some Aboriginal cultures dance is inseparable from the narrated story, and for many Polynesian societies to sing is to dance, to dance is to sing.

CONCLUSION

This chapter has sought to argue that, however unwittingly, many teachers of young children condone or ignore a classroom environment that, like its parent culture, presents dance as a discrete activity suitable primarily for obedient females. It has also endeavoured to argue a strong case for the power and effectiveness of certain strategies designed to counter the effect of this environment. The teacher of the young child is in a powerful and deservedly responsible position, sanctioned by educational authorities and implicitly seen as knowledgeable by a child. By presenting a full range of dance activities to all children in a variety of non-sexist contexts, the teacher can help children gain dance knowledge and understand that dance should help *all* of them to feel good about themselves and their bodies.

References

Adair, C. (1992) *Women and Dance.* London: Macmillan.
Biddulph, S. (1995) *Manhood.* Sydney: Finch Publishing.
Burt, R. (1995) *The Male Dancer.* London: Routledge.
Connell, R.W. (1995) *Masculinities.* Sydney: Allen and Unwin.
Conway, R. (1992) Sport, our national disease. *The Australian Weekend Review.*
Crawford, J.R. (1994) Encouraging male participation in dance. *Journal of Physical Education, Recreation and Dance,* **65**(2), 40–43.
Dempster, E. & Gardner, S. (1993) Thinking through feminism. *Writings on Dance,* **9** (special issue).

Department of Education and Science (1991) *Physical Education for Ages 5–16*. UK: National Curriculum Council.

Department of Education, NSW (1982) *K–12 Dance in Education Statement*. Sydney: Government Printer.

Department of Employment Education and Training (1992) *The Gen* (Gender Equity Network). Published by the Commonwealth by Susan Munter Communications.

Desmond, J.C. (ed.) (1997) *Meaning in Motion*. Durham and London: Duke University Press.

Exiner, J. and Lloyd, P. (1987) *Learning through Dance*. Melbourne: Oxford University Press.

Foster, S.L. (1995) *Choreographing History*. Bloomington and Indianapolis: Indiana University Press.

Gough, M. (1993) *In Touch with Dance*. Lancaster: Whitethorn.

Hanna, J.L. (1988) *Dance, Sex and Gender*. Chicago: University of Chicago Press.

Harrison, K. (1993) *Let's Dance*. London: Hodder and Stoughton.

Lehikoinen, K. (1997) Fragile masculinities and the sex role theory in dance for boys: A critical discourse. *Conference Proceedings of the Seventh International Conference of Dance and the Child International*. Kuopio, Finland, July 28–August 3, pp. 195–201.

Lowden, M. (1989) *Dancing to Learn*. London: Falmer Press.

McKay, J. (1992) Exercising hegemonic heterosexual masculinity: Sport and the social construction of genders. In *Society and Gender: An Introduction to Sociology*, edited by G. Lupton, T. Short & R. Whip. Sydney: MacMillan.

Meglin, J.A. (1994) Gender issues in dance education. *Journal of Physical Education, Recreation and Dance*, **65**(2), 26–7.

Morris, G. (ed.) (1996) *Moving Words*. London and New York: Routledge.

NSW Draft Creative Arts Syllabus (K–6) (1997). Sydney: NSW Board of Studies.

Plummer, K. (1995) The gender coding of modern dance: Its significance in the hidden curriculum of dance in education. MA Thesis, University of New South Wales.

Spurgeon, D. (1988) Imagery in dance education. *Conference Proceedings of Fourth International Conference of Dance and the Child International*, vol. 1. London: DaCi UK.

Spurgeon, D. (1991) *Dance Moves*. Sydney: Harcourt Brace Jovanovich.

Spurgeon, D. (1997) Keynote speech. Inaugural Ausdance Summer Forum, Sydney, January.

Stinson, S. (1988) *Dance for Young Children*. Reston, Virginia: AAHPERD.

Tankard, M. (1996) The fourth Ausdance Dame Peggy van Praagh Memorial address. *Ausdance Forum*, spring, 12–14.

Thomas, H. (1993) *Dance, Gender and Culture*. New York: St Martin's Press.

van Ulzen, K. (1994) Starved for success. *The Australian Weekend Review*, Jan. 29–30.

C H A P T E R

8

YOUNG CHILDREN TELLING IT LIKE IT IS

Insights for teachers

Jennifer Nicholls

In the past decade, there has been an increase in research relating to children's responses to theatre. The research includes investigations regarding children's dramatic literacy, 'theatrical sensibility' (Rosenblatt cited in Saldana & Otero, 1990), and understanding of characters' intentions and motives (Shantz, 1983). Klein and Fitch (1990) have studied children's abilities to recall non-linear plot structures and understand nonsensical characters, while Saldana (1996) has noted trends regarding young people's evaluative responses to theatre in the Arizona State University's longitudinal study of drama and theatre for children. How to measure children's aesthetic responses to theatre with semantic differential scales has occupied some researchers (Saldana & Otero, 1990; Cahill, 1991; Goldberg, 1977), while others, such as Saldana and Wright (1996), have given a useful overview of experimental research principles and analyses of common research tools, applicable to both qualitative and quantitative studies in drama and theatre for youth.

Research to date has concentrated on children's cognitive abilities in analysing plot structures, themes, characterisation, actions and emotional states. This study seeks to ascertain whether children can recognise various theatrical elements inherent in a production, and use them as signifiers for creating or enhancing the meaning of the play beyond the basic verbal narrative.

PURPOSE OF THE STUDY

The primary foci of the investigative study were (a) analysis of the diverse ways in which children create meaning for themselves within a theatrical production, and (b) to ascertain whether the choices the artists had made regarding theatrical elements had been recognised as signifiers by the children.

THE ROLE OF REM THEATRE

The REM Theatre Company, based in Sydney, is one of Australia's leading companies presenting theatre for children and young people. REM creates simple but strong theatrical productions that introduce children to stories drawn from many cultures and also to the elements that help create these stories in a theatrical context (Nicholls, 1996). This intelligent, sophisticated theatre allows children to draw widely on their own imagination and encourages children to create meaning for themselves by recognising theatrical signifiers within each performance. The theatrical production which was the vehicle for this study was *Changing into Animals* by the REM Theatre Company, presented at the Sydney Opera House in April 1996.

THE PRODUCTION

Changing into Animals is a simple story about a young girl called Becky who develops the power to change into animals whenever she wants to, and who uses this power to solve the mystery of her lost dog, Offenbach. By changing into animals, Becky is able to explore the forests, the skies, the caves and the sea, not to mention discovering what really lay below the mysterious crack in her bedroom floor. Essentially the play was depicted in a storytelling format. There were only two actors in the play, both male. The first actor not only narrated the story but also played the central role of Becky and numerous other characters throughout the story. The second actor was essentially the musician on stage, providing musical motifs and sound effects to accompany the action. Although not completely visible, the audience was certainly aware that he was making all the sounds which accompanied the action, and many children commented on his presence during the interviews. In addition to making music he played two characters: the Penguin, who was responsible for taking all the animals down the crack in the bedroom floor to rehearse the 'Big Song', and the nasty toad, who was not invited to sing.

The performance space (the Reception Hall of the Sydney Opera House) was small and intimate, and children were encouraged to sit on the floor quite close to the small raised platform area where the play occurred. Lighting was used throughout the performance and distinct states, such as night-time and daytime, as well as designated areas of light in the space, were created. Another visual effect used throughout the performance was slide projection. Sometimes the slides depicted actual animals and/or settings, such as a moth or a bird flying over the sea and rocks. Sometimes the slides were more abstract providing a suggested environment such as the inside of a cave or water. In this production, no props or character costumes were used.

BACKGROUND TO THE STUDY

The researcher spent a period of six weeks observing the creative process in the development and rehearsal of REM Theatre's production *Changing into Animals*. Extensive interviews were conducted with the actors, director, designer and composer, which highlighted the process each artist took in preparing for a production. By observing this developmental phase, the researcher noted the emergence of an integrated process, in which theatrical elements were constructed at the same time as the narrative.

For example, when introducing the character of the toad, a saxophone would be played to create a sound motif similar to the sound we associate with toads and frogs. Another example was when the central character ventured into the cave, a sequence of slides depicting an abstract cave effect was used. Thus the researcher grew familiar with the theatrical elements that would be incorporated into the production, and how those elements would be used to create layers of meaning or dramatic signifiers for the children in the audience. The researcher and director of the production were interested to see whether children would recognise dramatic signifiers and use these to enhance meaning.

The play used a number of theatrical elements which in effect became the signifiers for the story or narrative. These elements are shown in Table 7.1. These elements or signifiers formed the coding system that was developed by the researcher in conjunction with the theatre director for analysing children's responses to the production.

PROCEDURE FOR THE STUDY

The researcher and an assistant led focus group discussions with fifty-one children (aged 5 to 8 years) at the Sydney Opera House after the children had seen a performance of *Changing into Animals* over a period of three days.

Prior to each performance, an information sheet was distributed to adults, requesting child volunteers to participate in the focus groups, and informing adults of the purpose of the study. Parents signed a permission sheet and provided information regarding the child's name and age. The study targeted 5–8 year olds, but where requested permission was given for 4-year-old siblings to take part in the focus groups. Some of the most interesting and succinct comments came from these few 4 year olds eventually included in the study.

At the conclusion of each performance, the participants assembled in the foyer area, were allocated to one of two focus groups and moved to different places in the space for the interviews. There were 7 focus groups in total. The children were interviewed in groups of five to seven and asked a series of questions relating to their understanding and appreciation of the play. All interviews were audiotaped. The children and the interviewer sat on the floor in a circle. At the beginning of the interview, the children stated their names and ages. Each child wore a name tag which enabled the interviewers to identify the children as they responded to the questions, and provided identification for later transcribing of data.

On the day prior to the first focus group sessions, the questions developed by the researcher and director had been trialled with two children, to ensure that the wording and sequencing of the questions were clear and to ascertain responses likely to be elicited.

Table 7.1 Theatrical elements

Elements	Signifier	Signifier abbreviation
Narrated story or text	TEXT	(t)
Character's actions	ACTION	(a)
Lighting effects/projected slides	IMAGE	(i)
Sound and music effects	SOUND	(s)

RESPONSE MEASURES

Each focus group was asked the following questions by the researcher and assistant using the same order of questioning.

1. If we were to draw a picture of the play that you have seen this morning what would we put in the picture? (For these responses the children's answers were drawn on large butcher's paper so we had a pictorial representation of responses in addition to the audiotaped recording. This was designed as a positive introduction to the focus group process and allowed the children to feel that their answers were valued.)
2. Where did Becky go in the story?
3. How did you know where Becky went in the story?
4. What animals did Becky change into?
5. How did you know what animals Becky changed into?

This formed part of a larger study where children were also asked questions about their favourite moment in the play, least favourite aspect, and whether they could identify some of the musical sounds. They also had an opportunity to add anything else they wished to about the performance. Although data was collated on all questions, the present study focuses on children's responses to the five questions listed above.

CODING AND DATA ANALYSIS

Two basic approaches to analysing focus group data are a qualitative or ethnographic summary, and systematic coding using content analysis. Morgan described the two approaches as follows:

> The principal difference is that the ethnographic approach relies more on direct quotation of the group discussion, while the content analysis typically produces numerical descriptions of the data. A largely ethnographic approach may benefit from a systematic tallying of one or two key topics, while a basically quantitative summary of the data is improved immensely by including quotes that demonstrate the points being made (1988:64).

This paper will reflect both approaches in the analysis. For the ethnographic analyses, the researcher transcribed the audio tapes at the conclusion of the focus group sessions and coded the responses according to the categories agreed to by the researcher and director. For the content analysis the frequency of responses in each category, as identified from the transcription coding, was calculated within each group, as was the average across the groups. This decision to use the group rather than the individual as unit of analysis was taken due to the multiplicative nature of focus group methodology whereby participants may be influenced by the responses of other group members (Morgan, 1988).

The following section provides an excerpt from a transcription of one of the focus group interviews, as an illustration of both the protocol followed by each interviewer, and the quality of child responses. After each response a code was assigned corresponding to the system established from the rehearsal process ('t' for text, 'a' for action, 'i' for image and 's' for sound). This transcription indicates the range of children's free responses and shows the coding system on the right-hand side of the transcript in line with the child's response.

EXCERPT FROM TRANSCRIPTION OF FOCUS GROUP NO. 3

Participants were: Nicholas (7 yrs), Eric (4 yrs), Chloe (8 yrs), Adrienne (7 yrs), Nicola (6 yrs) and Julia (5 yrs)

Key: Focus question (FQ); Response (R); Subsidiary question (SQ)

FQ:	*Where does Becky go in the story?*	
R	Chloe: Down the crack.	
FQ:	*How did you know there was a crack?*	
R	Eric: They told us at the beginning.	(t)
	Nicholas: On those there ... (pointing to screens) you could see these things ... that looked like you went inside the floor.	(i)
	Eric: There was all these colours in the crack and he put this belt on to pretend he was a turtle.	(i/a)
SQ:	*Where else did Becky go in the story?*	
R:	Nicholas - Over the seas and the fields.	
SQ:	*How did you know it was a sea?*	
R:	Eric: They told us.	(t)
	Chloe: There were some sound effects.	(s)
SQ:	*Can you remember what the sound effects were?*	
R:	Chloe: I think it was the waves.	
SQ:	*How else did you know she was at the sea?*	
R:	Julia: You heard some whale sounds.	(s)
	Adrienne: You could see pictures of the sea and the moonlight and colours on them.	(i)
SQ:	*Where else does she go in the story?*	
R:	Nicola: She goes near the forest.	
FQ:	*How did you know it was a forest?*	
R:	Nicola: Because they had pictures.	(i)
SQ:	*What were the pictures of?*	
R:	Julia: Lots of green and trees.	(i)
FQ:	*What does Becky change into in the play?*	
R:	Nicholas: a cricket,	
	Chloe: a elephant,	
	Adrienne: a moth	
FQ:	*Let's start with the moth. How do you know she was a moth?*	
R:	Adrienne: She flies.	(a)
	Nicholas: There's a picture of a moth.	(i)
	Eric: She opened up the music box.	(a)
	Nicola: She opened up the music box and wished and then all the	

colours and the man twirled around and pretended to be a moth. (a/i)

Adrienne: She turns around and becomes whatever animal she
wishes. Like if she wanted to be a cat, all the colours would come
and the man would turn around and pretend he was a cat. (a/i)

FQ: *What else does Becky change into?*
R: Nicholas: A bird.

FQ: *How did you know she became a bird?*
R: Nicholas: There was a picture of a bird and also it sounded a bit
like a bird. They had sound effects all through, like "caw caw". It
sounded like a raven. (i/s)
Adrienne: She also changed into a dog.

SQ: *How do you know she was a dog?*
R: Eric: He said that I wish I could be a dog so I could sniff like a dog. (t)
Adrienne: You heard her barking. (s)

RESULTS

Ethnographic analysis

When recalling the events of the play, some children's first point of reference was remembering what was said by either the narrator or by one of the characters. Some children clearly recalled the actions of the various characters. Other children were relying on the visual images on the screen as their point of reference to locate the narrative in particular settings. Some children recognised and recalled the sound effects and the musical motifs used to depict characters, animals and settings.

Typical responses for text, action, image and sound were as follows:

Text

- Because they told us.
- They said over the rocks and over the waves.
- Because it told us in the story.
- The little girl told us.
- She said she wanted to change into a bird.

Action

- She threw up a web onto a rock and climbed up it.
- Because she flew into the cave to get all the animals back.
- She opened up the music box and wished and then all the colours and the man twirled around and pretended to be a moth.

Image

- They told us on the screen. They showed pictures of the toad and the cave and the pool.
- On the little screen there you could see rocks and the water.
- Because you could see her swimming on the screen.
- You could see pictures of the sea and the moonlight and colours on them.

Sound

- You heard some whale sounds.
- There were some sound effects.
- I think I heard the waves.
- They had sound effects all through like 'caw caw'. It sounded like a raven.

Some children used a combination of theatrical elements when reconstructing the story as follows:

- Because they said she was a moth and there was a picture of a moth, and the light.
- The picture and the narrator. Because the magic box changed her into a bird.

It is interesting to note the diversity of comments from the respondents when discussing each of the theatrical elements. While many statements, not surprisingly, reflect straightforward recognition of images, actions and sounds, some more complex and sophisticated analytical statements demonstrate interesting processes of deconstruction not normally expected from children of this age group. Furthermore these comments would indicate that children are capable of recognising and utilising theatrical signifiers within a drama experience, and would generally be able to construct a dramatic story from a range of theatrical elements.

Content analysis

The frequency with which the children identified theatrical elements in response to questions 3 and 5 is shown in Tables 7.2 and 7.3 below. Clearly image was the most commonly recalled signifier overall in responses to both focus questions, although the margin is much greater for the first than the second. Figures 7.1 and 7.2 depict the overall results of the content analysis, and clearly demonstrate image responses outweighing other theatrical elements.

Table 7.2 Group responses to Q.3, How did you know where Becky went in the story?

	text (%)	image (%)	action (%)	sound (%)	total responses (n)
group 1 (n=6)	26.7	46.7	13.3	6.7	15
group 2 (n=7)	0.0	100.0	0.0	0.0	4
group 3 (n=6)	25.0	50.0	0.0	25.0	8
group 4 (n=4)	33.3	16.7	50.0	0.0	6
group 5 (n=6)	0.0	28.6	14.3	57.1	7
group 6 (n=7)	30.0	50.0	20.0	0.0	10
group 7 (n=7)	36.4	54.5	9.1	0.0	11
group 8 (n=8)	33.3	33.3	25.0	8.3	12
average across groups (N=51)	23.1	72.1	16.5	12.1	73

Table 7.3 Group responses to Q.5, How did you know what animals Becky changes into?

	text (%)	image (%)	action (%)	sound (%)	total responses (n)
group 1 (n=6)	25.0	41.7	12.5	0.0	8
group 2 (n=7)	44.4	11.1	44.4	0.0	9
group 3 (n=6)	18.2	45.5	27.3	9.1	11
group 4 (n=4)	0.0	0.0	50.0	50.0	2
group 5 (n=6)	0.0	33.3	0.0	66.7	3
group 6 (n=7)	11.1	44.4	33.3	11.1	9
group 7 (n=7)	0.0	66.7	33.3	0.0	3
group 8 (n=8)	28.6	42.9	14.3	14.3	7
average across groups (N=51)	15.9	35.7	26.9	18.9	52

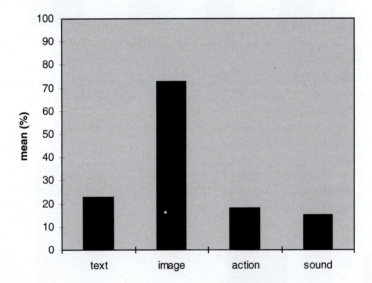

Figure 7.1 Summary of content analysis of Q.3 (How do you know where Becky went in the story?)

When asked to respond to question 1, 'If we were to draw a picture of the play that you have seen this morning, what would you put in the picture?' children's responses fell into two categories. The first category, 'depicted', delineates those elements that were actually represented in the play through slides or characterisation, such as the toad or the bird. The second category, 'imaginary', delineates those elements that children recalled that were not represented through visual effects or characterisation, such as Becky's parents, and the crack in the bedroom floor. These elements were generally only mentioned briefly as part of the general narrative, or occasionally mimed by one of the actors. The results are presented in Figure 7.3, and it is interesting to note that the 'imaginary' category is significantly higher than the 'depicted' category.

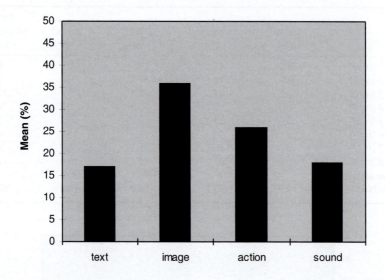

Figure 7.2 Summary of content analysis of Q.5, How do you know what animals Becky changes into?

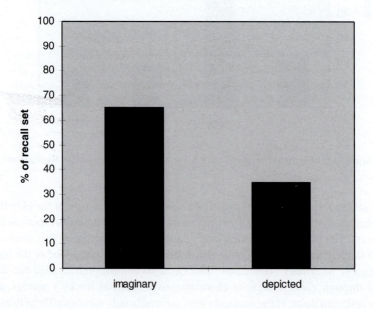

Figure 7.3 Summary of content analysis of 'If we draw a picture of the play, what would you put in the picture?'.

DISCUSSION

It is interesting to note that visual image-based responses were quite high in both questions (i.e. 3 & 5) particularly as many of the slides shown during the performance were an abstract representation of a place rather than a picture of a real place. Even though the story was told very clearly with simple text and plenty of actions, many children still relied on a visual image as their strongest point of reference to create meaning for themselves within the context of the performance.

Although reference to image was consistently high in response to both questions 3 and 5, the margin by which this was the case varied. An explanation for this may have been that in the course of the play, when Becky changed into animals, not only was there usually an image-based slide sequence depicting the animals, but the actions and sounds of the various animals occurred simultaneously with the slides. Though sound effects often accompanied a slide sequence depicting a place, they were not as readily identified as a signifier compared to the sounds and actions of animals that were identified as signifiers by the respondents.

Another interesting points to note is the fact that in many instances the images recalled were purely imaginary, and the children were obviously using their imagination to reconstruct a place, event or character.

When looking at the first question, 'If we draw a picture of the play ... what would we put in the picture?', 65% of the images and objects recalled are imaginary (Refer Figure 7.3). There were no props in the play, the actors did not wear character or animal costumes, and many of the images the children recalled were not depicted on the screen through the use of slides. They were either only briefly referred to or in some instances, such as with the crack in the bedroom floor and the music box, they are mimed. In the latter case, the actors set up a convention or ritualised movement sequence to signify the event or object, and they often returned to this a number of times throughout the play. The music box was an important element in the play's development because it was only when the music box was opened that Becky could change into an animal of her choice. The music box, then, was an interesting example of creating a powerful image in the imagination of the children. A number of theatrical conventions were utilised to create the imaginary music box:

- the actor moved to a particular stage area each time the music box was to be used,
- a particular lighting state was created,
- the actor mimed the opening of the music box,
- a particular musical motif was heard each time the actor approached the music box, and another each time the music box was opened.

This theatrical sequence of events created not only the image of the music box, but also the magic associated with it. This was highly successful, and arguably more meaningful to the audience than had a real one been used. This was an example of children clearly creating meaning for themselves, based on the theatrical signposts that were presented to them.

Q. Tell me about the music box. Where was it? How did you know it was a music box?

- It was over there in front of the curtain. (pointing to the place on the stage)
- It was in that white light spot down the front.

• Becky made a wish and then opened the music box and then she became a dog.
• It had music coming out of it when she opened the lid.

These sample responses clearly demonstrate that the young children interviewed were able to understand the concept of convention by:

• recognising the same location on the stage where the music box 'lived',
• recognising the musical motif that accompanied the music box being opened,
• realising that the lighting change helped locate the music box in a particular part of Becky's room,
• identifying the repeated sequence of events.

In the production and as part of the narrative, Becky was sometimes not sure whether she really had changed into an animal or whether it had been a dream. In these instances she returned to the music box where, on two separate occasions, she discovered a white feather, and a tiger's whisker sitting on top on the box. The music box, the feather and the whisker were completely imaginary. This had particular significance for a number of children as indicated by the following responses:

What was the best part of the play?

Eric: When it wasn't a dream. He just found a whisker and a feather on the music box and it wasn't a dream.
Marco: When she saw the gold tiger's whisker and the white feather.

Why was that your favourite part?

Marco: Because it wasn't a dream, it was real.
Elizabeth: Because when she thought it was a dream she always went over to the music box and the first time there was a golden tiger's whisker and the second time there was a bird's feather from a chook I think.

CONCLUSION

The results of this study were affirming for the artistic team responsible for *Changing into Animals*. It was reassuring for them to know that the theatrical elements they chose to incorporate into this production were interpreted appropriately by the young audiences and used as signifiers to help identify the various locations or settings, recognise the range of characters, and generally follow the events and actions that occurred. The study also demonstrated that elements of theatre can be used in simple ways to create a world that is entirely abstract yet very real in the imaginations of children.

IMPLICATIONS FOR TEACHING

Even the simplest drama created in the classroom can be enhanced in meaning by incorporating theatrical elements, and particularly by allowing children to make decisions about such aspects as music, costumes, props, use of space, sound effects, lighting and other visual effects, and the use of ritual and convention.

There has been much debate surrounding the dichotomy between the teaching of drama, and theatre in the classroom. In his important book, *Education and Dramatic Art,* Hornbrook (1989) discussed the problems associated with differentiating between the teaching of drama as an art form, and drama as a teaching methodology. He noted that dramatic art was a rich resource for creative exploration for children of all ages.

> The dramatic art curriculum offers opportunities for pupils and students at all levels to explore the expressive potential of theatre, as performers possibly, but equally as writers, designers, directors, technicians, *animateurs* and experimenters (Hornbrook, 1989:131).

One of the limitations of classroom drama, particularly with a teacher in role and a process drama format, is that it relies heavily on a verbal narrative, for example 'What shall we make a play about?' or 'What will happen if we go into the cave?' This study supports the view that not all children engage in or interpret drama through verbal cues, and although the analysis centres around the child as audience, the evidence would suggest that the child as a participator in the drama may not necessarily engage in the meaning of the drama through verbal, or text-based signifiers alone.

Incorporating theatrical elements or production techniques into classroom drama need not be an elaborate or costly proposition. It is cheaper to have an imaginary music box than a real one! Teachers should recognise the potential of theatrical signposts for creating meaning within a drama, and most importantly that text or narrative is only one potential signifier. This study and others show that not all children create meaning for themselves from verbal beginnings.

When making or devising dramatic stories with children, teachers should be encouraged to utilise theatrical elements. These elements should not necessarily be seen as an adjunct to the drama or a quick add-on at the end of a drama experience. Theatrical elements should be recognised and acknowledged from inception as integral to the narrative. As such, they should be incorporated and developed throughout the drama-making process. By introducing children to the elements of theatre as audience members and drama makers they are developing not only their cognitive abilities but their aesthetic abilities as well.

Goldberg (1985) believed that every human being should be offered aesthetic development as part of the education process. This development can be achieved by exposing children to arts techniques to teach them the vocabulary of making art, and by introducing children to arts processes through participatory experiences which exercise and develop cognition and aesthetic appreciation.

SOME PRACTICAL APPLICATIONS FOR TEACHERS

Some examples of theatrical elements that may be easily incorporated into a classroom drama situation are:

• When exploring through drama a topic such as life under the sea, teachers can provide children with the opportunity to create and play music and sound effects to enhance the setting of an underwater sea adventure.

- When making a drama about being trapped in an elevator, children can create the elevator by manipulating and reducing the space, using corners of the room and tables. By creatively utilising space the reality of a drama situation may well be intensified for those involved.

- Place curtains or black plastic over the windows to create a semi-blackout. Turn off the lights and shine torches on the ceiling. How might this impact on a drama experience about space travel? What can flashing torch lights represent? Stars? Planets?

- Use slides from holiday destinations to create simple backdrops on classroom walls. When dramatising the well-known children's story *We're Going on a Bear Hunt,* encourage children to create maps, and then design the indoor and outdoor environments according to the maps. Investigate simple but imaginative ways to represent a mountain, a river, a forest, or a cave.

- A basket of scarves can instantly be a range of simple costumes, a picnic table, a rowing boat or rockpools at the seaside.

- Recreate a deserted house by lighting imaginary candles, moving though thick cobwebs, making the sound of the creaky floorboards, and throwing old sheets over the tables and chairs, thus looking at the role of convention and ritual in drama.

SUMMARY

Children not only enjoy the power of theatre but are capable of deconstructing and recognising its signposts. Consequently they are also capable of investigating the elements of theatre and creating signifiers within the drama process. The elements of theatre are a rich resource not only for theatrical practitioners but also for educators. To ignore the theatricality of drama within the classroom is to deny children the rich historical and artistic heritage that is inherent in the artform. Its sources are limited only in so far as is one's imagination. It is time for teachers to acknowledge the power of theatre and recognise its place in classroom drama.

Acknowledgment

Thanks to Ms Helen Watt, research methodologist at the Institute of Early Childhood, Macquarie University, for her assistance with this study.

References

Cahill, C. (1991) An empirical study of proposed systems for measuring responses of children to theatre for young audiences. Unpublished dissertation, Southern Illinois University at Carbondale.

Goldberg, M. (1985) Aesthetic development: A position paper. *Children's Theatre Review,* **34**(1), 3–6.

Goldberg, P. (1977) Development of a category system for the analysis of the response of the young theatre audience. Unpublished dissertation, Florida State University.

Hornbrook, D. (1989) *Education and dramatic art.* Great Britain: Blackwell Publications.

Klein, J. & Fitch, M. (1990) First-grade children's comprehension of "Noodle Doodle Box", *Youth Theatre Journal*, **5**(2), 53–67.

Morgan, D. (1988) *Focus Groups as Qualitative Research.* USA: Sage Publications.

Nicholls, J. (1996) New directions in theatre for young people: A report on the recent work of REM Theatre in Sydney. In *Issues in Expressive Arts: Curriculum for Early Childhood,* edited by W. Schiller, pp. 23–30. Amsterdam: Gordon & Breach Publishers

Rosen, M. (1989) *We're Going on a Bear Hunt.* London: Walker.

Saldana, J. (1996) Significant differences in child audience response: Assertions from the ASU longitudinal study, *Youth Theatre Journal,* **10,** 67–83.

Saldana, J. & Otero, H. (1990) Experiments in assessing children's responses to theatre with the semantic differential, *Youth Theatre Journal,* **5**(1), 11–19.

Saldana, J. & Wright L. (1996) An overview of experimental research principles for studies in drama and theatre for youth. In *Researching Drama and Arts Education.* edited by P. Taylor, pp. 115–131. London: Falmer Press.

Shamdasani, P. and Stewart. D. (1990) *Focus Groups Theory and Practice.* USA: Sage.

Shantz, C.U. (1983) Social Cognition. In *Handbook of Psychology* (4th edn), edited by J. Flavell and E. Markham , pp. 495–555. NY: Wiley.

NURSERY RHYMES

Everything old is new again

Kathlyn Griffith

Included in a publication on children's literature (*Children's Literature Briefly*, Jacobs & Tunnell, 1996) is a table headed 'History and Trends Chronology'. Most of what is there is to be expected: the *Orbis Pictus*, Perrault's *Mother Goose, Household Tales, Alice's Adventures in Wonderland, The Tale of Peter Rabbit.* What is missing, however, is any mention of the oldest existing collection of what we now know as nursery rhymes, Mary Cooper's publication of *Tommy Thumb's Pretty Songbook Volume 11.* Is this omission indicative of the value people place today on nursery rhymes?

There is no doubt that at the beginning of the new millennium there are some who would question the relevance and value of nursery rhymes to children in the 21st century. Of what possible interest could a riddle about an egg sitting on a wall be? In a climate of debate about the future of the monarchy what point is there in reading rhymes that feature kings sitting in counting houses or queens baking tarts, or a Duke of York commanding ten thousand men? In these politically correct times how could society countenance such rhymes as one which has as its subject matter a man who keeps his wife in a pumpkin shell, one which features on old woman whipping her children, or one that has as its central character a person called Simple Simon?

Despite these doubts, anthologies of rhymes continue to be published, as do books which feature a single rhyme in picture book format. Go into any bookshop or bookseller, whether this be the local newsagency, specialist children's bookshop or supermarket, and it would be unusual not to find a volume of nursery rhymes or *Mother Goose* on the shelves. There is also no shortage of ways in which these rhymes are packaged to appeal and sell to an audience that is assumed to value them. There is always something new; always something to entice an audience already familiar with the rhymes but who perhaps crave difference and surprise, or to appeal to a new audience, one that has yet to encounter rhymes in their printed form. There can be no doubt that publishers see these rhymes as viable commodities. There is clearly a market for their continued production, a market created in part by their constant presence in our daily lives.

There are few adults who would fail to encounter aspects of rhymes in their normal activities. Nursery rhyme characters appear on greeting cards and wrapping paper, in television and print advertising; they often appear as a focus for political cartoons, satire or parody. An egg-shaped politician balancing precariously on a wall is an image often used in newspaper or magazine cartoons when elections are imminent. Nursery rhymes are alive in our culture. They are used as reference points for political, social and cultural comments. Inherent in their ubiquity in the commercial and political worlds is the expectation that they are 'known', that they will have an impact because the audience will be familiar with them. Lynn (1985:3) claims that 'Nursery rhymes are an overfamiliar phenomenon' and that knowledge of them is taken for granted. If this is the case then there is an implied assumption that they will continue to be shown and taught to each new generation.

This assumption of familiarity lies behind much of what is published today, and it can take many forms. The most obvious is in the production of new anthologies packaged for adults to buy for young children. These often have titles which highlight a particular well-known rhyme (e.g. *Jack and Jill: A Book of Nursery Rhymes*), or covers which feature characters from familiar rhymes (e.g. *The Orchard Book of Nursery Rhymes*). Such covers and titles jog the memory of the adult buyer who feels some obligation and responsibility to pass these on to the younger generation.

This assumption also underlies the writing of 'new' rhymes which put the form and rhythmic patterns of the original rhyme to another use. Again, no matter what the age of the reader or listener, recognition of the familiar occurs. This is the case with some of Dennis Lee's poems (1983), which clearly and humorously play with the prototypes, as in the following examples.

Little Miss Dimble

Little Miss Dimble
Lived in a Thimble,
Slept in a measuring spoon.
She met a mosquito
And called him my "Sweet-0",
And married him under the moon (p. 9) .

There Was An Old Lady

There was an old lady
Whose kitchen was bare,
So she called for the cat
Saying, "time for some air!"

She sent him to buy her
A packet of cheese.
But the cat hurried back
With a basket of bees

She sent him to buy her
A gallon of juice.
But the cat reappeared
With a galloping goose.

> She sent him to buy her
> A dinner of beef.
> But the cat scampered home
> With an Indian chief.
>
> She sent him to buy her
> A bowl of ice cream.
> But the cat skated in
> With a whole hockey team.
>
> She sent him to buy her
> A bite of spaghetti.
> But the cat strutted up
> With a bread and confetti.
>
> She sent him to buy her
> A fine cup of tea.
> But the cat waddled back
> With a dinosaur's knee.
>
> The fridge was soon bulging,
> And so was the shelf.
> So she sent for a hot dog
> And ate it herself (pp. 15–16).

Other uses are also made of such rhymes, which ensures their continued viability. In a recent publication, *The House that Crack Built* (Taylor, 1992), the nursery rhyme, 'The House that Jack Built' has been transformed 'into a powerful poem about the tragic problem of illegal drugs and all its victims' (book cover notes).

The opening line, 'This is the house that Jack built', has been changed to read 'This is the house that crack built' and the transformation continues as the highly recognisable cumulative pattern of the original rhyme is used to depict 'cocaine's journey ... from beginning to end' (book cover notes). The final page serves as a clear illustration of this journey.

> And these are the tears we cry in our sleep.
> That fall for the Baby with nothing to eat,
> born of the Girl who's killing her brain,
> smoking the Crack that numbs the pain,
> brought from the Boy feeling the heat,
> chased by the Cop working his beat
> who battles the Gang, fleet and elite,
> That rules the Street of a town in pain
> That cries for the Drug known as cocaine,
> made from the Plants that people can't eat,
> raised by the Farmers who work in the heat
> and fear the Soldiers who guard the Man
> who lives in the House that crack built.

In a 1996 reprint of a 1969 book *The Inner City Mother Goose,* it is clear that the author, Eve Merriam, has used the rhymes in a similar fashion, rewriting the original to create poems that convey powerful social comments, such as those in the examples below.

Jack Be Nimble

Jack be nimble
Jack be quick
Snap the blade
And give it a flick.

Grab the purse
It's easily done
Then just for kicks
Just for fun
Plunge the knife
And cut
And run ... (p. 21)

Solomon Grundy

Solomon Grundy
Born on Slumday ...
...This is the end
Of Solomon Grundy (p. 64)

Both books were written specifically for young adults (although the cover notes for *The House that Crack Built* claim that 'it is also accessible for even very young children'), who, it is assumed, know the original rhyme first heard as a baby or young child. These publications are clear examples of the way the rhymes can be used to say something new about the way we live. The fact that the content is based on a familiar rhyme, from a genre that is usually reserved for children, has a great deal to do with the impact of the 'transformed' versions. Readers are lulled into believing that they are going to hear something known, playful and quite innocuous but that is far from the truth. It is what makes these versions so powerful, so shocking; it is what makes them old and new at the same time.

Other 'new versions' of rhymes have been written to convey other messages about the times we live in. *Father Gander Nursery Rhymes: The Equal Rhymes Amendment,* most recently reprinted in 1995 to celebrate its tenth anniversary, is clear in its intention. Based on the premise that nursery rhymes can be used as a socialising force, the versions attempt to convey the message that adults have a responsibility 'to reinforce the message to our children that their own talents and the development of them will decide their success in life, not their skin colour' (book cover notes). To avoid children being exposed to the violence, sexism and racism inherent in many of the traditional rhymes the author (Doug Larche) has rewritten the rhymes to convey the messages of 'work, love and ethics' (book cover notes) as in the examples below:

Jack and Jill be Nimble

Jack be nimble, Jack be quick,
Jack jump over the candlestick!

Jill be nimble, jump it too,
If Jack can do it, so can you! (p. 8)

Ms Muffet & Friend

Little Ms Muffet sat on a tuffet
Eating her curds and whey
Along came a spider and sat down beside her
And she put it in the garden to catch insects (p. 42).

In a similar vein Loomans, Kolber and Loomans (1995) have written *Positively Mother Goose* which contains 'refreshing new version(s) of the traditional rhymes, promoting the values of self-esteem, conflict resolution, lifelong learning and innovative thinking' (book cover notes). Here are two examples:

Little Miss Muffet

Little Miss Muffet sat on a tuffet,
Eating her curds and whey;
Along came a spider, who sat down beside her,
And brightened Miss Muffet's whole day.

Solomon Grundy

Solomon Grundy, born on a Monday,
Looked on Tuesday, listened on Wednesday,
Learned on Thursday, loved on Friday,
Laughed on Saturday, leaped on Sunday.
This is the start of Solomon Grundy.

(Humpty Dumpty, in the light of the intentions of this book as described above, is fittingly illustrated as a jigsaw puzzle.)

Humpty Dumpty sat on a wall,
Humpty Dumpty had a great fall,
All the king's horses and all the king's men
helped to put Humpty together again.

Decker in *The Christian Mother Goose Big Book* (1992) has also attempted to use the rhymes to promote particular values. She has re-written the rhymes 'to lead little children everywhere, to know Him, the Author of the greatest Once upon a time ... story every told' (p. 300). Here are some examples of her rhymes:

Humpty Dumpty

Humpty Dumpty sat on a wall,
Humpty Dumpty had a great fall,
Humpty Dumpty shouted, "Amen!
God can put me together again." (p. 12)

Little Miss Muffet

Little Miss Muffet
Sat on a tuffet,
Thanking Jesus for curds and whey,
There came a big spider
And sat down beside her,
To listen to Miss Muffet pray.

She said ...
"Thank you, Lord Jesus,
For good things to eat.
For berries and nuts
And apples, so sweet.

I really can't see
How you feed this big world,
The lions and tigers
And pigs with tails curled.
The puppies and rabbits,
The birds in the air,
The horses and cows,
You give them a fair share.
The sheep and the cats
On your food they dine,
So thank you Lord Jesus,
For my kitty's food and mine."

Little Miss Muffet
Sat on a tuffet,
Thanking Jesus
For curds and whey;
And then that big spider
Who listened beside her,
Knelt down with Miss Muffet to pray (pp. 77–78).

In contrast to these explicitly didactic versions that are clear in their intention to socialise according to the authors' beliefs are those rhymes which have been re-shaped to offer a humorous comment on an aspect of contemporary society. This is clearly the case in John Yeoman and Quenton Blake's version of The House that Jack Built, *The Do-It-Yourself House that Jack Built* (1994). In this lighthearted interpretation of the original rhyme the additional text and the illustrations explore the current fascination of do-it-yourself building.

While the original text is recorded on the left hand page, the right-hand page has the characters extending the meaning visually and verbally in a dramatic recreation and re-shaping of the rhyme.

Nursery rhymes continue to be used to transmit messages about the culture we live in and that, in part, is why they continue to endure. And yet it is not the only reason. In the versions described above it is clear that the words matter. The audience is expected to make sense of the language, to understand the meaning and significance of what is being said. Whitehead (1993:45) talks of nursery rhymes working in ways 'which constantly leave the text open to questions, manipulations and re-working.' Each of the authors of the re-worked versions discussed above have used these characteristics of the rhymes to suit their own purposes. In Merriam's, Decker's and Taylor's versions is the sense that their 'manipulations' have produced versions that make unambiguous statements about culture and society, and there is perhaps an underlying assumption that these are definitive versions that offer a version of truth that is not open to question. There are some critics, however, who place little value on the meaning of the words and who fear the outcomes of relying too heavily on nursery rhymes to 'make sense'.

Nodelman (1996:194) in his discussion on nursery rhymes says '... what matters about "Humpty Dumpty" is less what it means than *how it says what it means*: the sounds of the words and the pictures they evoke rather than simple ideas about eggs or violent death that the words express.' This might well be true for those rhymes that are told to the very young in what Lynn (1985:9) has described as 'tightly circumscribed domestic environment(s)'. In such conditions, if the sense mattered, would anyone put a baby to sleep saying Rock-a-bye Baby, in which the cradle 'and all' falls out of the tree? Would anyone who was attempting to convey to children the importance of caring for animals sing Three Blind Mice?

For the very young child the sense is far less important than the sounds, the patterned language, the predictable rhythm and rhyme and the engaging character names. It is far less important than the interactive nature of the experience, in which adult and child share literature in playful, enjoyable circumstances.

It is not long, however, before the words, and the meaning or meanings generated by them, do matter. While not completely agreeing with Delamar (1987:23) who talks about 'the importance for these verses as part of early school training', or with Whitehead (1993:45) who argues against using '... the potentially most uncontrollable and wildly subversive of all literary genres' for 'controlled reading instruction', there can be little doubt that these rhymes can play an important role in the growth and nurturance of children's literacy skills.

References to nursery rhymes occur in many texts that children encounter in their before-school and school years. Recognising what the words say and, more importantly, what they mean matters. Maureen Roffey's *Let's Go* uses phrases from rhymes she clearly assumes children are familiar with:

> Let's go
> pat-a-cake
> pat-a-cake
> Let's go
> rock-a-bye
> baby

John Prater in his books *Once Upon a Time* and *Once Upon a Picnic* uses nursery rhyme characters in the visual and verbal texts to advance the action: 'There's an egg with a happy smile'. The narrative in each would lose much of its impact without knowledge of the rhymes to which references are made. It is more than just recognition of the characters, it is knowing the context in which they first appeared that matters here.

The success of Toni Goffe's *Mother Gooseville Stories* also depends on the audience knowing its nursery rhymes well if it is to make sense of them in the texts in which they now appear. These are stories for children who are competent readers and for whom the recognition of familiar rhymes brings pleasure and reading success. These books would lose much of their impact, humour and irony if readers were unaware of their complex intertextuality.

Research carried out over the past ten years has confirmed that knowledge of nursery rhymes has been linked to literacy success. Bradley and Bryant (1983, 1985) and Bryant, Bradley, Maclean and Crossland (1989, 1990) have demonstrated the strong link between knowledge of nursery rhymes and aspects of learning how to read. 'Children who play with rhyme not only break up words into a beginning and a rhyming part, but they also see that words that rhyme belong together in some way' (Clay, 1990). There is then a clear link between nursery rhymes and developing literacy skills.

Recognition of the value of nursery rhymes as early reading material is not new. There is considerable evidence to suggest that they have been used as reading material for centuries. In 1789 a book (by Tom Thumb, a Lover of Children) was published, the title of which was: *Reading Made Quite Easy and Diverting, Containing Symbolic Cuts for the Alphabet, Tables of Words of one, two, three and four syllables, with easy lessons from the Scriptures ... instructive fables and edifying Pieces of Poetry, with songs moral and devine ... with several entertaining Stories, Proverbs, Moral Sayings, Riddles ...*Significant here is the fact that this volume contained a group of what we now refer to as nursery rhymes, entitled 'Pretty Songs and Stories for Young Masters and Misses'.

In 1820 a small book was published entitled: *The Life and Death of Jenny Wren for the use of Young Ladies and Gentlemen Being A very small book at a very small charge To learn them to read, Before they grow large*.

Despite Whitehead's serious and very real concerns about the inappropriate use of nursery rhymes as a 'reading readiness resource' there can be little doubt that there is ample evidence to suggest that even a playful knowledge of them may have positive educational outcomes.

This discussion began by raising questions about the relevance of these rhymes in contemporary society. One aspect that must be mentioned is the fact that children themselves are partly and significantly responsible for keeping them culturally alive.

The playful subversion and often anarchic quality of the versions constructed, reconstructed and used by children can be heard in any school playground. Children play with and use the rhymes (which have been passed from child to child) for many reasons: to shock any adult who might overhear, to subvert the 'canon' passed down from adult to child, to accompany play, to exploit metalinguistic awareness or to include or exclude peers from play or friendship. Children's versions are an illustration of their often unconscious appreciation of how patterned language can be used to establish links with the past and create new meanings in the present.

Knowledge of such versions gives children power over parents and other authority figures. It allows them to defy authority 'through the corruption of a nursery rhyme, [which

has] almost always [been] taught by adults to children when they are small and helpless'
(Factor, 1988:158).

The 'humour, vulgarity, language play and fantasy' (Factor, 1988:153) contained in many
children's versions of traditional rhymes are meant to shock adults who naively believe
children could not understand the implications of what they are saying, and to impress
peers who believe perhaps they should not have access to what is being said. Some examples
of such versions are:

> Mary had a little lamb
> She also had a bear.
> I often saw her little lamb
> But I never saw her bare.
>
> Mary had a little lamb
> The doctor fainted.
>
> Ding dong dell
> Pussy's in the well.
> If you don't believe it,
> Go and have a smell (cited in Factor, 1983:40–43).

CONCLUSION

So what are we to make of this body of work that continues to fascinate children and adults
alike? Some have viewed their linguistic richness as reason enough for their continued
presence in any educational program. Others see nursery rhymes as either viable precursors
to the study of poetry (Lukens, 1995) or as the first examples of poetry a child experiences
(Nodelman, 1996). Rollin (1992) explores their potential in cultural and psychoanalytical
terms, and Opie and Opie have enlightened all with their comprehensive research into their
origins and place in the history and development of children's literature.

And yet perhaps what matters more than the result of such scholarly claims and
investigations is the fact that nursery rhymes are remembered and used by adults who pass
them on to children. Phrases and events are recalled and individual characters are used as
a form of descriptive shorthand for a range of actions. Nursery rhymes are said, sung and
read to children without the embarrassment that often accompanies the sharing of poetry.

Adults use nursery rhymes to soothe a restless child (Bye Baby Bunting), to accompany
children's play (Pat-a-cake in the sand pit); to distract and amuse (Ride a Cock Horse when
bouncing a child on the knee) and to label behaviour. They use the rhymes because they
have some memory of their own early encounters with them, those often spontaneous
interactions that characterise what is remembered from childhood. Such memories,
whether real or imagined, are stimulated no doubt by the efforts of many to retain the
rhymes' presence in the culture. And so the rhymes remain with us throughout our lives,
passed down from generation to generation in simple acts of sharing and pleasure that
ensure their continued relevance and their enduring appeal.

References

Bradley, L. & Bryant, P.E. (1983) Categorising sounds and learning to read. *Nature,* **301**, 419–421.

——(1985) *Children's Reading Problems.* Oxford: Blackwells.

Bryant, P.E., Bradley, L., MacLean, M. & Crossland, J. (1989) Nursery rhymes, phological skills and reading. *Journal of Child Language*, **6**, 407–428.

Bryant, P.E., Maclean, M., Bradley, L.L. & Crossland, J. (1990) Rhyme and alliteration, phoneme detection and learning to read. *Developmental Psychology,* **26**(3), 429–438.

Clay, M. (1990) Eggheads vote Humpty a winner. *Speld News*, **5**.

Delamar, G. (1987) *Mother Goose from Nursery to Literature.* Jefferson, N.C.: McFarland.

Factor, J. (1988) *Captain Cook Chased a Chook.* Melbourne: Penguin.

Jacobs, J. & Tunnell, M. (1996) *Children's Literature Briefly.* New Jersey: Merrill.

Lukens, R. (1995) *A Critical Handbook of Children's Literature* (5th edn) New York: Harper Collins.

Lynne, J. (1985) Runes to ward off sorrow: rhetoric of the English nursery rhyme. *Children's Literature in Education,* **16**(1), 3–14.

Nodelman, P. (1996) *The Pleasure of Children's Literature* (2nd edn). New York: Longman.

Opie, I. and Opie, P. (eds) (1980) *The Oxford dictionary of nursery rhymes.* Oxford: Oxford University Press.

Rollin, L. (1992) *Cradle and All: A Cultural and Psychoanalytic Reading.* Jackson: University Press of Mississippi.

Whitehead, M. (1993) Born again phonics and nursery rhyme revival. *English in Education,* **27**(3), 42–51.

Books Cited

Davey, G. (comp.) (1997) *Jack and Jill. A Book of Nursery Rhymes.* Australia: Hodder & Stoughton.

Decker, M. (1992) *The Christian Mother Goose Big Book.* Michigan: World Publishing.

Factor, J. (1983) *Far Out Brussel Sprout.* Melbourne: Oxford University Press.

Goffe, T. (1991) *The Dog with the Awful Laugh.* London: Walker Books.

Larche, D. (Father Gander) (1985) *Father Gander Nursery Rhymes. The Equal Rhymes Amendment.* California: Advocacy Press.

Lee, D. (1983) *Jelly Belly: Original Nursery Rhymes.* Sydney: Angus & Robertson.

Loomans, D., Kolberg, K. & Loomans, J. (1991) *Positively Mother Goose.* California: H.J. Kramer.

Merriam, E. (1996) *The Inner City Mother Goose.* New York: Simon & Schuster.

Prater, J. (1993) *Once Upon a Time.* London: Walker.

Prater, J. (1996) *Once Upon a Picnic.* London: Walker Books.

Roffey, M. (1993) *Let's Go.* London: Walker Books.

Spencer, A (Illust.) (1993) *Let's Go.* London: Walker Books.

Taylor, C. (1992) *The House That Crack Built.* San Francisco: Chronicle Books.

Yeomans, J. & Blake, Q. (1994) *The Do-it-yourself House that Jack Built.* London: Hamish Hamilton.

THINKING THROUGH PUPPETRY

Developing a quality puppetry curriculum in early childhood

Veronicah Larkin

Many young children enjoy the experience of making their own puppets. The design and construction of puppets can provide positive learning outcomes cognitively, physically and creatively for the young child. This element of the puppetry experience is widely addressed in published literature (see, for example, Rocard, 1979; Flower & Fortney, 1983; Hogarth & Bussell, 1985; Snook, 1985; Caruso, 1986; MacLennan, 1988; Robson & Bailey, 1990; Orton, 1993; Smith, 1996). Some of these authors have placed some measure of importance on children working towards a polished finished product, and have provided very specific guidelines and instructions related to puppet-making techniques. Other authors have more strongly emphasised the value of children experimenting with puppet making, such as Gammon (1993) who supported the view that children's puppet making should emphasise the processes of elaborating and adapting both the design and the construction, so that the children may experience success in creating characters from their own imaginations.

The use of puppets in children's own staged puppetry performance has been affirmed as a valuable addition to the child's experience of puppetry (Hodgson, 1984; Wright, 1986; French & French, 1991; Currell, 1992). Rump asserted that the experience of children planning and staging puppetry performances will 'nourish children's communication and social skills and demonstrate the benefits of concentration, self-expression and co-operative effort. As children are drawn into the project they will gain new confidence in their abilities, exercise their fertile imaginations — and have a lot of fun together' (1996:3).

Children's responses as audience members to a range of different arts performances have also been described in the literature (see, for example, Andress, 1980; Smigiel, 1993; Suthers, 1993; Suthers & Larkin, 1997), and the value of such performance encounters has been endorsed. A study undertaken by Suthers and Larkin (1997) provided evidence that a four-year-old child's attendance at a children's opera performance resulted in both immediate and long-term influences upon the child's artistic endeavours. The value of children experiencing staged puppetry performance has similarly been recognised (Kampmann, 1972; Vella & Rickards, 1989; McCaslin, 1990; Furman, 1992; Jalongo & Stamp, 1997), although how such performance attendance may specifically influence the young child's own receptivity, skill and interest in puppetry or in the wider arena of the performing arts has not been widely researched in the Australian context.

Any analysis of children as audience members of puppetry performances must concede that, for many young children, their first experience of seeing puppets in performance comes from viewing television programmes and television advertisements which utilise a range of televisual puppetry techniques. The global reach of television programmes such as *Sesame Street* support this view (Cameron, 1989). In describing the widespread influence of 'The Muppets', Richter de Vroe simply states 'Never before has puppetry achieved a comparable mass effect' (1989:183). The potential of televisual puppetry to entertain and educate the young child, as well as to inspire child-initiated puppetry construction and use, confirms the power and influence that this medium has had upon the development of puppetry as both an art form and a teaching tool (Richter de Vroe, 1989; Finch, 1993; Henson, 1994).

Incorporation of puppetry into early childhood programmes by teachers and caregivers has been less widely reported in the literature and has not been systematically researched and analysed to date. Much of the published literature on puppetry has come from practitioners sharing their ideas in the form of teacher resource materials, rather than from conducting empirical investigations. Some authors have offered spirited praise for the use of puppetry as a teaching tool and method for school aged children (Smith & Carre, 1984), while others have provided a range of strategies for the successful incorporation of puppetry into curricula designed for younger children (Rountree, Gordon, Shuptrine & Taylor, 1989; Jenkins, 1980; Hunt & Renfro, 1982; Sullivan, 1982). A paucity of published research describing and analysing the utilisation of puppetry in Australian early childhood programmes prompted the researcher to undertake a pilot study to explore the development of a puppetry curriculum for children aged between two and five years. The following questions formed the foci for the investigation:

• What kinds of puppets and puppeteering styles are favoured by teachers and caregivers?
• What kinds of puppets and puppeteering styles are favoured by children?
• What factors might influence the type of puppetry utilisation present in an early childhood setting? (Such factors might include prior experiences of children and adults, locations of puppetry experiences, contexts in which puppetry occurs, gender, group size, adult involvement and availability of materials and resources.)

THE STUDY

A collaborative research project was undertaken over a five-month period in 1997 at a community-sponsored long day-care centre located in Sydney. The subjects of the study were forty children aged between two and five years, located in three separate playrooms. The two-year-olds group consisted of ten children, and the three- and four-year-olds groups each consisted of fifteen children. Each playroom was staffed by a trained early childhood teacher and a teaching assistant who were all fully engaged in the research project. The average length of teaching experience for the teachers was three years, while for the teaching assistants the average period of service in child-care was seven years. The participating staff had been at the centre for two-and-a-half years, on average.

The research site was chosen on the basis that puppetry had not been a component in the curriculum prior to the commencement of the study. Additionally, all six participating staff members reported no particular specialist knowledge or skills in puppetry. While the setting had not previously incorporated puppetry into its programme, the director and staff responded positively to the opportunity to do so and were willing to accommodate any changes to routines or programmes the study might impose. These factors were considered necessary as the study sought to examine the introduction of a new puppetry curriculum into a mainstream, non-specialist early childhood setting.

The study involved the design, development, implementation and evaluation of a total of twelve puppetry experiences, devised by the researcher in consultation with the participating staff members. These puppetry experiences were designed to accommodate a range of current interests and skills levels of the children involved in the study. The staff in each playroom were required to implement and evaluate each of their four experiences on at least three occasions over a twelve-week period. It was agreed that staff members in each playroom would contribute to the teaching and evaluation processes and that the centre's existing evaluation instrument would be used, with slight modifications. The evaluation format used in the study is reproduced in Figure 10.1.

As the staff members participating in the study had no previous experience in puppetry, the researcher provided them with introductory instruction in puppet manipulation and puppetry evaluation strategies, and was available throughout the project for ongoing support and guidance. All puppets and related materials were provided by the researcher.

PUPPETRY CURRICULUM PROJECT: EVALUATION

Experience Number _____ Date _____ Staff initials _____

Number of times presented 1st _____ 2nd _____ 3rd _____ 4th _____ more _____

Starting time _____ Finishing time _____ Context_____

Puppets used _____

_____

Child/ren present _____

_____

Adult/s present _____

Description /evaluation _____

_____

_____

Figure 10.1 Pupperty curriculm project: Evaluation form

In addition to examination of the written evaluations recorded by the staff members, the researcher sought to gain additional data by conducting semi-structured interviews at the conclusion of the study. By a process of negotiation between the researcher and staff, it was determined that the two staff members from each playroom would be interviewed together. All three interviews were audiotaped and subsequently transcribed in full. The average interview time was ninety minutes. These interviews were designed to provide staff members with the opportunity to personally reflect upon the processes and outcomes of the project and to communicate their opinions in an informal and relaxed way. Staff were invited to bring to the interviews their written evaluations to help inform the discussion.

Prior to the interview, one staff member who spoke a first language other than English expressed some concerns related to her ability to communicate confidently in English where a detailed or technical discussion might be involved. She requested a written set of questions in advance of the interview to provide her with some general indication of the issues that might be discussed. To ensure uniformity, all six staff members received discussion questions in writing four days before the interviews took place. All staff members were reminded that these were simply general discussion ideas and that they were free to raise any other issues if they desired. These written discussion questions are reproduced in Figure 10.2.

Four contexts were selected to enable the puppetry experiences to take place in different locations within the setting and at different times throughout the day. The researcher encouraged the staff to modify the puppetry experiences in response to the children's expressed needs and to view the curriculum as flexible and dynamic. A summary of the puppetry experiences is reproduced in Figure 10.3.

RESULTS

The following summary of results was drawn primarily from data collected through the staff interviews, and from staff members' analyses of their written evaluations. A more detailed analysis of the findings generated from the written evaluations will be reported

---

PUPPETRY CURRICULUM PROJECT: DISCUSSION QUESTIONS

• What are your overall views of the puppetry curriculum project?

• Do you have a preference for a particular type of puppet? If so, what?

• Do you have a preference for a particular style of puppetry? If so, what?

• Do you have a preference for a particular context in which to facilitate puppetry experiences? If so, what?

• Do you have a preference for a particular location in which to facilitate puppetry experiences? If so, where?

• Do you have a preference for a particular puppetry experience? If so, what?

• Will you facilitate puppetry with your children in the future? Why/why not?

Figure 10.2 Puppetry curriculum project: Discussion questions

Figure 10.3 Puppetry curriculum project: The experiences

Two-year-olds group   Staff: Olivia and Rani*

Context	Experience	Puppet/s used
1. Indoors free play	Puppets suspended from a length of rope	Wooden spoon puppets
2. Indoors group time	'Do as I do' game: Children copy puppet's actions	Hand puppet
3. Caregiving routines	Puppet interacts with children at bathroom time	Face washer puppet
4. Outdoors play	Puppets placed on mat in the playground	Oven mitt puppets, hand puppets

Three-year-olds group   Staff: Leah and Stefan

Context	Experience	Puppet/s used
5. Indoors free play	Making homes for puppets using wooden building blocks	Finger puppets
6. Indoors group time	Storytelling: *Rosie's walk*	Hand puppets
7. Caregiving routines	Puppet used to settle children at rest time	Pillow puppet
8. Outdoors play	Puppets suspended from trees in playground	Rubber glove puppets, table tennis bat puppets

Four-year-olds group   Staff: Melissa and Sook

Context	Experience	Puppet/s used
9. Indoors free play	Learning centre: making and using puppet stages	Finger, hand, paper bag and stick puppets
10. Indoors group time	'Find the shape' game	Shapes stick puppets
11. Caregiving routines	Puppet used to remind children to place their shoes in their lockers	Shoe puppet
12. Outdoors play	Local walk: Children use natural objects to create puppets	Found puppets

* Staff names used throughout are pseudonyms. In acknowledgment of cultural sensitivities, each staff member was given the opportunity to select her or his own pseudonym.

elsewhere. All staff members were given the opportunity to read their summaries and to modify any responses as they wished.

The two-year-olds group

Olivia (teacher) and Rani (teaching assistant) summarised their responses to their four puppetry experiences in the following ways. (Please note that all children's names are pseudonyms.)

1. Indoors free play: Wooden spoon puppets suspended from a length of rope

While many children thought that this experience was a lot of fun, we noticed that it brought out some aggression in a few. We tried stringing the line at different locations in the playroom but we still found that Timothy (2 yrs 4 mths) and Ellie (2 yrs 2 mths) wanted to just punch at the spoon puppets and jiggle roughly on the rope to make the spoons move back and forth. We did notice that a longer line encouraged more aggression than a shorter line, and that Timothy seemed to encourage Ellie to copy him as he attempted to bat at the puppets. We also had one or two children who spent most of their time trying to swing from the rope and when they were told they couldn't do this these children seemed to lose interest in the activity very quickly. However, a number of children interacted very well with the puppets, particularly Lachlan (2 yrs 11 mths) who engaged in a rather lengthy conversation, where it appeared that he was lecturing the puppets for being naughty. We might use a short puppet line in future with a small group of children, however we would probably use hand or finger puppets rather than wooden spoons.

2. Indoors group time: 'Do as I do' game using a hand puppet

This was a great success as we have played a similar game before with the children, where the children copied our actions. Using 'Ralph' the dog puppet worked very well as we could move his arms, legs and head around in a lot of different positions for the children to imitate. The children believed that 'Ralph' had a life of his own and they always referred to him by name. The children especially loved it when 'Ralph' barked and praised the children and on many occasions individual children asked 'Ralph' to watch them, believing that he could actually see them as they attempted to copy his actions. On several occasions Lily (2 yrs 9 mths) became upset when she felt that 'Ralph' wasn't giving her enough of his attention. This is a wonderful puppet game and 'Ralph' is now a permanent member of the two-year-olds' room.

3. Caregiving routines: Face washer puppet interacting with children in bathroom

The whole group really loved 'Washy' the face washer puppet and, just like 'Ralph', the children seemed to believe that he was actually alive and that he could really see them when they were in the bathroom. The children didn't appear to notice that we were holding him and talking for him, as far as they were concerned he was a person in his own right. We were continually amazed at how important 'Washy' became to many of the children. Angelina (2 yrs 4 mths) and Frances (2 yrs 6 mths) frequently asked where he was and we soon found that we needed to bring him out at every wash up time, otherwise these two children became very upset. One day we had a casual teaching assistant in for the day who didn't know about 'Washy', and several children refused to wash their hands and face unless 'Washy' came for a visit. On another occasion we noticed that Hans (2 yrs 8 mths) and Luke (2 yrs 11 mths) started to deliberately splash water on the floor and when they were reminded about the bathroom rules they said 'Not you tell us ... "Washy" tell us to stop'. We feel that the use of 'Washy' has helped our bathroom routines work a little more smoothly as more children are co-operating with our expectations. 'Washy', like 'Ralph', is now a permanent fixture in our playroom.

4. Outdoors play: Hand and oven mitt puppets placed on mat in the playground

We didn't find that the puppet mat idea worked well outdoors. Many of the children simply took the puppets to the sand pit and filled them with sand. We also caught a couple of children dipping them in the water trough and another who thought it was great fun to go to the dough table and try to use his puppet as a rolling pin. The children seemed to prefer to use their puppets anywhere except on the puppet mat. We found that if one of us took just one puppet outside and sat on the grass with a small group of children they would interact happily with that puppet. This seemed to work much better than placing a set of puppets on a mat and expecting the children to stay there with the puppets. One rainy afternoon we had to pack up the outdoors equipment early so we brought the puppet mat inside and found that the puppets lasted a little longer on the mat, but again, the children wandered around the playroom with them and didn't seem to want to sit on the mat and use them there. We might use a puppet mat indoors in the future, however we won't set up a puppet mat outdoors again because our children are too young to sit in one place and use the puppets properly.

The three-year-olds group

Leah (teacher) and Stefan (teaching assistant) summarised their responses to their four puppetry experiences in the following ways.

5. Indoors free play: Using building blocks to make homes for the finger puppets

We have been talking recently about strategies we could use to encourage more of our girls to participate in block building. In our playroom the boys seem to dominate the blocks and many of the girls don't really try to compete with the boys here. We were keen to see if adding the finger puppets to the blocks would encourage more girls to have a go and we found the results very interesting, and the evaluations we did gave us a lot to think about. Every time we implemented this experience we noticed that the boys involved themselves in the actual building process, and when they announced the house was finished, the girls would take over and use the finger puppets in the same way that young children play with small-sized dolls in a doll's house. We tried to encourage everyone to have a go at everything but this didn't seem to make much difference. Even Stefan's presence, as a male playing with the finger puppets, didn't influence the boys. It is worth stating that the girls loved the finger puppets, especially the Alice in Wonderland and the Goldilocks puppets, and they created some wonderful adventures for these puppets in the block house constructions. Kelly (3 yrs 9 mths) took on the role of director and organised a number of the other girls to play the various characters in the Goldilocks story. These girls spent more than thirty minutes on this play. We wondered whether the boys didn't want to play very much with the finger puppets because puppets just can't compete with block building. We also wondered whether, in some subtle ways, the girls were sending messages to the boys that they were not welcome to play with the finger puppets. In the future we will use the finger puppets in other ways (away from the blocks) to see if the boys show more interest in them.

6. Indoors group time: Hand puppets used to tell the story of Rosie's walk

Most of the children in the group were familiar with the story and they enjoyed seeing a loved story brought to life with the puppets. The first time we presented the experience one of us (Leah) read the book while the other (Stefan) used both puppets, one on each hand. The children were delighted by this and seemed to look upon the experience as if they were attending a puppet play, spontaneously sitting in rows on the mat and clapping at the end of the story. The next time we did the story we used one puppet each and we more or less told the story off by heart. The children seemed to look upon this as a whole new experience and were just as delighted the second time around. On the third presentation we invited a number of children to come out in front of the group and use the puppets as we told the story. Some of the children simply held the puppet out in front of them, not moving it around or making the mouth speak, however the rest of the group didn't seem to mind this at all and still enjoyed the experience immensely. Over all, we found that it was easier for us to use just one puppet each and simply say the story rather than read it. This experience would work well if you had a third staff member who could read the story while the other two operated the puppets. This was the first time we have used puppets to tell a story and we are planning to look for other books and puppets we can use at story time.

7. Caregiving routines: Pillow puppet used to settle the children at rest time

Rest time can sometimes be a bit of a challenge in our playroom. We don't expect everyone to sleep but we do like all the children to have a little time after lunch where they are quiet and relaxed. We have mixed feelings about 'pillow puppet' being used to settle children down. The children absolutely adored it and laughed hysterically when it appeared and we think perhaps it may have over-excited some of the children and made it even more unlikely that they would lie down calmly and have a rest. We are sure that Dillon (3 yrs 4 mths) deliberately tried to keep awake for as long as he could because he was scared he would miss out on seeing 'pillow puppet' if he fell asleep. What was interesting was how easily the children believed that 'pillow puppet' was really talking and moving by itself and they all wanted it to come and visit them on their rest mat. We will use 'pillow puppet' at other times of the day, but it is too exciting to share with the children at a time when we are trying to encourage them to be quiet and peaceful.

8. Outdoors play: Rubber glove and table tennis bat puppets suspended from trees in playground

Initially we wondered if the children would be attracted to these puppets as they didn't seem as colourful or attractive as the finger and hand puppets we had been using in the other experiences. We need not have worried because we quickly discovered that the children thought these puppets were great fun too and they immediately took them down from the branches and started to play with them. The children enjoyed the novelty of searching through the trees to find the puppets and they seemed to think of it as a puppet treasure hunt. When we repeated this experience we chose different trees in different parts of the playground and this influenced where the children sat and used the puppets. When we stayed with the children and used one of the puppets ourselves we found that the quality of puppet play greatly improved and the children spent more time at the experience (see Figure 10.4). We were very impressed with some of the stories the children created and we found that one particular group of children often used the rubber glove puppets as the 'goodies' and the table tennis bat puppets as the 'baddies' in their puppet plays. As this experience worked well we plan to use other puppets in the playground, probably puppets made from odds and ends so it won't matter if they get dirty when used outside.

The four-year-olds group

Melissa (teacher) and Sook (teaching assistant) summarised their responses to their four puppetry experiences in the following ways.

9. Indoors free play: Making and using puppet stages for finger, hand, paper bag and stick puppets

We had thought the children would make small stages from the shoe boxes for the finger and paddlepop stick puppets and then larger stages out of the grocery boxes for the larger stick, hand and paper bag puppets. How wrong we were! The children became completely obsessed with making the larger stages, no matter how small the puppets were. We had situations like the one in which Casey (4 yrs 2 mths) and Theresa (4 yrs 7 mths) spent days cutting, taping, painting and decorating a cardboard box the size of a washing machine so they could use it for their two favourite rabbit finger puppets. On the days when we only put out the shoe boxes there was much less interest from the children. In the beginning it took a reasonably high level of adult intervention to help the children think of things in the playroom they could convert into puppet stages. Many children seemed to wander around the room carrying their puppet without coming up with any

Figure 10.4 The quality of the puppet play and the length of time spent at the experience increased when an adult was present and participating. Adult presence enhanced puppet play quality.

useable ideas. Then, without our help, Bertram (4 yrs 10 mths) and Samuel (4 yrs 10 mths) pushed the collage trolley almost against the wall and crouched behind it and started to use their puppets to call out to us to come over to see their puppet show. Possibly inspired by Bertie and Sam's efforts we found Cassidy (4 yrs 5 mths) recruiting children to bring their puppets into home corner to 'do puppet plays'. We then had four girls and one boy in home corner crouching behind the play furniture and using their puppets to interact with each other. This was very interesting play, as the children were not really putting on a puppetry performance as such — they were mostly engaged in home corner drama play, where the puppets were characters in their dramatic play. Building and finding puppet stages, while good fun for the children, didn't seem to contribute anything in particular to the quality of their puppet work — it seems the children saw the stage making and the puppet playing as separate activities.

10. Indoors group time: 'Find the shape' game using stick puppets

There's a game quite like this one which we have played with the children at different times where we hold up a foam shape and the children tell us the shape's name. So we found it easy to modify the game a little and use the shape puppets instead. We noticed that the children fell about with laughter when a puppet cheered or cried, according to whether the child named or matched the shape correctly. The children really believed the puppet's emotional reaction was genuine. We also found that using one of the shape puppets to ask a child to find that shape in the room worked well. Arthur (4 yrs 8 mths) especially seemed to try very hard to find the right shape because he seemed to want to please the puppet. We started to think that, for whatever reason, the children wanted to please or impress the puppets more than they appeared to want to impress us!

11. Caregiving routines: Shoe puppet used to remind children to place shoes in lockers

'Sneaky sneaker' was a great hit with the whole group and we found we used him in lots of different ways, not just for reminding the children about their shoes. We used him to greet children at the beginning of group time and sometimes trotted him out for transition games. When we looked back over our evaluations we have not really convinced ourselves that 'Sneaky sneaker' has made much difference to modifying any shoes-in-locker kind of behaviours. It seems to us that we are finding the same children are still dumping their shoes at the end of the sand pit or on the side verandah and we still have to remind them to put them away. So, while the idea of using a shoe puppet to ask children to do something has been great fun, for the children and for us, we're not sure it has really made a positive change to the children's behaviour. Still, we can see that the idea is a good one because it does feel better to have 'Sneaky sneaker' reminding the children instead of us doing it all the time. We'll keep him on our shelf and use him for the rest of the year because if we suddenly stopped bringing him out the children would be very disappointed and probably start to ask us where he'd gone.

12. Outdoors play: Local walk where children use natural objects to create found puppets

We have taken the children on different walks this year so the children are quite familiar with the area around the centre but this was the first time we had taken them on a puppet walk. At first we were both a bit sceptical, we didn't know whether the children would be able to look at something like a rock or a tree and see it as a puppet but we need not have worried. We took the stick-on eyes and mouths with us and the children thought it was wonderful applying these on things like fences, light poles, trees and walls. Martin (4 yrs 9 mths), Seamus (4 yrs 9 mths) and Chew (4 yrs 3 mths) particularly liked making the gate at the end of the car park into a moving puppet by opening and closing the gate as the rest of the children walked through. When one of us (Sook) used a funny voice and said "Thank you very much gate" the children thought this was hilarious and some children experimented with different puppet voices as the walk proceeded. On a later walk we decided to settle in one area of the park and we asked groups of children to collect items in their plastic containers and bring them back to the group to apply their stick-on eyes and mouth. We found that this encouraged the children to sit and use their found puppet, by themselves or with their friends. The children loved collecting things and creating their own individual puppets in this way and then placing the natural objects back where they had found them. We feel this experience is really unique and we'll definitely use it again this year and also in future years.

DISCUSSION

A review of the data generated from the staff evaluations and interviews suggests the emergence of some general issues regarding age appropriateness, physical location and context of puppetry experiences, the value of the experiences, use of materials, children's prior experiences, the role of adults and puppetry preferences related to gender.

Puppetry experiences with two year olds

Olivia and Rani indicated that two of their four puppetry experiences contained elements which made them somewhat unsuitable for the two year olds, with aggression (experience 1) and 'improper' use of the puppets (experience 4) being highlighted as matters of concern. The staff responses to these two experiences raises the issue of what is acceptable puppetry behaviour for two year olds, particularly in those circumstances where the children's ways of using the puppets do not accord with the expectations established by the staff. The successful introduction of a puppetry curriculum for two year olds might require a reasonably high level of tolerance of non-conventional patterns of usage of puppets, and a degree of latitude and acceptance of this fact might be necessary when facilitating puppetry experiences with very young children. The evaluation of experience 4 suggested that the presence and involvement of an adult with a small group improved the children's engagement in the activity and was a favoured modification to the original experience. Interestingly, those experiences in which the puppets were manipulated by an adult only (2 and 3) were rated as highly successful and worthy of future repetition. Linked with this, Olivia and Rani favoured the two experiences (2 and 3) which contained a single puppet and have suggested a modification for another experience (4) to change it to a single puppet activity. The children's belief in the independent existence of the puppet, as separate from the adult puppeteer, is highlighted in the evaluations of experiences 2 and 3, and may have contributed to the children's positive responses to these experiences. The children's prior experience of a 'Do as I do' type of game (without puppets) was cited as a possible contributing factor to the success of experience 2. Overall, Olivia and Rani's evaluations indicated a higher approval of those puppetry experiences where an adult was present and operating a single puppet (2 and 3) and a lower approval of experiences which involved the children manipulating the puppets in individual, undesired or unanticipated ways (1 and 4).

Puppetry experiences with three year olds

The descriptions provided by Leah and Stefan provided evidence of the emerging skills of some of their children to use puppets to tell their own stories (experience 8) and to participate in the telling of known stories (experiences 5 and 6). These observations might give rise to the suggestion that puppets which children strongly identify by character, for example Goldilocks, are more likely to stimulate puppetry play where the Goldilocks story is told. This might be compared to the non-specific characters of rubber glove and table tennis bat puppets (experience 8) where the children created their own, presumably original, stories. The presence and involvement of the adult during experience 8 was seen to have enriched this activity, in terms of both the quality of puppet play and the length of time the children engaged in the play. Like the staff in the two-year-olds playroom, Leah and Stefan commented upon their children's strong belief in the separate identity of the puppet when describing the children's response to 'pillow puppet'. However, the suitability of using this puppet as a rest time settling strategy has been questioned due to the children's excited responses. Leah and Stefan acknowledged the relationship that developed between the children and 'pillow puppet' as a reason for continuing the use of this puppet, in other contexts. The issue of gender was discussed in light of the children's responses to experience 5. It is noteworthy that this experience was implemented on three occasions, always with the same behaviours being present. It was considered noteworthy that even Stefan's engagement with the finger puppets did not motivate the boys to leave the block building and join in. Experience 9, in the four-year-olds playroom, was the only other experience involving finger puppets and the evaluations of this experience did not suggest a significant difference between girls' and boys' use of this type of puppet. This result might suggest that the three year old boys did not so much reject finger puppets as state a much stronger preference for block building. Overall Leah and Stefan's evaluations indicate a high approval of experiences 6 and 8, a desire to modify the context for experience 7 and a desire to re-present the puppets used in experience 5, without the addition of the blocks.

Puppetry experiences with four year olds

Melissa and Sook, like the staff in the two- and three-year-olds playrooms, commented on their children's belief in the identity of particular puppets who were seen to be capable of feeling genuine emotional reactions (experiences 10 and 11). The positive responses to the indoors group time puppetry experiences indicated by the staff in the two and three year olds playrooms was also shared by Melissa and Sook in their evaluation of experience 10. Here the staff believed it was easy to adjust a known game to incorporate a puppetry component. This issue of familiarity or prior experience (without the use of puppets) was mentioned in reference to experiences 2, 5, 6, 10 and 12. Staff who are in the early stages of acquiring skills and confidence in the implementation of a puppetry curriculum might relate well to those experiences which have familiar or known elements. In the evaluation of experience 11 there was an acknowledgment that while the children (and staff) enjoyed the addition of 'Sneaky sneaker' into the life of the playroom, the experience did not achieve its desired objective of encouraging children to remember where to store their shoes. This accords with the evaluations of experience 7 where 'pillow puppet' was popular with the children but ineffective in helping the children to settle quietly. These evaluations contrast with 'Washy' (experience 3) who was seen to be popular with the children and useful in creating a smoother bathroom routine. The evaluations of experience 9 provided some indication that puppetry staging devised by the children might have some measure of influence upon puppetry play. In home corner, for example, the observed puppetry play was influenced by the location. In terms of stage construction it may be likely that the novelty of large cardboard boxes contributed to the children's preferences and it is perhaps unsurprising that there was little attention given to constructing staging that reflected the type of puppets to be used. Melissa and Sook's positive evaluation of the puppet walks (experience 12) provided support for the view that some puppetry experiences which might not immediately appeal to adults can find favour with young children. Melissa and Sook's evaluations indicated a strong approval of experiences 10 and 12, a moderate approval of experience 9 and a belief that experience 11 was enjoyable but ineffective in achieving its objectives.

CONCLUSION

The evaluations provided by the six staff members in this study may assist other early childhood teachers and caregivers in planning a puppetry curriculum within their own settings. Some of the general issues that may inform practitioners include:

- Flexibility

    Young children may not always use puppets in ways anticipated by adults. A willingness to allow children to investigate puppets in their own ways can empower children to explore creatively without the imposition of strongly expressed adult expectations influencing the process.

- Time

    Young children need the opportunity to explore puppetry freely in their own time and to have the chance to re-visit and refine experiences over a period of time. The study showed that sometimes when children return to a puppetry experience they bring new insights and the desire to explore the medium differently.

- Context

    A puppet may become a loved addition to the playroom, but remain ineffective in fulfilling particular objectives, due to the context in which the puppet is presented. Matching the puppet to the context is important; for example a puppet that excites and enthuses children may be less appropriate when used at quiet times of the day.

- Location

    Where puppets are placed (or taken) can influence puppet play. Imaginative use of interior and exterior locations may offer children novelty, variety and new challenges, and encourage different forms of puppet play.

- Gender

  Subjects in the study raised the issue of puppet choice and its relationship to gender. While the findings here are inconclusive, it may be useful for practitioners to observe their own children's puppetry preferences and consider strategies that might promote a more gender-inclusive puppetry curriculum.

- Children's prior experiences

  All subjects in this study referred to the success of their indoors group time puppetry games and the possible link to the children's familiarity with a similar type of game. Practitioners, in planning their puppetry curriculum, might like to review their current repertoire of group time arts games and consider those experiences which may be suitably modified to incorporate a puppetry element.

- Selection of puppets

  The results of the study strongly support the view that children enjoy both commercially-made puppets and other types of home-made or found puppets. Practitioners considering the inclusion of puppetry into their arts curriculum need not incur large expenses in purchasing puppets. Using a little imagination, a face washer, pillow or shoe, for example, can quickly become a loved puppet.

- The puppet's own identity

  All six staff members in this study commented upon the children's strong belief in the separate identity of the puppet. While a practitioner who is just beginning to use puppetry may doubt the effectiveness of using rubber gloves, table tennis bats, wooden spoons, oven mitts and objects found in a local park, young children commonly do not have any such doubts about the 'reality' of the puppet.

- Confidence and imagination

  It may be useful for practitioners to enter into a puppetry curriculum without too many strongly held preconceptions. For example, a puppetry walk where natural objects become instant puppets may not immediately appeal to a teacher or caregiver, but may be warmly embraced by the children.

An important finding in this study suggests that while young children clearly enjoy puppetry incorporated into their daily routines, they also respond positively to small group puppet making and puppet play in which the emphasis is upon the children exploring puppetry in their own individual ways. A puppetry curriculum strongly directed towards the fulfilment of specific adult expectations may be a limited and constricting curriculum for young children.

Puppetry can be a powerful, educational, creative and highly popular art form within the early childhood curriculum. The development, implementation and evaluation of a puppetry curriculum can be challenging and rewarding for early childhood practitioners and provide a range of much-loved experiences for young children.

Young children can use puppetry to think through problem-solving issues associated with the design, construction and staging of puppet shows. They can also use puppetry to think through and resolve the challenges associated with shared dialogue, conversational interaction and narrative. Importantly, young children can observe, plan, debate, experiment, reflect, revise, reassess and revisit a range of puppetry experiences as they think through puppetry.

References

Andress, B. (1980) *Music Experiences in Preschool*. New York: Holt, Reinhart & Winston.

Cameron, D. (1989) Sesame Street's leading light. *Sydney Morning Herald,* Dec. 30.

Caruso, P. (1986) *Finger Puppet Fun*. Sydney: Ashton Scholastic.

Currell, D. (1992) *An Introduction to Puppets and Puppet-making*. London: Quintet.

Finch, C. (1993) *Jim Henson: The Works*. New York: Random House.

Flower, C. & Fortney, A. (1983) *Puppets: Methods and Materials*. Massachusetts: Davis.

French, R. & French, J. (1991) *Puppet Drama*. Sydney: ANZEA.

Furman, L. (1992) Celebrating theatre with puppets: An interview with Josef Krofta. *Youth Theatre Journal*, **6**(4), 13–15.

Gammon, J. (1993) *Easy to Make Puppets*. London: Anaya.

Henson, C. (1994) *The Muppets Make Puppets*. New York: Workman.

Hodgson, J. (1984) *The Australian Puppet Book*. Sydney: Real Books.

Hogarth, A. & Bussell, J. (1985) *Fanfare for Puppets !* London: David and Charles.

Hunt, T. & Renfro, N. (1982) *Puppetry in Early Childhood Education*. Texas: Nancy Renfro Studios.

Hutchins, P. (1970) *Rosie's Walk*. London: Bodley Head.

Jalongo, M. & Stamp, L. (1997) *The Arts in Children's Lives*. Boston: Allyn and Bacon.

Jenkins, P. (1980) *The Magic of Puppetry: A Guide for those Working with Young Children*. New Jersey: Prentice Hall.

Kampmann, L. (1972) *The World of Puppets*. London: Evans.

McCaslin, N. (1990) *Creative Drama in the Classroom*. California: Players.

MacLennan, J. (1988) *Simple Puppets You Can Make*. New York: Sterling.

Orton, L. (1993) *My Puppet Book*. London: Salamander.

Richter de Vroe, K. (1989) Puppets in cinema and television. In *The World of Puppetry*, edited by D. Szilagyi, pp. 182–184. Berlin: Henschelverlag.

Robson, D. & Bailey, V. (1990) *Rainy Days Puppets*. London: Franklin Watts.

Rocard, A. (1979) *Puppets and Marionettes*. Yorkshire: EP Publishing.

Rountree, B., Gordon, J., Shuptrine, M. & Taylor, N. (1989) *Creative Teaching with Puppets*. Alabama: The Learning Line.

Rump, N. (1996) *Puppets and Masks*. Massachusetts: Davis.

Smigiel, H. (1993) Rehearsing for life. *Australian Journal of Early Childhood,* **18** (1), 10–14.

Smith, T. (1996) *Finger Puppet Fun*. London: Lorenz.

Smith, B. & Carre, C. (1984) Elementary students' writing helps understanding of science. *Highway One*, **7**(3), 23–28.

Snook, B. (1985) *Puppets*. London: Dryad.

Suthers, L. (1993) Introducing young children to live orchestral performance. *Early Child Development and Care,* **90**, 55–64.

Suthers, L. & Larkin, V. (1997) An examination of a young child's responses to performance: Implications for arts curricula. *Journal of Australian Research in Early Childhood Education*, **1,** 115–122.

Sullivan, D. (1982) *Pocketful of Puppets: Activities for the Special Child*. Texas: Nancy Renfro Studios.

Vella, M. & Rickards, H. (1989) *Theatre of the Impossible: Puppet Theatre in Australia*. Sydney: Craftsman House.

Wright, J. (1986) *Rod, Shadow and Glove*. London: Robert Hale.

11

DYNAMICS, IMAGES AND IMAGINATION

Landscapes in cyberspace

Margaret White and Kathryn Crawford

Imagination has always been a critical part of human playfulness, learning and adaptation. Until relatively recently, nineteenth century scientific paradigms and technical metaphors influenced the ways in which people thought about the dynamics of imagination and human responses to the environment. For example, visualisation was understood scientifically in terms similar to the actions of a camera — the eye creating images of the object of focus (Metzler & Shepherd, 1974; Kosslyn & Pomerantz, 1997) which were subsequently stored and processed — with imagination integral to the process. After attempts to replicate these processes with computers, the limits of these kinds of models of human activity are now being recognised. Researchers now acknowledge the complex and interactive nature of the human imagination, and the ways in which all sensory information is interpreted and reinterpreted through an ever-changing lens of expectations, culturally acquired knowledge, and emotion-laden associations with experiences, people and places (Kosslyn, 1996).

In the post-modernist era, we have again remembered the knowledge of the ancient Greeks and Romans who understood the psychological importance of places and emotionally powerful images in the cultivation of imagination, and the importance of childhood memories. Yates (1966:26) provides the following account of methods used to stimulate imagination and long-term memory derived from *Ad Herennium* (86 BC):

> We ought then to set up images of a kind that can adhere longest in memory. And we shall do so if we can establish simultudes as striking as possible; if we set up images that are not many or vague but active [*imagines agentes*]; if we assign them exceptional beauty or singular ugliness; if we ornament some of them, as with crowns or purple cloaks, or if we somehow disfigure them, as introducing one stained with blood or soiled with mud or smeared with red paint, so that its form is more striking, or by assigning certain comic effects to our images, for that too will ensure our remembering them more readily.

The Ancients lived in societies in which few people could read or write, so remembering and reproducing (through forms such as drama, poetry and dance) what was said or done was important for effective government and cooperative activity. In this, the knowledge era, when information is so widely available and there is a greater need for imaginative adaptation and creative problem-solving in the face of rapid sociocultural change, the role of imagination in learning and human development is of particular interest. A central component of an educator's expertise is an understanding of ways to stimulate children's imagination, and to nurture their confidence and capability to learn through ongoing active and creative engagement with their environment. In the twenty-first century, learning that is creative, rather than reproductive, will be of primary importance.

In this paper 'imagination' and 'imaginative activity' are defined broadly as involving the dynamic processes through which understanding and awareness are explored and expanded. Psychologists such as Vygotsky (1978), Cobb (1977) and Rogoff and Lave (1984) suggested a view of human knowledge and awareness as emerging from engaging and personally meaningful experiences in a social context which may be mediated by cultural artifacts. Imagination is a critical component of learning and expanding awareness through play and other reflective, personally motivated activity. Like Vygotsky, contemporary educators are interested in the role of the creative arts as a significant part of the fluid and richly textured cultural context of human imagination, communication and development.

From this perspective, new knowledge (including scientific knowledge), and awareness are generated when people are:

- exploring new dimensions,
- imagining and experimenting as if the 'constraints' were removed,
- moving outside habitual, conventional or conformist views and awareness,
- emotionally involved,
- using words, thoughts, images, and all of their senses creatively to interact with and respond to objects and 'real' and imaginary places, people and actions.

Virtual reality now creates a new space — cyberspace — for human imagination, human awareness and dynamic interaction involving virtual objects and people. Computers have been used extensively by scientists but are increasingly becoming a 'children's machine' (Papert, 1993); whereas many adults are ambivalent about the changes resulting from the increased use of information technologies, children are powerfully attracted to and influenced by the dynamic images and new possibilities for exploration, representation and expression. Some preschoolers play with programmable toys or their parents' computers, and most watch videotapes or television. In particular, vibrant, dynamic and modifiable abstract images are an increasingly accessible part of a child's environment. Thus computers and multimedia technologies are changing the possibilities for childhood experiences and imagination. In the face of this substantial change, we need to understand the dynamics of imagination and human thinking, feeling and knowing in order to understand the impact of new technologies. As adults who were children of another era, we need to understand the sources, conditions and legacy of our childhood imagining and expanding awareness in order to mediate these processes for the children in our care.

This chapter will explore the ways in which adults remember imagination in their childhood, and report their children's responses to a theatrical production which uses powerful images and events enhanced by computer-generated images. We speculate about the new possibilities for learning through imagination and creative activities in technically and culturally rich environments.

SITUATING ADULT MEMORIES OF CHILDHOOD IMAGINATION

In childhood play, imagination can lead to unknown places, including refuges from the complexities of the world of adults. The cubbyhouses children create from the materials found in their environment, such as rugs, chairs, recycled timber and trees, provide such a refuge where children are removed from the gaze of adults, as Dovey suggests:

> [They are] places to find oneself, to think and to feel outside the assigned role within the family. [It is] important to understand that these places are not marginal to children's lives, they often figure strongly in the memory because of their crucial role in emotional development. (Australian Broadcasting Corporation radio transcript, Dovey, 1997)

Dovey acknowledges the role of imaginative experiences in emotional development though it must also be recognised that such experiences are central to other areas of development such as cognition. Imaginative experiences allow children to explore new and powerful roles that would not be 'appropriate' in their everyday lives. These new roles involve responsibility, power, courage, decision-making and judgment. These kinds of thinking are all associated with the development of expanded and more sophisticated and abstract schema or concepts that will enhance their thinking for the rest of their lives. This kind of cognition results in knowledge as a basis for action and new capabilities.

While adults are often aware of their conscious memories of imagining in their childhoods, the role of childhood imaginative experiences in the subconscious development of ways of seeing and behaving, which involves the embodiment of subtle interactions with the physical and human environment, is less evident to adults. Children's experience of landscapes of the imagination have been observed with some wonderment by adults, who are often seeking to recapture the memory of these experiences from their own childhood.

In a memorable vignette of children interviewed on audiotape in their cubbyhouse, the essence of their experience was captured, both through the apparently extraneous sounds of the rustle of clothes, the physical awareness evident in the breathless comment, 'There's lots of space but it's really, really hot because we've got lots of pillows', the footsteps signaling the approach of guests to the cubby, and through the dialogue with the interviewer:

Child:	We're building a space rocket house, this is the space rocket here [sounds of a mouth organ], maybe I could play it to the house.
Child:	I'll answer the door!
Interviewer:	Here I come!
Child:	We're all in the house.
Child:	All right, I'll be up here.
Child:	Where's that?
Child:	Just pretend we can't see.
Child:	I'll be looking at the bee tree.
Child:	Well I don't think there's very much room now.

[knock at the door]

Child: The door, the door!
Interviewer: Climbing in underneath the blankets, … it's hot under here isn't it?
Child: Yeah, it's sticky.
Interviewer: What's here in the house?
Child: Umm, there's TV, bed, toys, things we play around with.
Child: There's lots of space but it's really, really hot, because we've got lots of pillows.
Interviewer: What do you do when you go in your pretend house?
Child: There is a dressing room so … um, no one can see you when you're dressing up, so like, if you're going to pull down your pants to put some different pants on …
Child: We get some more peace from other people.
                  [Discussion about light and other facilities ensues.]
(Australian Broadcasting Corporation, Radio National, Comfort Zone, 1997)

With a genuine interest in the children's experience of their cubby, this adult was treated to an inside view of the significance of this setting for the children. Yet the temptation to raise an adult perspective (What's here in this house?) rather than picking up on the children's stated focus (We're building a space rocket house, this is the space rocket here) has resulted in a dialogue about the contents rather than any development of the imaginative impetus of the cubby building. With the best will in the world, adults cannot overcome children's conception of them as powerful beings who must be appeased. However, the sensitive approach of the interviewer allowed the children to articulate the entirely manipulable use of light and space in their imaginative world.

Adult imagination is an important part of development too. In 1902 George Mieles created an imaginative film titled *A Trip to the Moon,* in which he used special effects to simulate what at the time was a highly speculative narrative about space travel. When the Museum of Contemporary Art in Sydney showed this film as part of an exhibition titled 'Phantasmagoria' in 1996, Pryor (1996:41) wrote:

> … Mieles began to stage events specifically for the camera, using elaborate settings, fantasy worlds and magical transformations.

To a contemporary adult viewer, the imaginative conception of a scenario which has now been realised gives a rare historical perspective of a visual 'transformation' created from the imagination of an adult, which is also reminiscent of young children's dramatic play. The ability to transform objects and situations to build a narrative which explores the stretches of the imagination is a quality which we associate with childhood, and which for many adults becomes elusive.

There are examples of artists in the twentieth century, such as Picasso, who sought to use the inspiration of children's art in their own painting (White & Stevenson, 1997). These artists valued the 'qualities in children's art which appeared to be lacking in 'academic' art such as spontaneity, simplicity, unselfconscious expression of feeling through colour and line' (White & Stevenson, 1997:9).

It is important that much of the technical revolution had its beginnings in the fantasy and imagination of art (Leonardo da Vinci), science fiction (Jules Verne) and films such as that of Mieles. The roots and metaphors of these imaginings are often embodied in the design and applications of new technologies.

A contemporary example of adult imaginings being used to design and apply new technologies may be seen in a new theatre production for children. The Theatre of Image, an Australian theatre company which creates works for children and adults, adapted the successful children's book, *Jake and Pete* by Gillian Rubenstein (1995), into a multimedia production in a Sydney theatre.

BACKGROUND TO THE PRODUCTION OF *JAKE AND PETE*

The original story of *Jake and Pete*[1] describes the adventures of two 'Kit Kids' who are forced by their 'Mumcat' to leave home and seek a new life. It is essentially a story of a classic 'life journey' in which the audience is invited to participate in the Kit Kids' responses to their world and to watch their gradual maturing and 'toughening up'. A series of characters is introduced and they often create turning points in the Kit Kids' lives as they confront and overcome the particular challenges which each character presents. For example:

- Mumcat, who, weary of training the Kit Kids, decides to retire and leave them to fend for themselves;
- Crow, who experiences the death of a lizard as providing food (rather than a frightening experience). Crow also utters the memorable response to Jake's enquiry, 'How big is Road?' Crow: 'Road goes on forever ...'
- Snake who provides a glimpse into the world of nightclubs and drugs,
- Bog, 'boss of the dump and the garbage bin ...', who eventually provides the home they are looking for complete with ...

Figure 10.1 Transformation of *Fridge*

---

1. The multimedia production of *Jake and Pete* was developed through an Australia Council-funded partnership between the Theatre of Image and Macquarie University.

- Fridge, not the one full of food which they thought they were looking for, but an upturned fridge which, when lined with old newspapers and sacks, provided a warm, dry bed. This transformation is achieved through a powerful animated image of a sparkling blanket (see Figure 10.1).

The production was developed through an extensive series of rehearsals with the author, artistic director, actors, musicians, and a range of technical and production staff, in addition to members of the public, including children, who were invited to respond to the initial ideas at open workshops.

A partnership with Macquarie University enabled the Theatre of Image to collaborate with a specialised team of multimedia artists to develop the production on three levels:

- animated images[2] projected on to a 3 × 5 metre screen at the back of the stage (see, for example, Figures 10.1–10.3);
- actors performing on the stage, and
- a soundscape.

The animated images included a range of symbolic 'characters' such as *Road,* which is continually transformed as it moves through the 'life' of the production. Words and numbers are also used, such as the word *SPLAT* when a lizard is run over by a car (see Figure 10.2), and the words *6 months later* (see Figure 10.3) to suggest the passing of time. The writing is sometimes created on the screen by a mouse drawing the letters with its nose.

In terms of the methods used to stimulate imagination and long-term memory advocated in *Ad Herennium* (cited in Yates, 1966), these images certainly established striking simultudes.

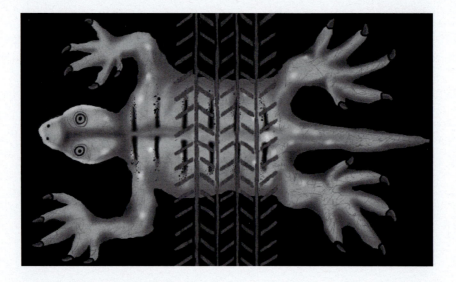

Figure 10.2 Road: Death of the Lizard

2. The multimedia images were created by Liane Wilcher and Perry Wong with overall design by Fabian Astore, Senior Multimedia Producer, Macquarie University.

Figure 10.3 Mouse writing

Characters included Bog, who epitomised the gutter-dweller 'soiled with mud', the exceptional ugliness of Boot, and the Kit Kids who were played by two comedians and clearly 'assign[ed] certain comic effects to [the] images'. That they were remembered readily was evident from the vivid recall documented here which occurred up to a month after the performance.

RESPONSES TO *JAKE AND PETE*: ACCULTURATION IN CONTRAST TO MAKING MEANING

Although direct access and interaction with children is desirable to gain insight into their responses, the data reported below have been gained, and therefore mediated, through the cooperation of parents. However this situation serves as an important illustration of how imagination, creativity and learning occur between people. In Vygotsky's terms, parents are often powerful gatekeepers who can either enhance or constrain a child in reflecting and imagining. A parent and a child create co-knowledge.

Six parents who had booked to see the production of *Jake and Pete* with their children were invited to participate in the project. Selection was based on the criteria of (a) prior intention to attend the production, (b) age range of children, and (c) parents' willingness to participate in the task. The children were aged from 4–8 years.

Each parent was given a notebook in which they were asked to recount any responses which their child made to the performance of *Jake and Pete* in the month following the performance. (The excerpts below are quoted directly from these notebooks.)

While the children's responses varied widely in relation to their age, gender, and other factors such as their position in the family, it was also apparent that the parents' responses had a significant bearing on the ways in which the children used the experience. Dialogues between parents and children build on past experiences and knowledge. Parents will also bring to any exchanges the values and beliefs which they have about their children's development and the ways in which their children learn.

For some children, the experience of *Jake and Pete* appeared to be linked to an acculturation process. In the following example, a character in the play is likened to a current visiting celebrity who has been of particular interest to children in this girl's peer group.

> Elizabeth (8 yrs) was discussing that her favorite character was Boot (whom she has renamed Sumo (in reference to a recent visit by Sumo wrestlers from Japan)). It is her favorite because he is big, fat and eats chips and burps.

In a contrasting response, two siblings were clearly using their experience of the theatrical production to make meaning, and showed how they were dealing with some profound issues as they joked about the dialogue and played with the voices. This spontaneous discussion took place between a mother and her two children, Kirsty (8 yr 6 mths) and Paul (11 yr 3 mths) as they were leaving the theatre and walking along the footpath :

Kirsty:	I like the way he said Road [deep voice with sweep of the arm]. They thought Road would solve everything!
Mother:	They did, didn't they! [pause, cross street]
	… and street is the Son of Road [deep voice]
Paul:	… and avenue is the Son of Street and alley is the son of Avenue! [deep voice]

[In the car driving home]

Kirsty:	I wanted them to find Mum cat when they found home.
Mother:	Yes, so did the little boy in front of us.
Paul:	But that's the way it really is Kirsty.

The parent appears to listen and to subtly support the children's imaginative exploration of the circumstances of the Kit Kids' lives in relation to their own psychological development towards independence, moving from the known into the unknown. There also seems to be an awareness of the children's sense of wonderment and the fact that the children have 'more to do' with the production. This connection between external stimulus and the child's participation in the unknown is made by Cobb:

> Wonder is itself a kind of expectancy of fulfillment. The child's sense of wonder, displayed as surprise and joy, is aroused as a response to the mystery of external stimulus that promises 'more to come' or, better still 'more to do' — the power of perceptual participation in the known and unknown (1977:27–28).

The third example shows how the experience provoked extended periods of dramatic play in a child who had experienced the production of *Jake and Pete*. As Helen's mother reported:

> Helen (6.8 years) decided to use some wood that we had which had white laminex on to create a picture of cats. She spent hours drawing the outline of cats on the wood. She rubbed them out many times until they were perfect. She arranged many cats around her and talked to them as she drew and formulated the plan of what she wanted to create.

She wanted her father to cut all the individual cats out of the wood but after discussing it with Helen her father pointed out that this would be too difficult given their size etc. Helen then decided to paint the cats and add various materials for collars etc. This whole process took approx 8 hours, [and] she worked continuously on her creation.

When she was finished she was obviously pleased with herself — with a big smile on her face she said:

This is not a 'dog snake' picture is it?

And on the following day:

Helen decided that she would like a friend over to play 'cats'. Lily came and they dressed up as cats in black skivy, black tights and white gloves. One had on one of her father's bow ties and the other a bow in her hair. [A] coffee table was covered in a rug and the 'cats' spent a long time in their new home acting out a game of exploring and having a family. The soft toys of cats became their babies. The game proceeded in various forms for hours, Helen wrote signs…

The mother's valuing of this process is evident in the language she uses. She appreciates the time which Helen has taken to make the drawings, to set up the play and her use of the word *creation* may suggest that she values the creative energy and conception of her playmaking.

She appears to have taken pleasure in observing her child's response and has described the scene carefully. We can probably conclude that her parents' facilitation of such play was an encouragement for Helen to extend her exploration and to draw another child in to collaborate with her. Speculate about a different relationship that was less supportive and valuing — would the child incorporate the language so easily had the experience not been shared?

LEARNING AND IMAGINING

The theatrical setting, with its archetypal images, larger-than-life costumes and characters, and an atmosphere which encourages the suspension of everyday reality, provides a setting in which children can explore new roles and kinds of thinking that are not part of their everyday lives (Rogoff & Lave, 1984). With new kinds of thinking and learning come new ways of knowing and new capabilities.

In Vygotsky's (1978) terms the setting is a 'zone of proximal development' which enhances the children's capabilities and awareness — extends their view and the quality of their thinking. The potential for new connections and new ways of thinking come through imaginatively identifying with the central characters of the play. The Kit Kids, although small and innocent, are also bold, independent risk takers who learn through overcoming obstacles, including their fears and doubts, using their growing understanding and capabilities to satisfy their needs. The audience experiences, through the vivid and powerful images that emphasise the smallness and vulnerability of the actors, an expanded awareness of familiar ideas such as Road and Fridge.

This is a play of the postmodern era. The audience experiences the juxtaposition of multiple perspectives as each incident unfolds and the different needs, motives and perspectives are illuminated. Fridge, which begins as a source of comfort and food, later becomes a safe dry bed. The audience experiences, through media images, the violent death of a lizard on Road, but the dead lizard is also seen as an available and valuable source of food by Crow and, eventually, by the Kit Kids. Children can explore the ways in which their own emotions, judgments and actions interact in rapid succession as they identify with the vicissitudes of the journey. There is one episode in which, just as a Kit Kid is about to expose his vulnerability and cuteness as a means of obtaining food, the audience recognises the grossness, violence and evil intent of the Boot character. In an instant, the softness and vulnerability of the Kit Kid's initial approach is transformed to an acrobatic and terrified flight. The power of the Boot character rests with the vivid and archetypally violent imagery that is used. As our data above indicate, the Boot character was vividly remembered although the incident occupied only a small amount of time during the play.

The processes by which imagination is used to extend a child's knowledge and awareness are complex and extended over time. Parent reports indicate the important role played by caregivers in supporting and encouraging further exploratory discussions (such as a play on words with Road), shared new expressions from the play (This is not a 'dog snake' picture is it?), drawing and playmaking. All of these processes allow the new capabilities and awareness to be consolidated and integrated into the ongoing reality of each child's life. In the above reports, it is clear that parents understood that each child needed to choose which incidents in their experience required further elaboration and the setting in which they felt they could explore them.

The data also indicate that through emotionally powerful experiences and simple, strong imagery, abstract ideas and connections were available to the children in the audience. Abstract ideas involving meta-cognition, such as the notion of home as an emotion rather than a place, seemed to be easily understood by the children. Similarly, the sibling-mediated comment about life, 'But that's the way it really is, Kirsty', suggests that these powerful and technically mediated experiences are giving young children early access to very abstract ideas and ways of thinking.

The kinds of thinking and feeling that were generated in the theatrical experience are not usually invoked in schooling. In many school settings, small children occupy a subservient role — they are expected to attend to, and follow, instructions. In such a role, it is not always seen as appropriate to act boldly and creatively to meet personal needs.

Many teachers believe that learning occurs only through positive, safe and explicitly directed experiences. However, research indicates that emotions are a powerful element of cognitive development (Mandler, 1980). In particular, conceptual development and changing awareness are usually accompanied by initial fear, vulnerability and uncertainty. As in ancient civilisations, it is now recognised that vivid and strong emotions are an important part of learning and remembering. A safe and practical way for children to gain these experiences is through imagination and imaginative activities in which they explore the full range of human thinking and feeling in a secure and stable context. Such experiences are enhanced when adults recognise and respond to children's explorations by listening, observing and being available to collaborate with the child in making meaning out of concepts which may at first be new and frightening or puzzling.

CONCLUSION

The importance of imagination and creative imaginative experiences in human development are now better understood (Cohen & MacKeith, 1991). Adults embody their childhood memories and imaginative thinking for the rest of their lives, although often they no longer have direct access to memories of the incidents and experiences that have created their continuing sense of reality. In order to respond sensitively to children's imaginative experiences, adults need to get in touch with the processes of learning (through imagination), but also to recognise that their own remembered experience and learning may well be different to those of today's children. Thinking and imagining are necessarily different from generation to generation, and this aspect of inter-generational change is particularly apparent now, when the experience of childhood includes virtual reality and potent images of new multimedia and information technologies, as well as personal interaction via networked communication.

The ease with which children engage in imaginative activity contrasts with the adult tendency to defend the status quo. Many parents feel ambivalent about change and wish to hold on to (and in some cases reproduce in their children) their own past experiences. In times of change it is particularly necessary for children to prepare for the reality of their adulthood by engaging imaginatively with the realities of their childhood.

Imagination and engagement are powerful tools in learning and expanding the awareness of children. Engagement in events such as the one described here suggests that in the interests of the sustainability of human cultures and communities, we need to explore the possibilities of using new communications and multimedia technologies to enrich childhood learning through access to the creative arts and thus access to the new and creative insights of the community, even at the most abstract level.

References

Cobb, E. (1977) *The Ecology of Imagination in Children*. New York: Columbia University Press.

Cohen, D. & MacKeith, S. (1991) *The Development of Imagination*. London: Routledge.

Dovey, K. (1997) 'Special places of childhood'. Australian Broadcasting Corporation, Radio National, Comfort Zone, 8 March .

Kosslyn S. (1996) *Image and Brain*. Cambridge, MA :MIT Press.

Kosslyn S. & Pomerantz J. (1997) Imagery, propositions and the form of internal representations. *Cognitive Psychology*, **9**(1), 52–76.

Mandler, G. (1980) The generation of emotion. In *Emotion: Theory, Research and Experience*, edited by R. Plutchik & H. Kellerman. New York: Academic Press.

Metzler J. & Shepherd R. (1974) Transformational studies of internal representation of three dimensional objects. In *Theories of Cognitive Psychology: The Loyola Symposium*, edited by R. L. Solso. Potomac MD: Erlbaum

Papert, S. (1993) *The Children's Machine*. New York: Basic Books.

Pryor, S. (1996) Interactive eye space. Phantasmogoria: Pre-cinema to virtuality. *Artlink*, **16**(2&3).

Rogoff B. & Lave J. (eds) (1984) *Everyday Cognition: Its Development in Social Context*. Cambridge, MA: Harvard University Press.

Rubenstein, G. (1995) *Jake and Pete*. Sydney: Random House.

Scardemalia, M. and Bareite, C. (1994) Computer support for knowledge-building communities. *The Journal of Learning Sciences,* **3**(3), 265–283.

Vygotsky, L. (1978) *Mind in Society*. Harvard: Harvard University Press.

White, M. & Stevenson, C. (1997) *Drawing on the Art of Children: An Historical Perspective of Children's Art of the Twentieth Century* (exhibition catalogue). Sydney: Macquarie University.

Yates, F. (1966) *The Art of Memory*. London: Routledge and Kegan Paul.

12

THINKING FOR THE NEW MILLENNIUM

The contribution of process drama

Kathleen Warren

Societies have always needed a thinking populace, people who are able to consider issues of importance, draw conclusions and make decisions that benefit society as a whole, while being considerate of the individuals within that society. This basic societal need is unlikely to change, thus it is the responsibility of all educators to foster children's ability to think productively, effectively and responsively when faced with problems. The future, however, offers few certainties. The children who will become the thinking adults of the new millennium must be encouraged to recognise that flexibility and change are likely to dominate the twenty-first century, and teachers need to be constantly on the lookout for strategies that will foster reflective and innovative thinking. Drama, and in particular process drama, has much to offer as it engages children in authentic problem solving within the safety of the drama experience and within the security of the classroom with a teacher they trust.

Young children intuitively recognise the power of exploring their world through dramatic activities, taking roles and dramatising situations in co-operative mode (Johnson, Christie & Yawkey, 1987:22). They create a play world, just as participants in drama create a drama world (Vygotsky,1978). The play world they create helps them make sense of the real world (Neelands, 1991:9), just as Harwood (1984:13) believes human beings have used theatre for centuries to expose or resolve human dramas present in the everyday world. The play impulse, says Habermas (1992:157) 'mediates form and matter.'

PROCESS DRAMA IN EARLY CHILDHOOD SETTINGS

Some of the forms of drama that can be effectively included in the early childhood curriculum are (in alphabetical order) circus skills, dance drama, dramatic poetry, improvisation (referred to at times as 'creative drama') mask and mime, performance, process drama, puppetry, role play, readers' theatre and story enactment. Each can contribute to children's learning and to their enjoyment and understanding of the dramatic form.

However it is those genres of drama which centre, as O'Toole (1992:2–3) suggests, on fictional role-taking, involving both children and adults in the process of negotiation, that will be of particular interest in this chapter. Of the drama forms listed above, it is the 'complex dramatic encounter' (O'Neill, 1995:xiii) known as 'process drama' which most accurately matches O'Toole's description. In process drama teacher and children embark on a voyage of discovery, working in concert. Each takes a role that is pertinent to the situation, interacting and co-operating in partnership to forward the drama's course, considering and discussing the issues raised, making suggestions, trying them out through enactment, and eventually developing and enacting a satisfactory (to the participants) denouement.

This process was exemplified in a drama conducted with a group of two and three year olds in role as experienced gardeners, who were approached by a woman (teacher in role) who was having difficulties with her own garden. All her plants had changed colour overnight: the grass was red, yellow daisies had turned blue, red roses were now purple and the leaves on the tree had become pink. The children decided that someone called Jack (another teacher in role) had come into the garden at night and painted the plants. They then thought about and suggested ways in which Jack could be caught in the act and dissuaded from his nocturnal activities, enacting the story as it developed from their ideas, suggestions and solutions. The teachers worked within their roles to forward the children's thinking, knowledge and understanding in ways that seemed to be developmentally appropriate for the group. Children and teachers worked together enacting various solutions to the problem until a peacable one on which all could agree, was decided upon.

Heathcote (1991) views the child as a crucible and sees the teacher's role as that of enabler. In this her views are closely aligned with those of the Reggio Emilia early childhood programs, in which children and teachers are regarded as partners in the process of learning (see Hendrick, 1997:19). Knowledge and understanding are not simply introduced by the teacher but are reflected upon and so constructed, developed and transformed through the children's engagement in the drama world, a world 'of wonderment, of inquiry, of adventure, of transformation, of narratives in the making' (Taylor, 1997:13). Children's awareness of issues is thus changed, expanded and strengthened (Fleming, 1994 :42) even if the issues concerned were not previously fully comprehended. Heathcote (1985) refers to the need for children to own their own knowledge. Process drama can act as the catalyst which enables them to own and so make use of the knowledge and understanding they already possess (Warren, 1996:87).

DRAMA FOR UNDERSTANDING

Process drama does not focus on the child as performer. It does not concern itself with a product to be shown to an audience, even the friendly and familiar audience of other children in the class, school or centre. It evolves without a script and 'its outcome is unpredictable' (O'Neill, 1995:xiii); in process drama, children and teachers live through 'moment-to-moment experiences' (Bolton, 1979:17). The immediacy, spontaneity, vigor and inventiveness (O'Neill, 1995:17) of the experience enables the participants to identify with imagined role situations and, through this identification and interaction, explore issues, events and relationships (O'Neill and Lambert, 1982:11). Bolton referred to 'drama for understanding', an involvement which can lead to real changes in insight: '... there must be some shift of appraisal, an act of cognition that has involved a change of feeling, so that some facet of living is given (however temporarily) a different value' (1979:41).

Drama is grounded in, and develops from, the socio-dramatic play of young children, and as such would seem to be an art form and an educative force that is closely aligned with child-centred curricula, using approaches which are developmentally and personally appropriate in cultural contexts. These elements are regarded as being central to quality early childhood education and care (Arthur et al., 1993:55).

The need for young children to think about their world and the people in it is an essential focus for early childhood educators, and process drama can contribute to children's developing understanding of other people, their feelings and situations. Early childhood educators should be concerned, Katz believes with enabling children to develop 'a deeper and fuller sense of events and phenomena in their own environment and experience' (1994:20). By taking children's ideas and interests seriously, early childhood educators create opportunities for them to become engaged in thought, examining in depth the diversity of the world around them. Drama allows children and adults to embark on that same quest, on a journey of discovery which may initially have no fixed destination (Hancock, 1995:21), but which has a shared direction. Kurth-Schai (1991:199) suggested that we have a limited understanding of the ways in which children 'discover, interpret and shape the world'. Yet children can give us valuable insights into their interpretations of reality if we are willing to listen. Process drama is a significant medium through which we can explore children's conceptual, experiential and emotional worlds.

LANGUAGE AND THOUGHT IN PROCESS DRAMA

Thinking and language are closely linked, language being the tool that human beings use to 'sort out' their thoughts (Bruner 1988:88). It is through the manipulation of language that people make sense of their world, or 'reproduce their lifeworld' (Habermas (1987:342). Makin et al. (1995:xx) define language as 'one of a range of symbols with which human beings express and manipulate their worlds ... sets of human-specific resources with which meanings are constructed and shared'.

Language is fundamental to children's conceptualisation of their own mental world (Astington, 1995:109), and the ways in which children talk about their own ideas is integral to our understanding of their thoughts. Language enables us to consider events from the past, and to talk about things that are not present; through language, children can build an imaginative world (Makin et al., 1995:xxiv). For example, in a process drama experience based on the Australian Aboriginal Dreamtime, a group of four year olds were in role as helpers of Biami, the spirit who created the land. The Aboriginal poet, Oodgeroo Noonuccal (Walker 1970), who originally published as Kath Walker, believed Biami to be the best known of the great Aboriginal ancestors who made the world and its people.

They were approached by a stranger (teacher in role) who wanted to know the story of the land. The children were able to relate these past events as if they had taken part in them and of course, being cast as Biami's helpers, that was exactly what the dramatic context assumed. When the stranger asked to be taken to one of the places Biami had created, but expressed fear of the dangers that might confront them all on the way, the children were able to describe rivers infested with crocodiles that the group would have to cross, trees they would have to climb and rocks that would block their path. They were also able to think about, and then enact, how each of these (imaginary) barriers could be overcome.

Habermas (1987:312) wrote of the three components of elementary speech acts: (1) the 'propositional' component represents or mentions the matter in question; (2) the 'illocutionary' component concerns the interpersonal relationships involved; and (3) the 'linguistic' components enable the intentions of the speaker to be expressed. Drama experiences, and in particular process drama, constantly involve children in these three elements as the drama proceeds. Drama both 'demands and embodies language', says Booth (1987:5). Language is at the core of the drama process (O'Neill and Lambert, 1982:18) and it is this that makes process drama such an effective learning and teaching medium. Process drama experiences provide children with many language opportunities to consider and form their own views of themselves and of the world (Booth, 1987:6), allowing them to develop control over those views and over their own use of language.

Tough's (1977) research on the development of children's language led her to postulate that three factors were necessary for children's language to develop to its full potential: dialogue with an empathic adults, opportunities for imaginative play, and an enabling environment in which children can encounter many language experiences. As Booth (1987:6) pointed out, all three conditions are likely to be met in drama experiences where the opportunities for rewarding language episodes can be unlimited.

THE ROLE OF THE TEACHER: TEACHER IN ROLE

The concept of teacher in role has already been introduced. By working with children within a drama experience, teachers have at their command a powerful educative tool (Warren, 1992:8). A teacher role of lower status relative to the roles assumed by the children can be especially effective, particularly if that character (i.e. the teacher in role) has a problem which needs solving. For example, in a drama with a class of four and five year olds, the teacher took the role of someone who had found a lost and distressed bird (another adult in role). The children were cast as ornithologists, who would obviously know a lot about birds and should therefore be able to be of assistance. The bird did not speak but expressed her unhappiness through posture, gesture and facial expression. The teacher in role simply said 'I don't know what is the matter with her', thus giving the children the freedom to think about the problem from many perspectives.

When it was finally decided (by the children) that this bird had somehow lost her family who had flown south to warmer climes for the winter (the drama was being conducted on a wintry November day in Ireland), the bird looked relieved, and the children who were monitoring her non-verbal behaviour closely were certain they were on the right track and began to think about where the bird's family might have gone and how they might facilitate a reunion. While the story was certainly enacted, each 'scene' was preceded by complex thought as the group wrestled with the problem at hand.

The opportunities for children to express their thoughts are influenced by a multitude of factors, but the way in which children are spoken to is, therefore, crucial; dialogue between teachers and children is critical to the learning process (Hendrick, 1997:19);

the teacher's most important language-related task is to help children communicate (Trim, 1992:xxi). In process drama, teachers encourage children to consider and express ideas by effecting a shift in the power relationships and by asking children questions as if they (the teacher/s) really want to know the answers. Carroll (1988:19) cites a conversation with Dorothy Heathcote in which she says:

> In drama you can't talk to the participants with a status attitude like teachers talk to children. You've got to use a language code of choice, and an amount of elaboration in the language that makes them feel like they know what they are doing.

The questions teachers ask children in process drama experiences are carefully framed to stimulate and encourage complex thought, for effective questioning on the part of the teacher enables children to explain their understandings (Makin et al., 1995:29). When teachers question as if they really want to know, children are immediately empowered, as they recognise that they are free to contribute a range of ideas and possible solutions without fear of disapproval or rejection. Such genuine requests for information or ideas are less threatening to children. There is a need for human beings to be open-minded and willing to construe knowledge and values from a variety of perspectives (Bruner, 1990:30). Process drama establishes fictional contents where difficulties are encountered which encourage children to consider a range of potential outcomes.

Bruner (1990:26) postulated the value of 'pragmatic, perspectival questions' in enabling people to understand their own culture. 'What would it be like to believe that?' or 'What would I be committing myself to if I believed that?' are exactly the sorts of questions that are often asked in process drama. Here are some examples of a teacher in role handing the decision making to the children:

- I don't know what we should do.
- Why would anyone want to steal Santa's sleigh?
- I went to check on Max's boat and there is a Wild Thing curled up in it fast asleep!
- I've often wondered what the sky is for.
- I don't know what sort of food they'd want for the wedding of Cinderella and the Prince.

Only one of these questions is framed in the traditional question mode, for the questions that are most effective at stimulating thought are not the questions that demand an answer but rather those that invite children to wonder about some aspect of the world or of behaviour.

The problems that arise in process drama can genuinely be considered as 'works of thought' (Foucault, 1984:390), throughout which both children and teachers can reflectively interact as true partners in the discourse. The language interactions between adults and children are interactions which foster a discussion of equals, emphasising associations in which the children's ideas and opinions are sought and accepted. Whenever teachers speak, they are faced with a choice (Barthes, 1977:191). Either they can accept the powerful stance of authority or they can speak in ways that will reject it. Bolton (cited in O'Neill, 1995:62) encapsulated the essence of teacher in role:

> The teacher in role has power but it is not of the conventional kind. It carries within it its opposite; a potential for being powerless ... the power relationship between pupils and teacher within the drama is tacitly perceived as negotiable.

To an observer of the dramatic action, it might seem as if the teacher is in absolute command (O'Neil, 1995:61), but the drama will progress most effectively when the teacher guides discreetly, encouraging the children to make the decisions that will forward its course.

Tough (1977:175) wrote of the importance of language in enabling human beings to exchange meanings. For this to happen, people must be able to use language to project into other people's needs (as listener), to reflect on their own meanings and find the language which will best express them. Through dialogue, children develop the language skills on which further education can build. The more teachers use strategies which demand the use of language, particularly through dialogue, the more will children's abilities to use language for thinking and communicating, flourish (Tough, 1977:178). The strategy of teacher in role is a perfect example of Tough's 'empathic adult'.

INTERACTIVE THINKING

Knowledge is less concerned with the simple recognition of objects than with the intelligence engendered through the mutual understanding which develops between subjects capable of speech and action (Habermas, 1987:295). When one person carries out a speech act another person takes up a position in regard to it. The two then enter into an interpersonal relationship which is structured by a system of perspectives amongst speakers, listeners and non-participants who are there at the time (op cit:296–7) . Drama educators will recognise in Habermas' argument, a lucid interpretation of process drama.

An example comes from a drama experience in which a class of six and seven year olds were in role as a search-and-rescue team. Their task was to deal with a dragon (teacher in role) who had been found asleep in an office. Although the first reaction from some of the boys in the group was to move in and capture the dragon (the girls were not so sure), the dragon's answers, or, more skilfully, non-answers to their questions forced the group to realise that here was a very frightened little creature. They decided that she must be a baby dragon who had got lost and that their task would be to discover just where she had come from and to take her home. The change in the children's perspectives and in their relationship with the dragon was facilitated by the skill and perception of the teacher who used her role to develop their understanding of the situation. Understanding is fostered "through discussion and collaboration" (Bruner, 1996:56) when children are encouraged to express their own ideas and to consider the sometimes opposing views of others.

SOME RESEARCH FINDINGS: DRAMA AND LANGUAGE

Claims regarding the capacity of drama to encourage children's thinking and language are based on experience, practice and research. Vitz (1984) investigated children's speech in a first- to third-grade classroom in the USA where the children were largely immigrants from Southeast Asia. Using a picture book she took examples of children's oral language as they retold the story, and found that children in the experimental group, who took part in creative drama experiences, used a significantly higher number of words per communication and showed a greater mean length of utterances, both indicating greater sentence or utterance complexity. The same complexity was not evident in the results from the control group who had taken part in an audio-lingual program. Snyder-Greco (1983:10) found that children who engaged in drama showed significant gains in the number of words used per utterance as well as making greater use of projective language to forecast events and relate possibilities of something that might occur. They also showed an increased ability to survey alternatives, anticipate consequences, recognise problems and predict solutions. It is these linguistic skills which are fostered in process drama and which require and facilitate complex thought.

The symbolic nature of language is emphasised by Foster (1990:26) who suggested that once children become symbolic their opportunities to communicate effectively expand. Wagner (1988: 48) referred to the work of Pellegrini (1980, 1982) who suggested that drama facilitates symbolic functioning because symbols and the concepts they stand for are necessarily separated in drama experiences. The work of Pellegrini and his associates focused on children in K-2 classes who were of low socioeconomic status. He maintained that when children are engaged in drama experiences they are using language orally to describe and discuss matters that they will later need to communicate in writing. At the beginning of their dramatic play episodes, Pellegrini (1980) observed that the children defined the roles they would play and identified the props they would use, and in so doing employed linguistic definitions of pronouns, explicitly introducing topics and clarifying any ambiguities about the roles they intended to portray.

Process drama extends this process. In the drama about the lost baby dragon (described above), the teacher explained prior to the drama that the children would take the role of people who help others. The group suggested possible characters and eventually decided on members of a search-and-rescue team. It was then suggested by the teacher that the drama would also involve a very strange creature and the children again were asked for suggestions. The ideas flowed — a monster, a tiger, a bunyip, a fairy, a ghost — but the group finally agreed on a dragon. Thus, before the drama even began, the children were enabled to make the sorts of decisions that Pellegrini had observed.

Tough's research (1977) found that children who were at risk educationally were those who were less efficient in using language to reflect, compare, imagine, predict, speculate and reason. Parsons, Schaffner, Little & Felton (1984) conducted research to investigate language in (process) drama lessons, as compared to language used in a control sample of non-drama lessons. They defined the (process) drama in which they were interested as 'being and doing within an imaginary situation' (Parsons et al., 1984:9). Drama forms such as dance, storybuilding, the speaking of poetry and the development and use of scripts were omitted, but the development of presentational drama, that is drama which is to be shown, was included.

Language samples from the process drama classes were analysed and compared to the samples from the non-drama classes. Parsons et al. (1984) found that process drama encouraged children to use higher abstractional discourse than was the case in non-drama classrooms, although presentational drama was not as effective in this regard.

In a discussion of the implications of their results, Parsons et al. (1994:19) referred to the educational benefits of drama, particularly experiential (process) drama. Their research indicated that in the non-drama classes the language used was 'overwhelmingly informational in purpose'. Process drama classes, on the other hand, enabled children to use the type of language that, as Tough (1977) has pointed out, advantages them educationally. Expressive language, that is language which expresses the feelings, opinions and thoughts of the speaker, occurred often during the process drama classes but rarely or never in non-drama classes. Informational language does not have the same complexity of syntax as expressive language; nor is it used to express abstract concepts or tentative and conditional propositions (Parsons et al., 1984: 20–21).

Process drama brings together thought and feeling, and this emotional engagement (Parsons et al, 1984:21) further stimulates intellectual growth. The use of reflection, which occurs both during and after good process drama, enables children to use language 'to express their evolving thoughts, opinions and feelings' (op cit:21). Children begin to use language to formulate theories about their developing morals and values as they discuss 'their own feelings, experiences and observations' (op cit: 21).

Carroll (1988:14) pointed out that process drama allows a wider range of language usage (for both teachers and children) than that found in non-drama classrooms. Carroll analysed and compared the patterns of discourse that occurred in process drama experiences with those of more conventional classroom interactions. Like Parsons et al., Carroll found that informational language was significantly higher in non-drama classrooms. In (process) drama classrooms, matter was included through 'role shifted discussion' (1998:16) in which children were enabled to engage in 'substantial discussions about abstract relations' (op cit:17). Such studies have shown that there is an interweaving of the cognitive and affective for the tasks and emphases planned in process drama classes, which enables children to utilise language to report, elaborate, give detail, sequence events, plan, predict, speculate, question others, persuade and reason, all of which require complex thought.

DRAMA AS SOCIAL PROCESS

The experience of considering issues from different points of view leads to the recognition that our actions affect the interests of others (Habermas, 1992:5). This realisation necessarily changes our view of the world, as through discussion and argument people search collaboratively for truth and, viewing issues from the perspectives of others, are motivated to find effective solutions for the propositions at hand (op cit:198) . Problems which arise in real life and which have to be resolved through discourse, require co-operation. Habermas (1987:67) refers to 'moral argument', which enables conflicts to be resolved by consensual means — a common will. He cites Mead (1934) who pointed out that taking the perspective of another person allows for self-reflection, which in turn leads to an understanding of why certain actions take place, and eventually allows human beings to develop internal control over their own modes of behaviour. Process drama allows children to experience this same passage of thought in what Heathcote (1984:130) referred to as 'a no-penalty area'.

For young children, there is much in their world that is new (Neelands, 1984), although they enter school with rich yet diverse backgrounds in terms of experience, knowledge, attitudes and language (Parsons, 1991:88). Process drama draws on this knowledge and understanding and extends it, enabling children to learn about the world in a remarkable way (Forehan, 1991:11). They learn through first-hand experience and are empowered to understand issues 'from within the experience of the participant' (Bolton, 1986:17). Drama harnesses the inner world of meaning to the outer world of expressive action (Morgan & Saxton, 1987:1), and enables children to learn by drawing on their knowledge of the real world and, through collaboration with teachers and other children, creating a parallel but fictional world (Simons, 1981:25).

IMAGINATIVE THOUGHT

The examples of process drama given in this chapter also imply an encouragement of imaginative thought. Through the power of the imagination, human beings develop a clearer understanding of the world and are able to consider a range of possibilities — 'the infinite horizons of essential knowledge' (Husserl, 1931:200). Reflective thought indicates that reflections are experiences which provide the basis for new reflections, which in turn provide the basis for reflecting even further. The simple retelling of what happened yesterday is an act of imagination (Booth, 1994:71). This is the essence of knowing and understanding and is based 'on the plane of imagination' (Husserl, 1950:133).

Process drama provides opportunities for children to use an imaginative approach to consider some of the primary human conflicts. The powerful, abstract, binary concepts of security/danger, courage/cowardice, cleverness/stupidity, hope/despair and good/evil (Egan, 1994:195) can be experienced through the imaginative engagement in process drama. This scaffolding of abstraction can, through imagination, make content understandable, attainable and significant even for very young children.

Casey (1991:36) discusses three acts of conscious imagining: 'imaging', 'imagining-that' and 'imagining-how'. 'Imaging' involves the contemplation of objects or events as they might relate to one or other of the senses, 'imagining-that' suggests that whole events or states of affairs can be conjured up, and 'imagining-how' refers to the contemplation of how an imagined circumstance takes place. Process drama places children in situations in which these passages of imagination must occur if the drama is to progress. In drama, children process the key events, images and themes of the story. What is happening is imagined, engaged with and interpreted (Booth 1994:71).

Certain images evoke imaginative experiences (Haine, 1985:188) which take children beyond what might normally be expected from them. Robertson (1982), researching the visual arts, found that certain 'themes' seemed to extend children's imagination, and this extension was demonstrated by the children's absorption in their work, the degree of satisfaction with what they were doing, and unusual, yet evocative ways of interpreting the subject. The same thing appears to take place in process drama (Haine, 1985:187–8), which is structured in ways that enable children to demonstrate a high level of thinking, a flow of fantasy, memory and speculation, and an almost mythical appreciation of the drama experience they are creating (op cit:190); what Janssens (1993:9) called 'an imaginative reality'. Through the use of imagination and intuition children can venture into the unknown as they explore the fictional process. 'The best dramas take place on planets or in caves' (Heathcote, 1985); in other words, children's imaginative thinking is stimulated more by the exotic than by the mundane.

Process drama requires imagination, but it is a disciplined and informed exercise of imagination (Degenhardt & McKay, 1988:246) in which the teacher and children work co-operatively and contextually as they anticipate a range of actions and develop and test a range of possible responses. Acceptance of the imaginative context — 'building belief' (Wagner, 1976:68) — is essential to the success of process drama. When this is achieved, participants can reflect on the meaning of what they are creating (Bolton, 1992:12).

CONCEPT DEVELOPMENT THROUGH DRAMA

When children are framed in a position of influence within a fictional drama context (Heathcote, 1984:168), they are immediately empowered to consider issues which might appear to be beyond their developmental level. Vygotsky recognised that the development of concepts is more complex than simply setting up associations between words and objects. Concepts develop as children consider solutions to problems, and as they work towards those solutions new concepts emerge (Vygotsky, 1962:54). Very young children group things together in their minds, using categorisations which may or may not seem to have logical bases. For example, a two year old might decide that all birds are ducks but may not include kookaburras in this category. Later, children are increasingly able to make abstractions and form stable groupings which lead to the formation of concepts. Between these two stages there is a phase in which children can operate with the 'functional equivalent' (Vygotsky, 1962:540) of the concept and are able to behave as if they have an adult's understanding of the idea. It is in this stage, in the zone of proximal development, that children, with adult assistance, are able to solve problems which might be expected to be beyond them given their level of actual development, and it is here that process drama has particular value. Bruner's (1988: 94) use of the term 'scaffolding' to describe the actions of the teacher in assisting children's entry into the zone of proximal development, implies that teachers should focus on 'manageable bits of the problem' (Simons, 1981:27), breaking it into parts so that children do not become confused by a multiplicity of issues.

Simons described a process drama experience in which primary-aged children were enabled to understand the concept of homeless youth. In a series of dramatic situations, the children worked through a sequence of strategies which put them in the position of considering the concept from several points of view. They were put into situations in which they had to deal with the betrayal of confidence, loss of security and powerlessness experienced by the homeless. At the conclusion of the drama, the children were given the opportunity to reflect on what had taken place. The reflective process (Simons, 1981:31) indicated that the children's understanding of the concept of homeless youth had broadened, and that they showed a deeper and more sophisticated understanding of the issues involved than had been the case in prior discussions which had set the scene for the drama experience.

FUTURE THINKING

Having just entered the twenty-first century, the concept of change seems less frightening than it did when Toffler's (1970) book *Future Shock* presented a description of a changing world which was greeted with trepidation and some dismay. We now see the new technologies which are moving the world forward 'towards a postmodernist culture of stimulation' (Carroll, 1996:16) as presenting a challenging and exciting future. Process drama can engage children in a 'fluid, negotiated sense of community' (op cit: 14) which encompasses and welcomes variations in meaning, situations and interpersonal interactions which will equip them with the skills they will need to cope with the changing future. Hancock (1995) suggested that drama is, and indeed should be, closely aligned with chaos theory because drama's unpredictability is also its power. It is the 'jumble of seeing disorder ... spontaneous and unforeseen interactions between individuals and ideas ...

collisions between actions and words' (op cit:17) which contribute to drama's excitement and potency. Evidence that children learn best when they have to contend with new ideas by comparing and contrasting them with ideas with which they are already familiar thus integrating the new ideas with those already held, has been extensively cited by Book and Putman (1992:20). Process drama experiences can engage children in predicaments in which such interactions and intricacies will occur (Hancock, 1995:17), and teachers' careful planning and handling of these situations provide a way through the chaos, out of which exhilarating dramatic moments may arise.

The risks of drama bring their own rewards (Morgan & Saxton, 1987:156). When teachers are able to welcome 'productive disorder' (Hancock, 1995:18) that is at the basis of vigorous drama, when they venture into the unknown, apprehensive about what might occur, but willing to take that risk, they can experience tremendous excitement when the gamble pays off and the children develop novel, exciting and challenging ideas. Teachers' confidence soars when they realise that what seemed a hazardous venture on their part actually enabled the children to break barriers in their thinking.

References

Arthur, L., Beecher, B., Dockett, S. Farmer, S. & Richards, E. (1993) *Programming and Planning in Early Childhood Settings.* Sydney: Harcourt Brace.

Astington, J. (1995) Talking it over with my brain. *Monograph of the SRCD,* **60**(1), serial No. 243.

Barthes, R. (1977) *Image, Music, Text.* London, Fontana.

Bolton, G. (1979) *Towards a Theory of Drama in Education.* London: Longmans.

Bolton, G. (1986) Freedom and imagination and the implications for teaching drama. In *Gavin Bolton: Collected writings on drama in Education*, edited by D. Davis and C. Lawrence. London: Longman.

Bolton, G. (1992) *New Perspectives on Classroom Drama.* London: Simon and Schuster.

Book, C. & Putman, J. (1992) Organisation and management of a classroom as a learning community culture. In *Power in the Classroom: Communication, Control and Concern*, edited by V. Richmond and J. McCroskey. New Jersey: Lawrence Erlbaum Associates.

Booth, D. (1987) *Drama Words: The Role of Drama in Language Growth.* Toronto: Language Study Centre, Toronto University.

Booth, D. (1994) Entering the story cave. *National Association for Drama in Education, J. (Aust),* **18**(2), 67–77.

Bruner, J. (1988) Vygotsky: a historical and conceptual perspective. In *Language and Literacy from an Educational Perspective,* vol. 1, edited by N. Mercer, pp. 86–98.

Bruner, J. (1990) *Acts of Meaning.* Cambridge, MA: Harvard University Press.

Bruner, J. (1996) *The Culture of Education.* Cambridge, MA: Harvard University Press.

Carroll, J. (1988) Terra incognita: Mapping drama talk. *National Association for Drama in Education J. (Aust.),* **12**(2), 13–20.

Carroll, J. (1996) Drama technology: Realism and emotional literacy. *National Association for Drama in Education J. (Aust.),* **20**(2),7–18.

Casey, E. (1991) *Spirit and Soul.* Dallas: Spring Publishing.

Degenhardt, M. & McKay, E. (1988) Imagination and education for intercultural understanding. In *Imagination and Education*, edited by K. Egan and E. McKay . New York: Teachers College Press.

Egan, K. (1994) Tools for enhancing imagination in teaching. In *Teacher Development and the Struggle for Authenticity*, edited by P. Grimmet and J. Neufield. New York: Teachers College Press.

Fleming, M. (1994) *Starting Drama Teaching*. London: David Fulton.

Forehan, B. (1991) Drama with visually impaired children. *National Association for Drama in Education J. (Aust.)*, **15**(2), 11–15.

Foster, S. (1990) *The Communicative Competence of Young Children*. London: Longman.

Foucault, M. (1984) Polemics, politics and problemizations. In *The Foucault Reader*, edited by P. Rabinow. London: Penguin.

Habermas, J. (1987) *The Philosophical Discourse of Reason* (translated by F. Lawrence). Cambridge, MA: Polity Press.

Habermas J. (1992) *Postmetaphysical Thinking: Philosophical Essays* (translated by W. M. Hohengarten). Cambridge, MA: Polity Press.

Haine, G. (1985) In the labyrinth of the image: An archetypal approach to drama in education. *Theory into Practice*, **24**(3), 187–192.

Hancock, A. (1995) Chaos in drama: The metaphors of chaos theory as a way of understanding drama process. *National Association for Drama in Education J. (Aust)*, **19**(1),15–26.

Harwood, R. (1984) *All the World's a Stage*. London: Methuen.

Heathcote, D. (1984) Signs and portents. In *Dorothy Heathcote: Collected Writings on education and Drama*, edited by L. Johnson and C. O'Neill. London: Hutchinson.

Heathcote D. (1985) Personal tutorials with Dorothy Heathcote, University of Newcastle-upon-Tyne.

Heathcote, D. (1991) 'Drama and Curriculum' (videorecording). Newcastle-upon-Tyne: University of Newcastle upon Tyne.

Hendrick, J. (1997) *First Steps towards Teaching the Reggio Way*. Columbus, Ohio: Merrill.

Husserl, E. (1931) *Ideas: General Introduction to Pure Phenomenology* (translated by W.R. Boyce Gibson). London: Allen and Unwin.

Husserl, E. (1950) *Ideen I*. Den Hague: Nijhoff.

Janssens, L. (1993) The realm of imagination. Paper presented at the International Conference to Celebrate the Work of Dorothy Heathcote, University of Lancaster, July.

Johnson, J, Christie, J. & Yawkey T. (1987) *Play and Early Childhood Development*. Illinois: Scott Foresman.

Katz, L. (1994) *Reflections on the Reggio Emilia Approach*. Urbana, Ill. Eric Clearinghouse on Elementary and Early Childhood Education.

Kurth-Schai, R. (1991) The peril and promise of childhood: ethical implications for tomorrow's teachers. *J. Teacher Education*, **42**(3), 196–204.

Makin, L., Campbell, J. & Diaz-Jones, C. (1995) *One Childhood, Many Languages*. Sydney: Harper Educational.

Morgan, N. & Saxton, J. (1987) *Teaching Drama: A Mind of Many Wonders*. London: Hutchison.

Neelands, J. (1984) *Making Sense of Drama*. London: Heinemann.

Neelands, J. (1991) The meaning of drama, Part 1. *The Drama Magazine: Journal of National Drama*, November 6–9.

O'Neill, C. (1995) *Drama Worlds: A Framework for Process Drama*. Portsmouth, NH: Heinemann.

O'Neill, C. & Lambert, A. (1982) *Drama Structures: A Practical Handbook for Teachers*. London: Hutchinson.

O'Toole, J. (1992) *The Process of Drama: Negotiating Art and Meaning*. London: Routledge.

Parsons, B., Schaffner, M., Little, G. & Felton, H. (1984) *Drama, Language and Learning* (paper No.1). Hobart: National Association for Drama in Education.

Parsons, B. (1991) Storymaking and drama for children 5–8. In *The Arts in Early Childhood*, edited by S. Wright. Sydney: Prentice Hall.

Pellegrini, A. (1980) The relationship between kindergarteners' play and achievement in prereading, language and writing, *Psychology in the schools,* **17,** 530–535.

Pellegrini, A. (1982) The effects of thematic-fantasy play training on the development of children's story comprehension, *American Educational Research Journal,* **19,** 443–452.

Roberson, S. (1982) *Rosegarden and Labyrinth* (2nd edn). Dallas TX: Spring Publications.

Simons, J. (1981) Concept development and drama: Scaffolding the learning. In *Drama in Education: The State of the Art,* edited by J. Hughes .Sydney: Educational Drama Association of New South Wales.

Snyder-Greco, T. (1983) The effects of creative dramatic techniques on selected language functions of language disorders children. *Children's Theatre Review,* **32,** 9–13.

Taylor, P. (1997) Australian research: on-line and on-top. *Australian Drama Education Magazine,* **3,** 10–17.

Tough, J. (1977) *The Development of Meaning.* London: Unwin.

Trim, J. (1992) Language teaching in the perspective of predictable requirements of the twenty-first century. *AILA Review,* **9** (edited by J. Matter), 7–21.

Toffler, A. (1970) *Future Shock.* London: Bodley Head.

Vitz, K. (1984) The effects of creative drama in English as a second language. *Children's Theatre Review,* **33,** 23–26.

Vygotsky, L. (1962) *Thought and Language.* MA: M.I.T.

Vygotsky, L. (1978) The development of higher psychological processes. In *Mind and Society.* Cambridge, MA: Harvard University Press.

Wagner, B-J. (1976) *Dorothy Heathcote: Drama as a Learning Medium.* Washington DC: National Education Association.

Wagner, B-J. (1988) Research currents: Does classroom drama affect the arts of language? *Language Arts,* 65(1), 46–51.

Walker, K. (1970) *My People* Brisbane: Jacaranda Press.

Warren, K. (1992) *Hooked on Drama.* Sydney: Institute of Early Childhood, Macquarie University.

Warren, K. (1996) Empowering children through drama. In *Issues in Expressive Arts: Curriculum for Early Childhood,* edited by W. Schiller, pp. 83–97. Amsterdam: Gordon & Breach Publishers.

13

CHAPTER

UNCOVERING THE
POTENTIAL OF RHYTHM

Education through arts

Kathleen Kampa

What implications does our rapidly changing world have on the educational needs of children? As educators continue to search for strategies to enhance students' learning potential in order to prepare them for the changing world, current research gives us insights into the ways in which our brain functions, the different types of intelligence we possess, and how children learn best.

Education is already making changes to incorporate what current research is teaching us about how children learn best. Early childhood educators, dancers and musicians have been uncovering parts of this secret for many years. Orff, Laban, Dalcroze and Kodaly are among those dancers and musicians who have focused on the use of music and movement in the development of the young child, and a principle common to all of their work is the element of rhythm. Rhythm is a natural element in our world and is consequently at the heart of a child's everyday life. Rhythm is part of the cosmos or nature (Nash 1974; Findlay, 1971). Children see the patterns of day and night, the seasons and the ebb and flow of the tide. A child's own body provides a 'biological' sense of rhythm in his or her heartbeat, breath, and digestive system. Daily activities such as jumping rope or throwing a ball become efficient when performed in rhythm. Child's play, from its very earliest manifestations, draws out rhythm in game chants, songs, and rhymes. Cultures have used rhymes or chants to introduce young children to rhythm. Even memory itself demands rhythm as it manifests itself in many forms: number patterns, pictures, graphs, movement patterns, song lyrics, melodies, stories, poetry, language phrases, travel routes, and so on. Rhythm provides us with immeasurable pleasure and security, not just in the arts, but in our everyday lives.

This chapter focuses on rhythm in the context of an arts-based programme to develop English language skills, using Howard Gardner's 'multiple intelligences' approach to guide the mode of instruction. Other curriculum areas can be nurtured as well through a combined multiple intelligences approach within an arts-based program. The nature of instruction in many of the arts-based programs begins from the child's perspective, with topics relevant to young children. As in other successful early childhood programs this approach is integrated, drawing out each element for particular focus, rather than beginning with separate parts. The importance of developing an understanding from the whole picture to its parts is echoed in constructivist approaches such as Brooks (1993:47) who proposed that '... students seek to make meaning by breaking the wholes into parts that *they* can see and understand'. As John Dewey (1902, 1990), an early critic of modern education, wrote:

> ... the child's life is an integral, a total one. He passes quickly and readily from one topic to another, as from one spot to another, but is not conscious of transition or break.

Our goal as educators then is to create an environment in which children can easily discover the natural rhythms of the world in which they live. Children must be able to construct an understanding of their world and develop a personal way to respond to it through language. The connections between language and rhythm are apparent. Through an arts-based approach, children explore concepts through both the body and mind. Using the senses, they *hear* music and stories. They *see* pictures. They *smell* the rain, clean hands, autumn leaves, and freshly baked cookies. They *taste* a vast array of food. They physically *touch* their world when they use their bodies to interact with the many images surrounding them. Through multi-sensory experience, children reflect, discuss and refine their impressions of the world. Rhythm features in these sensory experiences and its appeal to children means that a rhythmically engaging classroom is full of joy and discovery.

In such an atmosphere, both teachers and students sense that learning is taking place. Recent brain research by Robert Sylwester in his book *A Celebration of Neurons* states:

> ... joyful classroom behaviors ... create an internal chemical response that can increase the possibility that students will learn how to solve problems successfully in potentially stressful situations (1995:39).

Educational brain consultant Pat Wolfe (1996) suggests that rhythm, music and rhyme are also powerful hooks to memory. Hence, activities utilising music, rhyme, and/or rhythm have the potential to either stimulate or calm children.

THE RHYTHMIC POTENTIAL OF THE BRAIN

Discovering how the brain learns best can greatly enhance the learning climate. The brain itself is rhythmical; Sylwester (1995) suggests that the human brain is similar to a jungle with tens of millions of neural networks or nerve cell connections. The brain sifts through the multitude of incoming sensory information and must decide what is important to keep and what will be dropped. Short-term memory is at work. In effect, the brain decides what is necessary to pay attention to. The selection criteria for retaining information relies heavily upon how emotionally relevant and useful the incoming information is. Information that is emotionally laden will command attention and be processed by the brain's 'emotional centre', the limbic system. According to Juan Pascual-Leon, because short-term memory space (referred to as M-Space) is limited to holding a small amount of information in young children, we must 'chunk' related pieces of information into larger units (Wolfe 1996). Fortunately, this 'M-Space' increases from just two spaces (plus or minus two) for children at the mental age of five and increases by one unit every other year up to age fifteen. Long-term memory begins to form. During the next stage of processing, neurotransmittors are produced. These are chemicals that carry information across the gap, or synapse, from one neuron to another. When this occurs, a connection is being made. The more rehearsal that occurs in the short-term memory, the stronger the connection becomes, and in turn the stronger the memories that are stored. In these ways the brain itself actually works in rhythm to create patterns which in turn create memory (Wolfe, 1996; Sylwester, 1995).

What 'brain-friendly' strategies are recommended for the classroom? Sylwester's view of a healthy learning environment would be a classroom filled with:

> sensory, cultural, and problem layers that are closely related to the real-world environment in which we live ... the environment that best stimulates the neural networks that are genetically tuned to it (1995:23).

Sylwester's suggestions point to the need for the child to create his or her own reality through personal construction of categories, development of existing abilities, and individual solutions to challenges. Moreover, he suggests that the arts and humanities are conducive to expanding and integrating stimuli in the environment. An arts-based program encourages children to explore, experience, play, and celebrate their world in brain-friendly ways.

THE POTENTIAL OF MULTIPLE INTELLIGENCES

As we reflect on students' learning processes, it is evident that students develop skills and come to understand a topic in many different ways. Howard Gardner (1983) proposed that students do not learn in the same way; they each learn in their own, unique way. The *ways* in which students learn and demonstrate understanding can be grouped into various 'intelligences'. Gardner labelled eight of these intelligences and is currently working to define a ninth one.

Everyone possesses varying amounts of each of these intelligences, but the combination is unique to each person. Sylwester cited Gazzaniga's suggestion that genetics play a role in the way the brain processes information, with various 'modules' of the brain '... interconnected, semi-autonomous networks of neurons ... specializing in a limited cognitive function' (1995:39). Since the modules focus on a particular area of learning, this may give us some insight into how the brain develops the various intelligences. Gardner (1983) holds the view that the realisation of these inborn capacities or potential intelligences is influenced by the culture into which one is born.

In what ways are your students smart? Gardner defines intelligence as:

- the ability to solve problems that one encounters in real life,
- the ability to generate new problems to solve, and
- the ability to make something or offer a service that is valued within one's culture (Gardner, 1983:60–61).

By looking at the ways in which students solve problems, we can better understand their preferred 'intelligence' for learning, as well as discovering ways to enhance their weaker modes of intelligence. A brief summary of the multiple intelligences for use in teaching follows.

- *Linguistic intelligence* consists of the ability to think in words and to use language to express and appreciate complex meanings, as in the work of authors, speakers, and journalists. Schools most often rely on this form of intelligence. Students working in this intelligence prefer to solve problems by talking or writing about them.

- *Logical/mathematical intelligence* involves inductive thinking and deductive reasoning, awareness of patterns and symbols, and the ability to judge and form hypotheses. Again, schools focus on this type of intelligence and can easily test for it on standardised tests. Students preferring this mode tend to enjoy number puzzles and games of logic.

- *Visual/spatial intelligence* suggests keen observation skills along with the ability to transform the mental images to reality, as in the work of an artist or navigator. In schools, these students tend to like to see pictures, or utilise a graphic organiser for information retention.

- *Bodily/kinesthetic intelligence* is quite evident in dancers, athletes, surgeons, and craftspeople with their ability to manipulate objects and use their finely tuned physical skills. Students with strong bodily/kinesthetic intelligence like to move, using their whole body and deftly handling props or tools.

- *Musical intelligence* is evident in composers, conductors, musicians, music critics, and sensitive listeners. Students preferring this mode enjoy content which is taught with music as a strong linking mechanism.

- *Interpersonal intelligence* is the capacity to work effectively with others, as in the work of a teacher, social worker, or politician. Such students like to discuss and collaborate on projects, during school and even out-of-school hours.

- *Intrapersonal intelligence* involves knowledge of the self and the ability to look within. Philosophers, theologians, and psychologists all have strong intrapersonal intelligence. Students with this intelligence like, and need, time for reflection and metacognition, time to think about their thinking or learning.

- *Naturalist intelligence* is a new intelligence still being explored. This intelligence involves the ability to see patterns in nature, such as the ability of the late Jacques Cousteau.

As we reflect on a student's preferred way of learning, or intelligence, we can structure experiences designed to nurture his or her preferred intelligence as well as to draw out the less favoured intelligences. Arts-based activities can open the door to a wealth of experiences in many different intelligences so that students can 'enter the classroom' and engage in meaningful learning through different 'windows', or intelligences rather than within an approach directed at only one type of intelligence. Topics are more effectively reinforced with a variety of approaches or 'intelligences'. Caine and Caine suggest that '. . . if the same message can be packaged in several ways, the receiver has a much better chance of grasping what is actually happening' (1991:120). They go on to suggest that every experience has the 'seeds of many, and possibly, all disciplines' (1991:119) . Therefore, topics presented through a variety of approaches give all students a 'way in' to the material as well as a comprehensive view of the topic.

THE RHYTHMIC ASPECT OF MULTIPLE INTELLIGENCE THEORY

Each intelligence also has a rhythmic potential. Linguistic activities utilise rhythm in poetry and in the gentle rhythms of each culture's spoken language, as well as in music such as rap. Logical/mathematical activities rely on the development of number patterns. Counting and multiplication demonstrate number patterns along with a sense of rhythm in saying the number aloud. The development of logical thought, such as thinking through a move in a chess game, goes through the rhythmical process of remembering the strategy. Visual/spatial activities define rhythm through picture patterns, such as graphs and maps. Even written language has a rhythm of letters which are tall or short, spaced together or apart. Bodily/kinesthetic activities allow the body to move with various rhythms, some sporadic, others steady or constant. Activities such as throwing a ball or executing a ballet step develop a particular rhythm, which when refined produce consistency in performance. Musical activities obviously include rhythm as a musical element. However, they also involve the development of another sense of rhythm or pattern, such as the harmonic chord changes from a major chord to its 'opposite' in many familiar songs, or the pattern used in defining a scale by whole steps and half steps. Interpersonal activities have a sense of rhythm in the manner in which two or more people can successfully share ideas in turn. Intrapersonal activities require rhythm for enhancing the rehearsal of information which produces short-term and eventually long-term memory. Naturalist activities search for rhythmic patterns in nature, such as the multi-point shape of the maple leaf or, on a larger scale, changes in weather or climate. Music and movement can draw together all of these intelligences with an emphasis on the rhythmic potential of each type. Music has proven very useful in providing the 'memory hooks' necessary for allowing content to pass from short-term to long-term memory and be stored successfully.

PLANNING AND DEVELOPMENT

In my work at Seisen International School in Tokyo, Japan, I develop integrated curricula with the kindergarten and elementary staff. Units are planned together, using dance and music to reinforce subject content as well as to create a complete dance and music experience in the classroom.

In the kindergarten programme over the past two years, ideas and topics have focussed on the themes of 'Learning About Myself' [body parts, locomotor (movements that go from one place to another)/non-locomotor movements, emotions, taking care of myself], 'Animals and Their Habitats/Life Cycles' (life cycles of the butterfly, frog, and bird, animal movements, habitats of the forest, pond and desert), 'Seasons and Their Special Signs' (autumn leaves, winter snow and hibernation, spring growth and birth, summer fun), 'Health Week' (healthy food and lifestyle, safety), International Day (songs, chants, games, and folk dances from around the world) and Multicultural Holidays [Japanese Sports Day (*Undo Kai*), Halloween, Seven-Five-Three Day (*Shichi-Go-San*), Thanksgiving, Christmas Around

The World, Bean Throwing Day (*Setsubun*), Valentine's Day, Girls' Day (*Hina Matsuri) H*, St. Patrick's Day, Cherry Blossom Viewing (*0-Hanami)*, Easter, and Children's Day (*Kodomo no hi)*] (see Figure 13.1).

In Grade One, the overarching goals have linked the child's view of the world with musical concepts such as tempo, melody and rhythm, and expanded these concepts in creative dance contexts. Explorations are linked thematically to classroom topics as well as to holidays and seasonal events. Grade One topics include Cooking In The Kitchen (process of cooking, food groups, favourite foods), Multicultural Holidays — cultural background and purpose of each holiday, such as Autumn Equinox Day, local harvest festival (*Nakamachi Matsuri)* and procession, Halloween, Seven-Five-Three Day (*Shichi-Go-San*), International Day, Thanksgiving, Christmas, Japanese New Year (*O-Shogatsu*), Vernal Equinox Day and Earth Day — and 'Animals in Many Habitats' (interdependence and dependence of animals and their environment, animal groups, animals in various environments, such as the desert, farm, and rain forest). Students culminate their animal study with a performance integrating spoken language, original songs, creative dance, and instrumental accompaniment.

Through integrated studies in Grade Two, students review and expand their knowledge of music and dance concepts in relation to new topics about their world. Integrated studies incorporate study of 'The Human Body' (Systems and their interaction in the body — naming body parts, special functions, energy qualities), 'Understanding Cultures Around The World' (diversity and variation — folk dance and music, international instruments, songs in various languages, qualities of various countries' terrains), 'Dinosaurs' (evolution and equilibrium — names and descriptions of dinosaurs, movement and energy qualities, timeline, song-writing projects), and 'Oceans' (change and conservation — names and descriptions of animals and plant life, phases of the ocean, energy qualities).

Thus, the goal of the music and dance curriculum is to complement the child's search for understanding of the world. Through dance and music, children are actively engaged in exploring each topic, and constructing their own personal understandings of the world.

A RHYTHMICAL INTERPRETATION OF AUTUMN: KINDERGARTEN LEVEL

This section outlines a series of kindergarten lessons on the subject of autumn which utilise an arts-based focus on rhythm and multiple intelligences. Over the course of three or four lessons, we explored the topic of autumn with a focus on the dance elements of level, flow, shape, balance and tempo. Background information was built up from a field trip to a local park during autumn as well as from observations of the trees in the school playground. Autumn is a beautiful season in Japan and there are so many different leaf shapes and diverse types of trees. Students often carried dried leaves to class and I displayed many of their leaves on the bulletin boards around the room. I also took many walks to find interesting and unusual leaves from gardens and parks to share with the students.

Our first lesson looked at the way leaves fall to the ground, or in dance terms, 'level' (vertical height of movement) and 'flow' (fluidity of movement). First we observed different kinds of leaves falling. We wrote words on construction paper leaves to describe this movement, such as float, tumble, drop, twirl, rock, curve. We used single body parts as well as our whole body to recreate the same movement. With some gentle music ('Behind The Waterfall' by David Lanz and Paul Speers, 1985), students began to explore

Figure 13.1 Children celebrating International Day

Figure 13.2 Children carrying the 'o-mikoshi', a portable shrine, during Nakamachi Matsuri (harvest festival)

the movements in one place, throughout the room, and with a partner. They experimented with varying the place where their leaf would land, such as on their shoulder or their foot. They would say, 'My leaf landed on my foot', or 'My leaf tumbled down to my elbow'. We looked at beginning at a 'high' level and ending at a 'low' level close to the ground. We finished our lesson with a song employing a descending melody, 'Down, down down, the leaves are *falling* to the ground'. We substituted new verbs in the song, such as *twirling* or *rocking,* and danced the many ways that the leaves fell to the ground.

The second lesson brought a wealth of leaves to the room. 'Look at how this leaf falls!' the children exclaimed. This prompted the question of why different leaves fall in different ways. Shape and size were the two qualities the children suspected might change the way the leaves fell; the colour did not make any difference in their leaf explorations. As they experimented with the leaves, we reviewed their leaf song. Then we looked at the qualities of the leaves, such as rounded edges, points, curved and heart shapes. The students made leaf shapes by themselves and then with a friend. We created larger leaves with groups of four, eight, and even the entire class. The students made leaf shapes that were still on a tree (high level) and leaf shapes that had floated to the ground (low level). They tried balancing and holding their shapes. We incorporating balancing leaf shapes into our dance from the previous week, dancing again to 'Behind The Waterfall''. The students took time to reflect on the way in which the dance had changed, and discussed this with a friend.

Colour changes in the leaves were important for the children. Together we created a song to the tune of 'Shoo Fly' to reflect the 'magic' in the changing colours. The lyrics were:

Chorus	Leaves change so magically (sung three times)
	Guess what kind of leaf I'll be?
	Spoken by teacher or child: *momiji* (a red maple)
Verse	I'll dance, I'll dance, I'll dance like a *momiji* (red maple) (sung three times)
	An autumn forest leaf I'll be.

[Repeat song and substitute other colours and leaf names, such as *ichoo* (ginkgo leaf), *sasa* (bamboo leaf), *sakura* (cherry leaf), *matsuba* (pine).]

Figure 13.3 Kindergarten children in the shape of a leaf

At the chorus, students made various leaf statues with their bodies in a designated spot (see Figure 13.2). Each time the children heard 'Leaves change' they made one statue, and thus made three statues with each chorus. At each verse, the students moved around the room making the shape of that specific leaf.

The last lesson took place after several windy days. The children observed leaves and twigs blowing all around the playground. We wondered what we would do with all of these leaves and twigs, so we created a song about autumn to the tune of 'Row, Row, Row Your Boat'. Students were seated on the floor, pretending to be in the park or on the playground. The lyrics were:

> Throw, throw, throw the leaves, up into the sky,
> Tumbling, tumbling to the ground,
> Let's make an autumn pie!

We discussed the ingredients of our 'autumn pie,' such as leaves, dirt, twigs, bugs, grass, rocks, and dried flowers. Children loved the nonsense element introduced and the new possibilities for rhythm. They also noted that the words of the poem, when written, formed a descending pattern.

We also experimented with ways of moving quickly (allegro) and slowly (adagio). Using instruments such as a drum and a triangle to keep the tempo, students had to adapt their movements to the change in tempo. We also added a song (see below) and an 'allegro' section to our dance.

> Adagio (slow; with triangle):
>
> Falling, falling, autumn leaves are falling.
> Falling, falling, falling to the ground.
>
> Allegro (fast; with drum):
>
> Whirling, whirling, autumn leaves are whirling.
> Whirling, whirling, whirling all around.

Now we had a song, a dance, and a story to tell:

> The trees are standing proudly in the forest. It is autumn, and the leaves on the trees are brilliant colours. Red, orange, yellow, brown, and even green leaves cover the trees. But because it is autumn, the leaves begin to fall off the trees, floating gently to the ground. They don't all move in the same way Some tumble. Some dance. But they all move from high upon the branches down low onto the ground. A gentle breeze blows some of the leaves. Is your leaf shape rounded like the basswood tree leaf or the cherry tree leaf? Is it frilly like the ginkgo tree leaf? Or does it have points like the momiji, or maple tree leaf? Is it long and thin like the matsuba, or pine needle? Is it big? Do you need a friend or two to make your leaf? Balance so carefully on your tree! Oh! The wind is starting to swirl, blowing many leaves off the trees, whirling them around and around. They're tumbling and twisting! Twirl around other leaves. It's so windy! Everything is moving so fast — allegro! Perhaps we should rake our leaves together in a pile. Shall we play with them? Let's toss them all together on the count of three—1, 2, 3! Again! And again! The forest is quiet again. There are still some leaves on the trees. They are still very proud with shimmering brilliant colours.

I told this story with and without the music, 'Behind The Waterfall'. After the dance experience we talked about new 'leaf words', as well as what was difficult and what was fun. We clarified the dance elements which were discussed in the story. We also looked at what we had learned about learning, such as making ideas on our own, or creating with a friend, or learning about different observations made by different children.

This movement experience reflects rhythm in many ways. Rhythm is a part of the year's seasons. I will continue exploring the seasons with the children throughout the remainder of this year. Rhythm is present in the movement of the leaves. The many musical experiences have varying rhythm experiences, from the steady beat in the songs which the children have sung, to the gentle pulse in 'Behind The Waterfall'. A sense of rhythm develops through the repetition and development of an autumn dance. With further practice, students might even set a rhythmic pattern to the spacing in the room and the partners they dance with. The rhythm itself seems to keep drawing them in, inviting them to dance this piece again and again.

LINKING 'EXPLORATION OF AUTUMN' WITH A MULTIPLE INTELLIGENCE VIEW

The opportunities for the use of multiple intelligences in this experience are extensive. Links are listed below.

- *Linguistic:* leaf verbs, song lyrics, discussion, talking about where the leaf is falling.
- *Logical/mathematical:* drawing conclusions about leaf similarities and movements, writing song lyrics within a specific metre.
- *Visual/Spatial:* interpreting leaf movements, moving about the various parts of the room, creating leaf shapes alone and with a friend.
- *Bodily/Kinesthetic:* interpreting each leaf's 'dance' with arm and whole body movements, creating leaf shapes, dancing fast and slow in various ways, balancing, dancing alone and with a friend, dancing high to low, moving with different energy qualities (i.e. floating, tumbling, whirling).
- *Musical:* interpreting recorded music with body movement, singing, moving in response to instruments playing fast or slow.
- *Interpersonal:* dancing and creating shapes with a friend, sharing the space with the entire class, creating a dance piece with the class, discussion.
- *Intrapersonal:* creating individual leaf shapes, individual choices in the dance — who to dance with, where to dance, which leaf shape, level and floor pattern — metacognition (thinking about our thinking).
- *Naturalist:* leaf shapes, leaf movements, connection made to the type of tree, qualities of autumn, patterns on the floor of light and shade, and patterns in the air.

Thinking about autumn using a myriad of approaches challenged students to think creatively, work cooperatively, and feel confident about what they had learned. The focus on multiple intelligences assured every child an opportunity to engage fully in the lessons and further construct his or her personal understanding of autumn.

PLANNING AND DEVELOPMENT OF THE RAINFOREST UNIT: GRADE ONE

Our elementary programme has also benefited from an integrated arts-based curriculum, especially for our students who speak English as their second language. We discovered that the children in Grade One class were particularly interested in rainforest animals. We began by asking them what they knew about the rainforest and what they would like to know. As teachers, our major goal was to guide the students to discover the dependence and interdependence of life. Together with the students, we discussed what we would like to know more about, such as plant and animal life in the rainforest, the four levels of the rainforest, cooperation and struggles, and dangers in the rainforest. With these goals in mind, I looked for natural connections between the topic material and dance concepts, such as locomotor movements, levels, shapes, energy and relationships. I looked at music links in the same manner, choosing form, rhythms, pitch, and tempo as specific focus areas in the curriculum. With the topic at the core of the lesson, it was easy to expand children's knowledge of dance and musical concepts beyond these initial focus areas. The content material was woven into the arts experiences. Songs were written and dances were created. Our final goal was for the students to share their creations in an 'informance', a performance which informs the audience about a specific topic.

A RHYTHMICAL INTERPRETATION OF THE RAINFOREST UNIT

We began the rainforest study with the story of *The Great Kapok Tree* by Lynne Cherry (1990). This story shows the rainforest animals' struggle to save their kapok tree from destruction by a logger. The children were fascinated with the animals and wanted to explore animal locomotor movements. They were also sensitive to each animal's speed and shape. They discussed animal pathways, animal dispositions and the ways in which each animal traveled alone or in a group. We integrated language to describe the way the animal moved, though their bodily/kinesthetic understanding of the movement was much richer. Since the prose in the book lacked a strong sense of rhythm, the students utilised ideas for the verses from their locomotor movement brainstorming. They used their movement explorations to elaborate on the verses. As a class, we decided to create a musical chorus to express the animals' message. The purpose of this message was to tell the man in the story (as well as the world) about the importance of the rainforest. They chose the melody of 'Shoo Fly' because of its strong syncopation. This is what they created:

Chorus	Stop, sir, don't hurt this tree (sung three times) We need it to live happily.
Verse 1	Boas: We slither, we slither around this kapok tree, We slither, we slither around this kapok tree, We slither, we slither around this kapok tree, We slither, we slither around this kapok tree.
Other verses	(each line is repeated four times) Bees: We gather, we gather, the pollen from the flowers.

Tarantulas: We scurry, we scurry, through the herbs on the forest floor.
Monkeys: We swing, we swing, on the branches of the canopy.
Butterflies We fly, we fly, up over the treetops.
Sloths: We crawl, we crawl, so slowly upside down.
Hummingbirds: We fly, we fly, we dart from flower to flower.
Frog: I jump, I jump through the understorey plants.
Anteater: I creep, I creep and eat up all the ants.
Birds (toucan/ indigo macaw): We soar, we soar so high in the sky.
Jaguars: We prowl, we prowl, in search of our next meal.
Child: I play, I play, in the rainforest with my friends.
All: We pray, we pray that God will save this tree.
(Sung after the last verse.)

Final chorus   Trees give us oxygen ,
Trees are a place to sleep,
Trees are a home for all,
What a treasure for us to keep.

The movements developed hand in hand with the song-writing process. Many children shared the ways in which they gesture to 'stop' and 'go' in their own countries. We generalised that most of us use sharp, bound movements to show 'stop', and flowing movements to show 'go'. The students stood in a circle as if they were protecting the tree, and performed the chorus with sharp, bound movements on various levels. We added instruments to enhance the sharp sound in the chorus. On the verses, each child moved like a particular rainforest animal.

In *The Great Kapok Tree*, Cherry illustrates the various layers of the rainforest. Realizing that the animals live in different places in the rainforest, the students created a multi-level frieze to demonstrate the four levels of rainforest vegetation. Using chairs, the children were able to show the animal life at every level — the emergents (high), canopy/umbrella (middle), understorey (low) and forest floor (floor). To simulate the complexities of a real rainforest, each student decided to become a particular rainforest animal and research its habits, disposition, relationships and habitat. Playing music of sounds from the Amazon rainforest, they created a dance reflecting early morning in the rainforest. The students clearly showed their own animal movements in a specific layer of the rainforest, as well as the other animals with which their animal would interact. We extended the use of the rainforest levels in a song sung to the tune of 'Over in the Meadow,' and revised it for the rainforest animals. During the song, students demonstrated animal movements, relationships (various group sizes) and level changes.

In the Rainforest

In the rainforest in the top layer near the sun,
Lives a mother harpy eagle and her baby eaglet one.
'Fly,' said the mother, 'I'll fly,' said the one,
And they flew and were happy in the top layer near the sun.

(In groups of four)
In the rainforest in the canopy of trees,

Lives a mother sloth and her little sloths three.
'Swing,' said the mother, 'I'll swing,' said the three,
And they swung and were happy in the canopy of trees.

(In a large group)
In the rainforest in the understorey,
Lives an arrow poison frog and her little frogs forty.
'Hop,' said the mother, 'I'll hop,' said the forty,
And they hopped and were happy in the understorey.

(In groups of five)
In the rainforest on the forest floor,
Lives a mother tapir and her little tapirs four.
'Walk,' said the mother, 'I'll walk', said the four,
And they walked and were happy on the forest floor.

The children also learned animal folk songs from South America to expand their knowledge base of the Amazon rainforest as well as to build on their understanding of that culture. Each song was enhanced by movement and instrumentation.

Many activities developed in the course of this unit. Over the six-week period the classroom teachers expanded their animal knowledge base with stories, drawings, games, creative writing and poems. Since we wanted to showcase the rainforest activities in an informance, each student painted their rainforest animal on the front of a T-shirt and rainforest vegetation on the back. As the unit progressed and the topic was broken down into smaller chunks, students constantly referred back to the overall picture of the rainforest, continually reorganizing the new information in an original way. They utilised their past knowledge of dance and music concepts to fully reflect their understanding.

A MULTIPLE INTELLIGENCES VIEW OF THE RAINFOREST EXPERIENCE

- *Linguistic:* animal movement verbs, song lyrics, discussion, talking about the qualities of animals and their habitats, metacognition (thinking and talking about the thinking process), story, poems and game activities

- *Logical/mathematical:* comparing and contrasting animal characteristics, categorising animals and plants, writing song lyrics within a specific metre.

- *Visual/Spatial:* interpreting four levels using classroom items, moving to various parts of the room or near certain people in dance pieces, creating animal and plant shapes alone and with a friend, painting a picture.

- *Bodily/Kinesthetic:* interpreting each animal's movements using a wide range of creative movement elements, creating plant and animal shapes, dancing on various levels, balancing, dancing alone and with one or more people, moving with different energy qualities (such as creeping, pouncing, slithering and darting), dancing to a variety of musical metres (such as 3/4 and 4/4 timing).

- *Musical:* interpreting recorded music with body movement, singing several songs, choosing a melody to suit the emotion of the written lyrics, embellishing songs with pitched and unpitched instrumentation, interpreting the rainfall in an instrumental improvisation.

- *Interpersonal:* dancing and creating with one or more people, sharing the space with the entire class, creating a dance piece with the class and taking part in various discussions.

- *Intrapersonal:* creating individual animal shapes and movements, individual choices in the dance — who to dance with, where to dance, which animal or plant shape to be and at what level, creating an individual interpretation of rain and metacognition (thinking about our thinking).

- *Naturalist:* animal and plant shapes and movements, interdependence of life in the rainforest, qualities of each level in the rainforest, patterns in plant life.

The students alternated between seeing first the entire rainforest and then just one small portion of it. Each experience presented a new way of looking at the rainforest. As they developed their song and movement ideas, the children not only revised the lyrics but refined their understanding of the 'total concept' of the rainforest. The varied approaches ensured that content information would be processed and reinforced in many different ways. The magical, game-like quality of the activities increased the student's desire to repeat the experience, reinforcing topic, dance, and music content.

A RHYTHMICAL INTERPRETATION OF THE BODY: GRADE TWO

The topic 'The Human Body' also lends itself perfectly to the exploration of rhythm through a multiple intelligence, arts-based approach. Combined with activities in the Grade Two classroom, students delved into the study of their body and its systems through an integrated teaching approach. As the music and dance specialist, I concentrated specifically on arts activities intended to develop their understanding of the body. After eight exciting weeks, the students shared the conclusion of the learning experience through an informance. The goal of our informance was to share information about the body through arts activities. We performed for the Kindergarten to Grade Five students, as well as for the Grade Two children's parents. The response was outstanding! Kindergarten students could describe various components of the human body and its systems after attending the informance. Grade Five students who were also studying the human body were able to 'see' and 'hear' the same information through a different approach. The Grade Two children's parents were thrilled to see their children's use of the multiple approaches. Many said that even they themselves better understood particular elements of the human body after they had experienced it in the informance. Rhythm was a key feature in providing 'memory hooks' for the content language in this study.

The teaching of language through rhythm was a key focus of this unit, and the opportunities for language development through rhythmic activities were particularly strong throughout the entire project. Since our students represent over fifty different countries, development of English language proficiency is extremely important to our curriculum. This bodily/kinesthetic experience allowed students to process and store new vocabulary in exciting and meaningful ways. This in turn provided them with strong 'memory hooks' which enabled them (and will continue to enable them) to retrieve this information quickly and effectively.

In addition to the bodily/kinesthetic intelligence being utilised, the remaining seven intelligences were nurtured and developed throughout the unit with reference to each body system. Careful emphasis was placed on ensuring that students experienced the topic through both their prominent and less favoured intelligences. Even more attention was given to ensuring that every child felt successful in each intelligence. In particular, students were encouraged to develop skills in their less favored intelligences, and this proved to be a healthy challenge for all involved.

Classroom teachers provided a wonderful link with artistic endeavours, group projects, model building and individual projects. Their classrooms were filled with skeletons, body books, poetry and many other projects. Students studied each body system in its entirety, including the brain, muscles, skeleton, respiratory system, circulatory system, digestive system, and excretory system. We looked briefly at various cultural perspectives of the body, especially as they related to health. Several parts of the 'Body Project' which took place in my dance and music class, as well as in the students' regular classrooms, are described below.

Part one: Introduction — our body

We began by looking at who we are and what we use our bodies for. In music and dance, we looked at how we are able to move and how we use our voices. Students learned some simple jazz isolation exercises by moving each body part separately. The songs 'Body Rock' and 'Warm-up' from *Kids In Motion* by Greg Scelsa and Steve Millang (1987) are both useful for an introduction to the body. We also learned a Spanish song called '*Mi Cuerpo*' (Share the Music) which explains in both Spanish and English how our bodies 'make music.' The children exchanged names of selected body parts in their own languages in a game called 'People to People.' As each body part was called out, pairs of students joined that body part together with 'magic glue' and stated it in their own language; their partners then repeated the word. Students continued to connect body parts together. When 'People to People' was called out, students changed partners. Students created several language variations of 'Head and Shoulders, Knees, and Toes' and learned other body-part songs in Akan, Zulu, and Spanish.

Part two: The skeleton

Our study of the skeletal system began with the creation of life-sized body tracings made out of paper in the Grade Two classroom (see Figure 13.3). Students added drawings of some of their bones. As each new body system was introduced, students added it to the skeleton.

Together we discovered a variety of ways our bodies can move. We wanted to find out why our bodies moved in these ways. We began by exploring the various ways that our bones help move our body. As we began to isolate each bone type or joint, we brainstormed a chant to remember that bone's purpose. We finally set the chant to the song 'Dem Bones', and added group locomotor movements to the chorus (see Figure 13.4). Each verse was a self-space dance, using non-locomotor movements. The lyrics below represent the students' understanding of bones, joints, and the importance of the skeleton in our daily lives.

Figure 13.4 Girl with body cut-outs

Figure 13.5 A group of children doing 'Dem bones' dance.

Dem Bones

(in circles)

Chorus	My bones in my body help me ... walk around My bones in my body help me ... walk around My bones in my body help me ... walk around My bones help me walk around!
Verse	My skull, my skull protects my brain (line to be sung three times) Dem bones gonna walk around!
JUMP!	(around the room)
Chorus	My bones in my body help *me* jump around ...
Verse	My ribs protect my heart and lungs (line to be sung three times) dem bones gonna jump around!
SKIP!	(in circles)
Chorus	My bones in my body help me skip around...
Verse	Ball and socket joint moves so much (line to be sung three times) Dem bones gonna skip around!
MARCH!	(around the room)
Chorus	My bones in my body help me march around...
Verse	My pelvis protects intestines and bladder (line to be sung three times) Dem bones gonna march around!
SLIDE!	(in circles)
Chorus	My bones in my body help me slide around...
Verse	Elbows and knees hinge like a door (line to be sung three times) Dem bones gonna slide around!
HOP!	(around the room)
Chorus	My bones in my body help me hop around...
Verse	My vertebrae zip up my back (line to be sung three times) Dem bones gonna hop around!
	(to go individual places)
DANCE!	My bones in my body help me dance around ...

Part three: Respiratory system

After a vigorous warm-up, we looked at the first line of a song about the respiratory system. 'First you take a deep breath, get some oxygen and send it down to the lungs.' We discussed the process of breathing, noting that we experienced a change in our chest size when we breathed. We experimented with various ways to change our chest size: quickly/ slowly, alone/with a friend, with one part of our body, with a prop (such as a balloon or a piece of plastic). We related these expanding and contracting movements of our bodies to the steady flow of oxygen and carbon dioxide in and out of the lungs. We recreated the respiratory system in the following activity.

Students were divided into two groups. One group formed the shape of two oval lungs. Each oval held hands to maintain the shape. A better simulation resulted when students held onto a large lightweight scarf, to simulate the inhaling and exhaling. We counted together — 'INHALE, 2, 3, 4, EXHALE, 2,3, 4' — while the students 'expanded' and 'shrank' in size, raising the scarf on the inhale and lowering it on the exhale. Students added a chant with the movement: 'Inhale the good air! Exhale the garbage!' and 'Inhale oxygen! Exhale CO_2!'.

The other group became the free-flowing oxygen and carbon dioxide. They went inside the lung shape on 'INHALE, 2, 3, 4' and held a white scarf high in one hand to represent the fresh oxygen. On 'EXHALE, 2, 3, 4' the students went outside of the lung shape and held a gray scarf high in their other hand to represent carbon dioxide. We set this movement experience to the music 'Slip Of The Tongue' by Kenny G (1986). In addition, the students learned the song 'How The Beat Goes On' from *The Organic Puppet Theatre* by Terry Louis Schultz and Linda M. Sorenson (1984). The content material in the lyrics reinforced the overall classroom model of the respiratory system. The students further created movements to collaborate with the song lyrics. Because the movements were derived from the students' own reflections and understanding of the language content of the song, they had yet another 'way in' to learning about this system. In their classrooms, they added lungs to their body drawings. Once again the multiple intelligence approach and its rhythmic potential greatly enhanced the children's ability to retain this information.

Part four: Circulatory system

Our integrated study of the circulatory system looked at characteristics of the heart and the flow of blood through the body. In music and dance class, we focused on the action of the heart and the pathway the blood takes through the body. Later, we integrated the circulatory and respiratory systems into one movement piece.

We began the circulatory system with students working in small groups. Two children formed the shape of one chamber of the heart, 'expanding' and 'squeezing' the shape in a steady beat while I counted 'EXPAND, 2, 3, 4, SQUEEZE, 2, 3, 4.' Using bound flow (movements that stop, such as a punch, jump or hop), the other children became the blood that flowed in when the heart expanded and flowed out when the heart contracted.

Our classroom really began to come alive when we combined the circulatory system and respiratory system in the following movement activity. The materials used included:

- red and blue scarves or ribbons to represent the blood and the chambers of the heart;
- white and grey scarves or tissues to represent oxygen and carbon dioxide;
- bed sheets to represent the lungs; and
- Foot drawings, stomach drawing.

Two pairs of children formed the right side and left side of the heart. For simplicity, we only simulated two chambers. The children representing the right side of the heart wore blue to symbolise the lack of fresh oxygen in the blood. The children representing the left side wore red to symbolise blood rich with oxygen.

Two groups of children formed the pair of lungs. The children raised and lowered the sheet as they counted 'INHALE, 2,3,4, EXHALE, 2,3,4,' as in the prior respiratory system experience.

Several children represented the oxygen and carbon dioxide, moving into the lung shape with the white scarf held high (on the inhale) and moving out with the gray scarf held high (on the exhale). The remaining children represented the blood. With red and blue scarves, they travelled throughout the entire body. They began in the right chamber of the heart with their blue scarves held high. (They formed a line near the right side of the heart so that they could anticipate their turn to move.) The heart expanded and contracted as before. The blood travelled first to the right to one of the lungs and exchanged its waste products for fresh oxygen. The red scarf was now raised to show the fresh oxygen in the blood. The blood then travelled through the left chamber and then on to the rest of the body.

Part five: The digestive system

The digestive system offered a wide range of activities to explore. We learned about the digestive system as a whole and the role each part plays in the process. These lessons also built upon the students' study of nutrition in Grade One. In music and dance class, we integrated content gleaned from the various classroom activities. We created a 'Digestive System' dance, revised a song, and learned a nutrition dance called 'You Are What You Eat'. We began by dancing our favourite food words. For example, children in Japan eat *onigiri* (rice balls). Students improvised movements to demonstrate the sound of the word. Favourite Japanese foods were *miso shiru* (a kind of soup), *o-sembe* (rice crackers) *umeboshi* (pickled plums) and *aisu curimu* (ice cream). Word favourites from around the world were *paella* from Spain, *pakora* from India, *spaghetti* from Italy, and *pizza* from America. With a dance content focusing on the contrasting qualities of 'smooth energy' and 'sharp energy', we explored foods such as smooth whipped cream versus exploding popcorn. Students danced 'smooth energy verbs' such as float, glide, press, melt, and flow, and 'sharp energy verbs' such as punch, kick, slash, crush and explode. In this way, students had a bodily/kinesthetic understanding of the innate energy critical to the functioning of the digestive system.

Students developed background information by matching digestive system vocabulary (such as mouth, teeth, saliva, oesophagus, stomach, acids/digestive juices, small intestine, large intestine, rectum) with a diagram of the digestive system. This provided a visual/ spatial and linguistic 'way in' to the digestive system. Students discussed the sharp and smooth energies used in each part the digestive process. We decided to recreate the digestive process in two groups: the various parts of the digestive system, and the food group. The various parts of the digestive system dictated the way that the students utilised the space in the room. At the far end of the room, they first created the shape of the mouth and teeth. When that process was finished, they transformed that shape into the next part of the system, the oesophagus. These individual parts of the digestive system guided the amount of time spent in each space, to show how each part of the system functioned. Students later switched roles to experience both parts. Students representing the food group moved through each part of this system. They reacted to the change in shape and energy quality of each part, moving through the room as each part transformed. All of the students shouted out rhythmic chants they had created for each part of the digestive system. This rhythmic pulse and language structure helped the students to gauge how long to remain in each part of the system.

The entire music/movement experience is detailed in Table 13.1. Each part of the digestive system is listed, together with the reaction of the food group. The whole food group transforms with each digestive system change.

Table 13.1 Details of the music/movement experience

Mouth	Food group
Children formed a circle and created tooth shapes. They used sharp, crushing movements to show how the food would be broken up into small particles. They chanted 'Chew! Chomp! The food gets smaller and smaller'. Students repeated this chant three times. They then changed to the smooth movements of the saliva saying 'The saliva helps to soften the food'.	Children created food shapes with their body within the 'mouth' or circle. As the teeth chewed, these food shapes moved sharply, becoming smaller and smaller. Food pieces stuck to other food pieces. A few children carried clear plastic streamers and smoothly oozed through the food as saliva.
Oesophagus	**Food group**
Children moved from the circle into two lines facing each other. They moved their arms in smooth, wavy patterns to help the food along its journey. They chanted 'The oesophagus squeezes the food!'	Children squeezed, slid, slithered, or rolled through the 'oseophagus tunnel'. The saliva continued to ooze through the food. This group moved to the area where the stomach would be.
Stomach	**Food group**
Children formed their stomach shape around the partially digested food. They became the digestive juices, moving in sharp, slashing movements around the food in the stomach shape. They chanted 'Acids attack!'.	Children 'melted' becoming smaller as the digestive juices circled. They made a big, flat shape together in the middle of the stomach.
Small intestine	**Food group**
Children moved into a curving line, all facing forward in one direction. They stood at arm length from each other, creating a distance of approximately three feet from student to student. With this measure, seven students were needed to accurately represent the length of the small intestine at 21 feet, and these seven students curved back and forth forming a narrow tunnel. They chanted 'The small intestine grabs the vitamins; the small intestine grabs the minerals.'. The children gestured with their fingers as they chanted to show the movement of the small intestinal 'fingers' called *villi*.	The children slithered one after another through the 'small intestine tunnel'.
Large intestine	**Food group**
Several pairs of children formed the large intestine by joining their arms in an arch, as if to play 'London Bridge'. They chanted in a low voice, 'The large, the large, the large intestine!'. They formed a pathway which circled around the edges of the small intestine (vinyl tape was placed on the floor to make it easier for them to find their place).	The children followed the taped pathway on the floor, moving under the arches.
Rectum	**Food group**
We used a extendable Galt tunnel to end our digestive journey. Two students held the end of the tunnel and chanted 'This is what we don't need'.	The students pushed their way out of the tunnel.

The students decided to use recorded music ('Add-On Machine' by Eric Chappelle, 1993), so that they could all participate and accurately represent the size of the digestive system. The steady beat of the music, along with the acceleration in the tempo, lent itself well to the use of chant and the build-up at the end of the activity. This multiple intelligence, arts-based experience easily utilised the various ways children learn in a rhythmically engaging and enjoyable lesson.

Students also created a dance about food groups and healthy eating to accompany the song 'You Are What You Eat' by Cathy Fink and Marcy Marxer (1990). The message in the chorus 'You are what you eat' is a rhythmical reminder for students to eat well. Children asked to dance to this jazzy piece again and again, enhancing the opportunity for this content material to be stored in long-term memory.

Part six: The grand finale, 'The Informance'

The Grade Two students gathered up all of their projects and covered the walls, ceilings and windows of their performance space. In addition to the group activities, each child had an opportunity to do something special during the informance, and in the process the audience was informed about the entire body.

Parents and other Seisen students commented that they could actually see and feel how the human body worked. The performance space had a 'joyful hum' as parents and students alike discussed the informance and perused the wonderful artwork, poetry, models and songs posted around the room. Later, the students were treated to 'Skeleton Sweet Tarts'.

Teachers' reflection

Rhythm, along with language, was evident in nearly every body activity to clarify content or process. The chants and songs provided great motivation for the students, especially because they themselves had helped to create them. The need to move was always fulfilled through the dances, which had been created with wonderful rhythms so students had the opportunity to see and experience their own biological sense of rhythm.

During the reflection process, we considered the variety of intelligences we had utilised and appealed to in the unit. We categorised the experiences into a chart which mapped the subject groupings and the major 'intelligence' or approach used (see Table 13.2). This merely illustrated some of the examples that were prevalent in this project. As teachers, we continue to see the project as integrated, rather than separated into boxes and categories. However, this chart (illustrated in Table 13.2) gave us an opportunity to see how an arts-integrated project can draw upon all intelligences to thoroughly expand a student's knowledge and understanding of a particular concept or topic.

SUMMARY AND CONCLUSION: THE SUCCESS OF RHYTHM IN A MULTIPLE INTELLIGENCE, ARTS-BASED TEACHING APPROACH

I believe that the use of rhythm in presenting content material contributed significantly to the success the children experienced throughout this unit. This is because chants and movement are: a natural extension of play; a fun way to engage in rote rehearsal of specific content language; an approach which helps the brain see patterns and organise information; and a rhythmic and kinesthetic way into the brain.

The musical activities form another link. Just think of how many songs to which we know the lyrics. We have a lot of information stored musically in our brains. Memory for music goes straight to the limbic centre of the brain. Because of music's connection to emotion, its power to create memory links is very strong. Kanel (1997) cites Murphey as describing this as the SSIMH, or more precisely the 'song-stuck-in-my-head' phenomenon. Music, as well as chants, can produce involuntary replaying of the song (a song or

Table 13.2 'Body Works' unit and multiple intelligences

	Maths	Science	Reading	Writing	Movement	Music
Linguistic	Reading maths problems involving measurement.	Talking about the basic functions of the body.	Reading *The Magic School Bus Inside The Human Body* and similar books.	Writing stories, poems and songs about the body.	Creating phrases to describe movements, e.g. 'Acids attack!'.	Changing words of a known song to 'Body Song' words.
Logical–mathematical	Problem-solving measurement problems.	Experiments involving body parts with puppets.	Critical thinking activities related to reading.	Writing word problems.	Using body parts as a 'measure', creating a full-scale model of the digestive system.	Students expanding and contracting in 4/4 time.
Visual–spatial	Sketching body measurements.	Drawing organs of the body.	Viewing videos and CD-ROMs relating to the body.	Labelling parts of the body and writing the functions.	Creating a moving model of the respiratory, circulatory and digestive system.	Notate the song using music symbols or created symbols.
Bodily	Measuring pulse before and after physical activity.	Experiencing the 'feeling' of major body qualities.	Reading words to songs and creating a dance.	Writing a journal response to movement activities.	Moving throughout the respiratory and circulatory system as the 'blood flow'.	Create an instrumental (accompaniment) to the digestive system dance.
Musical	Evaluating the metre of the body songs. Writing chant rhythms using notation.	Learning a song about the function of the circulatory and respiratory system.	Read words and notation to songs, especially noting the foreign words.	Writing chants about about the body and its systems.	Creating a song to reflect the body movement of the skeleton based on the chants.	Learn a body song as a round.
Interpersonal	Group work in measurement.	Group work making body puppets.	'Buddy reading' of body book resources.	Writing a play with a friend about the function of a body part.	Moving together with classmates to create a body system dance. Dancing with a friend.	Singing a round. Co-ordinating instrument sounds with groups songs and dances.
Intrapersonal	Individual measurement of body parts.	Placement and functions of organs on 'big body'.	Journal responses to reading.	Writing own poem, story, play or song about the body.	Discovering individual range of bone and muscle movement.	Creating your movements to 'Body Rock' and 'You are What You Eat'.

melody we just cannot get out of our heads). Sylwester (1996) explains that music may be our first language and means of communication. As educators, we can harness the power of the natural rhythmic predisposition of the brain and use it .

Together with dance, arts activities involve the child in thinking with the body. Children learning through their many intelligences have opportunities to personalise their learning. They have the opportunity to develop their own ideas and their own language, both oral and written. The connections with their peers provide outlets for sharing ideas, and developing vocabulary. Students focus on asking their own questions and inquiring *with* their teacher. Through arts-based activities, they create and construct layers of rhythms, music, rhymes, movement, and images that clarify their world views.

References

Allen, J., McNeill, E., and Schmidt, V. (1992) *Cultural Awareness for Children*. Menlo Park, CA: Addison-Wesley.

Brooks, J. & Brooks, M. *(1993). Search of Understanding: The Case for Constructivist Classrooms.* Alexandria, VA: Association for Supervision and Curriculum Development

Caine, R.N. and Caine, G. (1991) *Making Connections: Teaching and the Human Brain.* Alexandria, VA: Banta.

Campbell, B. and Campbell, L (1992) *Teaching and Learning through Multiple Intelligences.* USA: New Horizons for learning.

Cherry, L. (1990) *The Great Kapok Tree.* San Diego, CA: Harcourt, Brace and Co.

Coelho E. (1994) *Learning Together in the Multicultural Classroom.* Scarborough, Ontario: Pippin.

Dewey, J. (1990) *The School and Society. The Child and the Curriculum.* Chicago, IL: University of Chicago. (Original work published 1902.)

Findlay, E. (1971) *Rhythm and Movement: Applications of Dalcroze Eurhythmics.* Miami: Summy-Birchard Music.

Gardner, H. (1983) *Frames of Mind.* New York: Basic Books.

Gilbert, A.G. (1992) *Creative Movement for All Ages.* Reston, VA: The American Alliance for Health, Physical Education, Recreation and Dance.

Gilbert, A.G. (1977) *Teaching the Three R's.* New York: MacMillan.

Jacobs, H.H. (1989) *Interdisciplinary Curriculum: Design and Implementation.* Alexandria VA: Edwards Brothers (ASCD).

Kanel, K. (1997) Teaching with music: A comparison of conventional listening exercises with pop song gap-fill exercises. *JALT Journal, 19*(2), 219.

Nash, G. (1974) *Creative Approaches to Child Development with Music, Language and Movement.* Van Nuys, CA: Alfred Publishing Company.

Schultz, T.L. and Sorenson, L.M. (1984) *The Organic Puppet Theatre: Children's Activities in Health Awareness.* White Bear Lake, MN: Night Owl Press.

Share the Music. Music Text, Grade Two. (1995) New York: MacMillan McGraw-Hill.

Sylwester, R. (1995) *A Celebration of Neurons.* Alexandria VA: Association for Supervision and Curriculum Development.

Wolf, P. (1996) *Mind, Memory, and Learning: Translating Brain Research in Classroom Practice.* Napa, CA: Self (workshop presentation).

Discography

Chappelle, E. (1993) *Music for Creative Dance: Contrast and Continuum,* Vol. 1. Ravenna Ventures Inc. (Add-on Machine).

Fink, C. and Marxer, M. (1990) *Help Yourself.* Rounder Records. (You Are What You Eat).

Kenny G. (1986) *Duotones.* Arista. (Slip of the Tongue).

Scelsa, G. and Speers, P. (1985) *The Cities' Sampler.* Originally from Narada Equinox album 'Natural States'. Nara Music. (Behind the Waterfall).

14

CHAPTER

DRAWING

Making thinking visible

Janet Robertson

In this chapter I hope to add a further dimension to our understanding of the role of drawing in children's learning. While not asking early childhood educators to disavow past (and dearly held) beliefs about the roles of drawing, this added dimension is in agreement with newer theories of how children learn, and explores the possibilities these theories afford the educator and child for collaborative learning (Forman, 1996; Kolbe, 1996a).

CHANGING THEORIES, CHANGING PRACTICE

The theories which inform our practice as early childhood educators are changing as new philosophies, research results and cultural changes alter the way we see young children's learning. Currently postmodern and constructivist theories hold sway over the previous theories of Piaget and post-Piagetians (see Elliot, 1995; Fleer, 1995; Light et al., 1991; MacNaughton, 1995; Mallory & New, 1994; Rogoff et al., 1993). These new theories propose that children gather knowledge from the world and culture which surrounds them, and that they do this in conjunction with others. 'Others' include parents, friends, caregivers, teachers, television, walks, books, radio, music, and religion and nature. It is also recognised that this is an interactive process and that children are thus active participants.

In the city of Reggio Emilia in Northern Italy, there is an exciting vision of what these new theories look like in practice. One of the central tenets of this complex and extraordinary educational experience is the notion that children have 'a hundred languages' (Commune di Reggio Emilia, 1987; Edwards et al., 1993; Malaguzzi, 1993; New, 1990; Vecchi, 1993). These graphic or symbolic languages are a vehicle through which children can '... communicate their ideas, feelings, understandings, imagining and observations' (Katz, 1993:25). Katz (1993) and Kolbe (1996a) have commented that we have vastly underestimated very young children's ability to use such symbolic languages skilfully and with meaning. Such visual materials and experiences in symbolic languages are provided on a daily and ongoing basis in the Reggio Emilia schools, so the common misconception that these schools are art-based is understandable when one is confronted with often alluring and bewilderingly beautiful major pieces by very young children. But to indulge in this belief is to 'miss the point' as Katz (1993:27) dryly states.

FORMS OF COMMUNICATION BY ADULTS

Given the metaphor of a hundred languages, drawing can be considered a form of communication. If this is the case, it holds that, as with any form of communication, drawing can take on many guises and tasks. For example, written language has many forms. Poetry is a distinct form of written language and not easily confused with an annual report. Often several written forms are combined, such as in a novel which includes libretto or prose interspersed with poetry, or in a well-crafted research report, which makes sense of figures and condenses years of work into two or three pages of tightly written prose.

When we use spoken communication we utilise many forms, from the terse to the loving, from the eloquent to the monosyllabic, and it is our facility with the spoken form which makes such nuances possible. Although it is reasonable to say that we assume we are expressing our thoughts clearly when we speak, the proliferation of 'communication' workshops and courses may indicate that communication processes are more complex and multifaceted than we often recognise.

Transfer this notion of communication to drawing. What can we see and understand in each drawing? Take Leonardo da Vinci whose paintings are well known centuries after he painted them. We are given a glimpse into how these paintings were created by the sketches in which he sorted out questions of style and form before committing himself to paint. In these drawings we can see da Vinci thinking aloud and solving problems. These preliminary sketches not only illuminate the problems he struggled with, but also show us the changes he made as he worked through various solutions.

By looking further we can see the mind of da Vinci at work. A man of prodigious intellect, he was an inveterate inventor. His notebooks are peppered with sketches of ideas such as battlements, water works and flying machines. He seems to have used these sketches to commit an emerging idea to paper, to be able to think about it some more. We can almost see him flipping through his sketch book a few weeks later, pondering, and then refining the idea in a further drawing.

Consider the many guises and tasks attributed to drawing. Da Vinci, in his sketches for *Mother, Child and St John,* strives to make a crayon capture love, adoration and world-weary sorrow. Or consider the technical drawing an architect gives to a builder, usually devoid of colour and movement, an idea on paper which can be replicated in three dimensions by those who know how to read the conventions. However, technical drawings like this do not have to be stripped of beauty. As with written communication, there are many occasions on which several forms of drawing are combined. Botanical drawings and paintings, achingly exact in their physical description of the plant, also have beauty in form and colour, and so the idea of the plant is enhanced by the construction of the drawing or painting and by the artist's perspective.

Comic strips, political cartoons, maps, technical drawings, even drafts for dress patterns are forms of drawing readily accessible to children. Surrounded by this multitude of examples, it is reasonable to expect children to have some knowledge of diverse drawing conventions at an early age.

All these forms of drawing have one thing in common: because the drawer put pen to paper, ideas are made visible. Thought has moved from the drawer's mind to paper and can now be shared with others. In much the same way, written or spoken ideas are shared once spoken or written. Jerome Bruner discusses this product of thought:

> Externalisation produces a record of our mental efforts, one that is outside of us rather than vaguely in memory. It is somewhat like producing a draft, a rough sketch a mock up... it relieves us in some measure from the always difficult task of thinking about our own thoughts (1996:23).

DRAWINGS IN EARLY CHILDHOOD SETTINGS: MEANING AND METAPHOR

For many years the role of drawing in Australian early childhood settings has been at worst an 'activity', and at best a process owned by each child as they step through stages in some autonomous forward motion (Kolbe, 1996a, 1996b; Derham, 1970). The concept of children moving mystically through stages, their fragile creativity emerging, has perhaps constrained us from seeing the many tasks and guises children attribute to their graphic expression.

Young children's self-expression in the visual arts is something of a 'holy cow'. This early childhood inner sanctum of burgeoning creativity and therapeutic emotional release is one which I challenge with some trepidation. Francis Derham, doyen of Australian early childhood visual arts in the 1950s and 1960s, sternly admonished:

> I deprecate any discussion of a child's work by the adult in the presence of the child or other children ... not until past adolescence are children ready for public discussion of their work, and even then, unless delicately handled, it will block their progress (Derham, 1970:74).

So firmly held are our beliefs about self-expression and creativity as the central tenets of the purpose behind providing young children with experiences in the visual arts, that we may not always question the cognitive possibilities such experiences afford them. If a child is *thinking* on paper, the desire to communicate this idea to others must be respected. Other children quite easily recognise such ideas and utilise them to further understand and build on their own ideas. On one occasion I observed three toddlers — Mike, Wendy and John — drawing together. Wendy and John were engaged in drawing a picture of Dorothy the Dinosaur, the subject of a song much loved by toddlers in Australia. Mike, listening to their conversation, glanced across and said in a puzzled tone, 'Where's Dorothy'? Wendy and John took no umbrage at his question and pointed to various parts of their pages, saying 'In the middle'. Mike looked more closely and said 'her spots is yellow, no green spots'. Indeed he was right. Their round shapes with green spots were incorrect, but the two children were unmoved, and continued to construct a jointly understood story about rain at a Dorothy concert. In this instance, Mike's questions moved him no closer to the idea they were constructing, but in fact clarified matters for the other two children. It appears to me that there is a role for both teachers and children to think through the ideas which are sometimes inherent in a child's drawing.

While talking recently with three three-year-old boys about dinosaurs, I realised that they were constructing a hypothesis that a 'bone' dinosaur was not as frightening as a 'skin' dinosaur. In other words a skeleton of a dinosaur ('bone' dinosaur) is not as potentially dangerous as one with skin, because 'skin' would mean that the dinosaur was alive. This idea was shared between the boys and mulled over, becoming one of their collectively held notions of dinosaurs. My role as the adult was to clarify each step of the discussion with questions attempting to make things clearer for the children — to act as a sort of partner/intrepreter. The other boys soon took up this technique and asked each other clarifying questions, which both affirmed and elaborated on the speaker's idea. This construction of an idea, based on sketchily held bits of information, led the boys to further and more elaborate ideas about the differences between being alive and dead.

In this instance the boys were using the spoken word as a means of communication, so my role as partner/interpreter would be acceptable early childhood practice (Nimmo, 1994). However these three boys had previously tackled making maps together, via the medium of drawing. The story of their journey from individually held ideas and knowledge to a commonly agreed graphic convention and understanding of maps was an exciting process to observe.

MAPS: AN EXTENDED INVESTIGATION

Individually held information and interest

The three boys noted above, on separate occasions, had expressed interest in maps. Ben (3 yrs 1 mth), while reading a book with an adult, explored a road on a map with his finger. Upon reaching the graphic for the ocean, his finger stopped and he asked, "What is this?'. Told it was the ocean, he nodded and said 'I've stopped'. He appeared to understand one of the cartographic conventions of maps. Craig (2 yrs 10 mths), while driving with his parents, announced that a street sign said 'Turn here for Grandpa's house'. In this case it seems Craig understood the convention of road signs even though he was not yet reading, familiarity with the route had given him the clue. The third child, John (3yrs 2mths) whose favourite reading material in the car is the street directory. John puzzles over this material, attempting to make sense of it in much the same way as Forman (1996) describes children wrestling with the written word.

Identifying knowledge bases

Given this evidence of the boys' interests and abilities, I decided to videotape them discussing maps together. The maps proved to be a physical focal point in the discussion, used frequently as a visual reference. After Ben identified a road on the map, John jabbed his finger on another road and said 'this is one too!'. This use of visual material as a basis to discover what each boy knew also provided an opportunity for them to teach each other individually held information. For example, Craig, on considering the map, announced to the other two, 'the blue is the sea and the green is the grass'. The other two nodded and Ben announced 'these are roads'. John nodded saying 'and these is corners'. Hunting through the map they discovered examples of this newly acquired information. They then asked a few questions, such as what a blue squiggle meant (the symbol for a river) and constructed some of their own theories, such a 'this is a windmill' for the graphic indicating a lookout. It was using these maps that they started to announce place names and destinations. Both Ben and John talked about Sydney and Melbourne and 'my house'. Craig pointed to a place on the map and said it was 'Grandpa's house'. There was also considerable tracking of roads with fingers, indicating 'going' somewhere.

Attempting to give the boys as much scope as possible, I included weather maps. They proved to be very proficient with these, indicating that they understood the graphic for rain (rain drops), storms (lightning) and sunshine (sun). John decided that it was 'Raining in Melbourne, here'. From this observation it is possible to see that the boys understood what maps were for, and were prepared to construct theories, and give and accept ideas from the others.

Putting ideas on paper

The following day I gave three boys a large piece of paper and asked them to draw me a map. Seated on the floor they each started to draw directly in front of them and, as is the way with such young children, circular shapes dominated. Ben made a small mark on one of his lines and said it was 'my house', and then moved the pen along making a mark that was 'the road to the shops'. Craig, glancing at Ben's work, nodded, made a mark on a line, 'my house', moved the pen along and marked another spot 'Grandpa's house'. Kim (3 yrs 2 mths), who had joined the other two as John was away, watched closely, and stopped his wild circular movements to make one mark, 'my house'.

Cognitive narrative

It is at this point, what I will call a cognitive narrative began. Each boy was no longer 'talking to himself' within the drawing medium, instead they began a shared conversation of both spoken and drawn concepts. Ben leant over the paper and made a long straight mark, saying 'Blaxland Road' (Blaxland Road is one of the roads leading to our school). The other two started to make more straight lines, but did not name them. Then Ben, lifting his pen, made a mark in the middle of the sheet of paper, saying 'The park'. I asked him if there was a road from his house to the park. Without hesitation he placed his pen on the previously named 'my house' and drew a line to 'the park'. He asked me to write 'Ben's road to the park', and as I was doing this Craig drew a line from his own house to 'the park'. Kim watched closely, then drew a road, again from his graphic symbol for house to that for 'the park'. The boys all waited until I had finished writing the names of their roads, then Ben drew 'the beach', another small mark isolated from the other marks. Again, he and Craig drew roads from their houses to the site. Kim managed to draw a line to the site, but stopped short of the actual mark. Ben leant over and with his pen completed the road, joining it to 'the beach'.

Shared meanings

It was during this process that the boys create shared meanings, the narrative including jointly held understandings. They went on to create another site called 'Mum's work'. In drawing their roads to this site, Ben invented a variation. Instead of creating a new road from 'home' to 'Mum's work', he traced his finger down his existing 'park road' and then drew a line at a 90° angle to 'Mum's work', thus utilising an existing road graphic. He then drew several more of these secondary roads, not naming them. Deciding he needed another destination, he made a mark near his house calling it 'the pool', and drew a connecting road.

Kim, glancing across and seeming daunted by the physical distance between his house and the pool, made a mark near his house, called it 'the pool', and drew a short road to it.

On completion of their work I talked to them about the graphic convention of the legend on a map. I asked if they wanted one on their map and upon their agreement, I drew a small legend in the corner of the paper, using the colours they had used for their roads.

Revisiting the narrative

The next day, Kim and Craig asked me if they could draw another map. With John and Ben, they first reviewed their previous map, remarking on the legend. 'See, that's you', said Kim pointing to Ben's green marks; 'Yeah, and that's me' said Craig pointing to his ochre marks. They then sat around another large sheet of paper. Each boy drew his house, then Ben announced that this was a map about the park. He drew a mark separated from the others and each boy drew a road from their house to the park. In this map there were none of the extraneous marks which characterised their first map. It appeared that they were consolidating their understanding of common destination and routes to and from. Finding some toy cars they drove them along the roads, talking about the park and constructing a verbal picture of the park's swings and slides. They played on the map for a further thirty minutes, 'driving' back home to get food and toys.

Together these boys constructed a map, creating common sites or destinations, and using common graphic conventions such as a line for a road and a mark designating a particular destination, also requiring that the adult write road names and places. Together they constructed a cognitive narrative, aided by the visibility of their ideas through the drawing. This map was a vehicle for the boys to demonstrate their understanding of maps, as well as a tool with which they taught each other further ways in which they could communicate these ideas. Most salient was the fact that without each other, they would not have been able to construct such a sophisticated concept. Ben's role as destination maker, Craig's quickness in picking up the ideas and Kim's willingness to learn, all combined to create the cognitive concept of a map which was clear to its creators and to us, the observers. The boys made their thinking visible.

The interactions between the boys, both gestured and spoken, supported the intellectual development of the concept, clarifying each leap forward with a graphic, which was then practised until grasped by all. I am mindful here of George Forman's words:

> At times I think we are downright Puritans, that is, we think learning must involve struggle and pain to be worthy. However quality teaching does involve a subtle form of help, a response that is leading but not pushing, a response that is suggestive but not final, a response that is descriptive, but not necessarily directive (personal communication, 1997).

In this instance it was Ben who was the teacher, communicating an idea which the others took and used to construct an agreed convention, which then became a vehicle for dramatic play, and a verbal and graphic interplay of ideas.

Teacher's role

The previously held image of the child whose delicate creative ability matures slowly and who is immersed in 'self-expression' has given rise, perhaps inadvertently, to the role of the teacher as observer. Teachers have been relegated to providers of opportunities, rather than as collaborators, investigators and questioners within an interaction with the child and the ideas embodied in their drawings. (Not all drawings children create are an idea which can be discussed, it is for the discerning teacher to know what type of drawing being produced is; see below).

What is the role of the teacher in understanding these ideas? The teacher's role is complex. Terms which describe this role include: provider, observer, partner, collaborator and provocateur.

Firstly, the role of provider as dictated by Derham still stands. Providing time, good quality materials and opportunities to use them is essential. Drawing should not take a back seat to other visual arts. The role of drawing in forming thought needs to be honoured by its prominence in the arts programme.

Secondly, as teachers we need to observe children. Honouring the child's right to decide whether indeed the drawing they are doing represents a particular idea or not is essential. Identifying whether a drawing represents an idea is difficult and depends on a sound knowledge of the child and excellent observation skills. This observation is not casual, it is direct and structured. Recording sequentially each stroke a child makes, the conversation while the action takes place, as well as the actions and speech of the companions will provide data for further analysis. It also offers children a visual memory of how they constructed a drawing. I often have children check to see whether I am making appropriate marks on the observation sheet. This has one pertinent advantage: it shows children that what they are doing is important. Believing that their work processes are held in high esteem underlines the point that it is the process rather than the product that is important. Toddlers often overlay their work with other marks, either random or figurative. Noting the sequence and appearance of each shape can uncover several recognisable symbols within a 'busy' page.

Thirdly, as a partner in the process the teacher takes a more supportive and companionable role, accompanying the children as they work and being a supportive presence taking an interest in their work as it unfolds. We must acknowledge our involvement in the construction of an idea, and in this acknowledgement place ourselves as a partner in the creation of the idea. Our place in the interaction or communication, and our role in constructing the context in which the interaction takes place is part of the planning process. In our role as participant/ observer, offering knowledge, listening to, watching and recording children's understanding of knowledge and designing the context in which this knowledge is shared, all assist in the process of making thinking visible.

Collaboration may involve offering suggestions and the loan of knowledge. From the teacher, technical assistance such as simply showing a child how to grip the pen efficiently or reminding them about a previous experience, means that this collaborative role is one in which the teacher is embedded within the cognitive narrative of the work.

Finally as provocateurs, teachers can 'push the edges' of children's thinking, through offering pertinent questions and suggestions. Recently, Virginnia (4 yrs) painted a picture of a house. Virginnia is a careful painter and more inclined to be innovative in other work. The house seemed to be a stereotypical house, sitting on a line for the ground and under a line for the sky, with two windows, a door and a chimney with smoke spiralling out of it. We looked at it together and she explained parts of the painting. Then I asked her what happened between the sky and the ground. She considered this and then filled in the space with birds. As her ground line was halfway up the page, I asked her whether anything happened underneath the ground. (I wondered whether she would suggest underground pipes.) Her eyes lit up and she said, 'Dirt and worms'. Working for another fifteen minutes she carefully illustrated a worm family in black dirt.

I do not advocate all teachers using the above form of questioning with all children. However, I know Virginnia very well, our relationship is strong and we often discuss complex ideas. A strong relationship, combined with a context and history of discussion, is essential. There is a fine line between provocation and criticism. Peers often ask far more searching questions than I feel comfortable, as noted above when Mike asked, 'Where's Dorothy?'.

DRAWING AS COMMUNICATION: THINKING TO DRAW, DRAWING TO THINK

We need to offer drawing as a means of communication. Within the interaction surrounding drawing, the skill level of the child is important. Very young children may not be ready to draw symbols recognisable to adults, but their verbal outpourings are available to us and to their peers. Listening and watching encourages the notion of drawing as communication. Offering the child the notion of drawing as 'ideas on paper' — of drafts — begins very early and encapsulates the belief that it is the process rather than the product which is important.

Additionally, the role of peers in the process of drawing and idea generation is a resource we have often underestimated (Nimmo, 1994). It is possible to say that within Australian early childhood literature the rhetoric that children are individuals has led us towards a pedagogy focused too much on the individual child, in isolation from others (Bruner, 1996; Fleer, 1995). We may have undervalued the importance of peer teaching, interaction and cognitive narrative within the newer theoretical umbrella of social constructivism. Drawing, such a natural yet complex act, is an important tool for children to clarify, communicate and generate concepts within an interaction between paper, mind, peers and adults.

Drawing is a communication tool which children can use to express ideas, not only in externalising their own thoughts but as a mean of clarifying for others what it is they are thinking. Within each early childhood setting there are various cultural tools. Drawing, when handled skillfully and respectfully, is one such tool. In an increasingly visual world, giving children drawing as a tool recognises that the visual representation of ideas is part of the symbol system of our wider culture. Practice and skill in using this tool will enable children to make their thinking visible to others.

References

Bruner, J. (1996) *The Culture of Education*. Cambridge, MA: Harvard University Press.

Commune di Reggio Emilia (1987) *The Hundred Languages of Children*. Reggio Emilia: Commune di Reggio Emilia.

Derham, F. (1970) *Art for the Child under Seven* (4th edn). Canberra: The Australian Pre-School Association.

Edwards, C., Gandini, L. & Forman, G. (eds) (1993) *The Hundred Languages of Children: The Reggio Emilia Approach to Early Childhood Education*. New Jersey: Ablex Publishing Corporation.

Elliot, A. (1995) Scaffolding young children's learning in early childhood settings. In *DAP Centrism. Challenging Developmentally Appropriate Practice*, edited by M. Fleer, pp. 23–34. ACT: Australian Early Childhood Association.

Fleer, M. (1995) Challenging developmentally appropriate practice: An introduction. In *DAP Centrism. Challenging Developmentally Appropriate Practice*, edited by M. Fleer, pp. 1–10. ACT: Australian Early Childhood Association.

Forman, G. (1996) Design documentation and discourse: cornerstones of negotiated learning. Paper presented at 'Weaving webs: Collaborative teaching and learning in the early years curriculum conference'. University of Melbourne.

Katz, L. (1993) What can we learn from Reggio Emilia? In *The Hundred Languages of Children: The Reggio Emilia Approach to Early Childhood Education*, edited by C. Edwards, L. Gandini & G. Forman, pp. 19–40. New Jersey: Ablex Publishing Corporation.

Kolbe, U. (1996a) Redefining 'art': A perspective on the Reggio Emilia approach. Paper presented at the 'Unpacking Reggio Emilia: Implications for Australian early childhood practice conference'. Macquarie University, Sydney, 4 May.

Kolbe, U. (1996b) Towards collaborative learning through visual arts experiences with three and four year olds. Paper presented at 'Weaving webs: Collaborative teaching and learning through the early years curriculum conference'. University of Melbourne, 11–13 July 1996.

Light, P., Sheldon, S. & Woodhead, M. (eds) (1991) *Learning to Think*, vol. 2. London: Routledge.

MacNaughton, G. (1995) A post-structuralist analysis of learning in early childhood settings. In *DAP Centrism. Challenging Developmentally Appropriate Practice*, edited by M. Fleer, pp. 35–54. ACT: Australian Early Childhood Association.

Malaguzzi, L. (1993) History, ideas and basic philosophy. In C. Edwards, L. Gandini, & G. Forman (Eds.), *The hundred languages of children: The Reggio Emilia approach to early childhood education*. New Jersey: Ablex Publishing Corporation., 41-90.

Mallory, B. & New, R. (eds) (1994) *Diversity and Developmentally Appropriate Practices. Challenges for Early Childhood Education*. New York: Teachers College Press.

New, R. (1990) Excellent early education: A city in Italy has it. *Young Children,* Sep., 4–10.

Nimmo, J. (1994) Building community to realise the potential of children: The challenge of Reggio Emilia. Paper presented at 'The challenge of Reggio Emilia: Realising the Potential of Children Conference', Melbourne University, 25–27 September.

Rogoff, B., Mistry, J., Goncu, A. & Mosier, C. (1993) *Guided Participation in Cultural Activity by Toddlers and Caregivers* (vol. 58). Chicago: The University of Chicago Press.

Vecchi, V. (1993) The role of the atelierista. In *The Hundred Languages of Children: The Reggio Emilia Approach to Early Childhood Education*, edited by C. Edwards, L. Gandini, & G. Forman, 119–127. New Jersey: Ablex Publishing Corporation.

15

VISUAL THINKING IN TECHNOLOGY EDUCATION

Marilyn Fleer

A National Statement on Technology for Australian Schools was released in 1994. This national document focussed upon the technological process of *designing, making and appraising*. Of interest was the requirement that children visualise images from a *plan view* if they are to effectively engage in the design element of the technological process illustrated in this document. Visualising from a plan view is not common among young children. The cross-cultural analysis detailed in this chapter suggests that this perspective is culturally determined and hence learned rather than being developmentally defined. A case study of young children being introduced to a plan-view perspective is presented. It is argued in this chapter that technology education provides another medium through which children can visually think and learn about their world.

> Do you know how I think? I close my eyes so no light can get in; like I'm underground. I've got the book in my head. I close my eyes and then I can see the book with my hands and the pictures and then I open my eyes and let a little bit of some light in and then I'm thinking (Rowan, 4 yrs).

The process of thinking is described by some children in visual terms. Rowan presents a compelling case that he is a visual thinker. There is an established body of literature which demonstrates that some people 'hear what you are saying' or 'see what you mean'. However, when the key learning areas are analysed for their emphasis on visual processing, a number of surprising results emerge. In the area of technology education, the *design, make* and *appraise* emphasis is closely tied to visual processing. Children are actively encouraged to visually represent their thinking through design work and three-dimensional (3-D) modelling. Why are children being asked to do this? There is a belief that such an emphasis on technology education will yield future citizens who will be able problem solvers, citizens who will be able to think divergently and contribute to the notion of a clever country (Australian Education Council, 1992).

This chapter considers the visual thinking that emerges when children engage in technology education. In the first part of this chapter, elements of the visual thinking process are considered through a cross-cultural analysis of children's approaches to drawing. In the second part of this chapter, a case study is presented which illustrates children being explicitly taught a plan-view perspective as they engage in technology education.

DESIGNING, MAKING AND APPRAISING

The *National Statement on Technology for Australian Schools (1994)* and *Technology — The National Profile* (1994) both place importance upon the design, make and appraise process. However, little guidance is offered on how to help children re-orient their drawing or design work from a front view to a plan view. Similarly, variations in children's visual thinking across cultures have not been considered in these documents. This is understandable, since the release of these documents marks the formal beginning of teaching in this area, and details regarding cross-cultural variations have not yet been identified.

Front-view orientation

A front-view orientation evident in many children's drawings and designs prior to and at the commencement of school is common. This can be understood when the cultural practices of many societies are examined. The images presented to children in books are mostly front-view illustrations (as opposed to other perspective such as plan view), with stylised figures of animate and inanimate objects (See Figure 14.1). As a result, it is not difficult to see how young children, when asked to design or draw a house, will represent the image as shown in Figure 15.2. The children's experiences tend mostly to be of front-view perspectives, and hence children will draw in this manner themselves.

Figure 15.1 Spot: The central character in a popular children's book

Evidence confirming this proposition was noted in an orientation-to-drawing study by Fleer (1995) in which nineteen Anglo-Australian children aged five and six years (with a mean age of 6 years 2 months) were asked to do three drawings. Instructions were given as follows:

1. Draw a picture of anything you like.
2. Draw a picture of where you live.
3. Draw a picture or design of the Lego/Duplo house you have just made.

The results are shown in Table 15.1. Of the nineteen children, seventeen drew a front-view perspective when asked to draw anything they wished, with only one child showing a plan-view perspective in part of her drawing. Seventeen of the nineteen children drew their house in a similar style to that shown in Figure 15.2. The stylised drawing of a two-storey house featured in most children's work. Even after the children had participated in Lego/Duplo construction, only one child drew her design from a plan view. Most drew their construction in a stylised manner similar to their second drawing. Although this was a numerically small group, the results were consistent with earlier research (see Fleer, 1993).

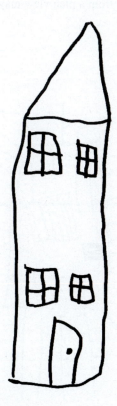

Figure 15.2 Rowan's drawing of his house

Table 15.1 A summary of children's drawings/designs

	Front view	Plan view	Combination (plan & front)	Insufficient detail	No response
Free drawing	17	–	1	1	–
Drawing of their home	17	–	–	1	1
Drawing design/ Lego house	15	1	–	2	

Figure 15.3 shows a plan view of an Aboriginal child's home and vehicle. This drawing by Brendan (8 yrs), who lived in a community within the goldfields region of Western Australia was done in response to 'Draw me a picture of where you live' (Fleer, 1997). The drawing demonstrates similarities with data collected earlier by Lendon (1973).

The different perspective shown in Figures 15.2 and 15.3 can be better understood when family storytelling practices are considered. For example, the plan-view orientation in Figure 15.3 is evident in sand drawings shown to children by adults (Figure 15.4) during storytelling in many traditional Aboriginal communities. These sand drawings can be represented on paper, as illustrated in Figure 15.5 (Gray, 1982). The ability or inability of young children to intuitively draw from a plan view may well be influenced by cultural practices.

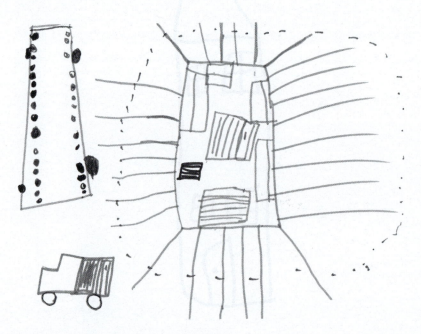

Figure 15.3 Brendan's drawing of where he lives

Stylisation of objects

The stylised nature of objects in many cultures can be seen not just in book illustrations and drawings but also in children's toys, games and jigsaw puzzles. For example, consider Figure 15.6 which shows toys designed for infants. The representation of a dog would clearly not be seen as a dog by an infant. An infant's life experiences would not allow him or her to easily associate the toy with the real thing, since it only vaguely looks like a real

Figure 15.4 Sand drawing of a camp and truck

Figure 15.5 Paper representation of a sand drawing: 'The women getting ready to go collecting yams' (Gray, 1982)

Figure 15.6 Infant toys

dog. The association between the stylised object and the real item occurs as a result of adult–child interactions. The social context gives meaning to the objects for the child. Hence, cultural associations become defined early, but a full understanding of this association occurs over time.

Similarly, stylised images from an Aboriginal culture may be seen in the paper representation of a sand drawing in Figure 15.5. The symbols of the women can also be seen in the sand drawing of the family members sitting in the truck and around the campfire (Figure 15.4). Children come to understand these stylised images through early and repeated exposure to them in the social context of storytelling. These images can also be seen in a large number of traditional indigenous Australian art works.

The power of these stylised objects to influence children's representation of things in their environment, particularly the perspective taken, should not be underestimated. It can be speculated that cultural factors play an important part in children's perspectives in drawing and hence in their ability to participate in design work in technology education. Introducing non-Aboriginal children to a plan view is as challenging as focusing predominantly on a front view for some Aboriginal children from traditional communities. In the following section, a case study of a teacher introducing non-Aboriginal children to the design, make and appraise process is presented.

INTRODUCING DESIGN TO YOUNG CHILDREN

In the previous section it was shown that many children have a tendency to draw from a front-view perspective, making it difficult for them to utilise the design aspect of the technological process approach. It can be speculated that three aspects contributed to this challenge: (1) young children's representational skills are rudimentary; (2) limited experience of drawing from a bird's-eye perspective (plan view) is likely; and (3) the cultural practices of the family do not emphasise a plan-view orientation. As a result, a carefully sequenced and cognitively oriented approach to technology education must be planned.

Case study

The children who participated in this technology education program over a two-week period were between the ages of 3 and 5 years. The majority of children were between 3-and-a-half and 4 years of age, from an Anglo-Australian background, and attended a child-care centre featuring a technology education program. The attendance of the children over the two weeks was variable because some children attended child care only two days a week. On most days the group size ranged from twenty to twenty-five children, with a core of 8 regular attenders. Group time and free-choice time included elements of the design, make and appraise process. The teacher used the block area and the drawing and collage materials to implement the technology program, beginning the program by telling the story of *The Three Little Pigs*.

Theoretical foundations of the teaching program

Vygotsky's (1978) notion of socially constructed learning was the paradigm adopted for this programme and Bruner's (1987) scaffolding metaphor was the learning strategy used to introduce technology education to these children. The teaching sequence was developed with the premise that the technology experience should be introduced for a social purpose and should continually focus on extending the children's development, so as to maximise potential learning (the zone of proximal development) through the adult and child working together on tasks deemed too difficult for the child alone. Vygotsky's socially constructed learning orientation was also supportive of research which emphasised the importance of a social perspective for encouraging and maintaining girls' involvement in technology education (Beat, 1991).

Children working technologically: The challenges

Curriculum material in the area of technology education assumes that children have skills in visual processing that will allow them to design and make as well as appraise. However, the young children in this case study had many difficulties with the orientation expected for accurate design work. The children's representational skills were not yet at the level that would allow them to design a building. In addition, the children could not be expected to draw a design and then use it for construction. This was an unfamiliar process for them and outside their everyday experience. Similarly, the children in the case study drew from a front-view perspective. Prior to the teaching program, they had not drawn from a plan-view orientation. These observations of children's abilities were at odds with the requirements of the technology curriculum material as presented to teachers. As a result, two challenges emerged:

- introducing children to a plan-view orientation, and
- encouraging children to design, make and appraise.

The simple yet unfamiliar approach advocated by the *National Statement on Technology for Australian Schools* (Curriculum Corporation, 1994), namely the design, make and appraise approach, required the early childhood teacher to take an active role in modelling and scaffolding each stage of the process. First, it was deemed important to orient the children's attention to the bird's-eye view (plan view) when drawing and constructing. This was done through the teacher modelling this perspective for children (see Transcript 1). The second area which needed to be modelled for the children was drawing their design prior to construction. Once again this focus was unfamiliar to the children and needed to be carefully introduced. The appraisal phase of the approach was deemed too problematic for children of this age and was not considered in this case study.

Transcript 1   Scaffolding: A bird's-eye view

Teacher: This house is special because I can see right down inside that house.
Charlie: 'Cause you didn't have a roof on that house.
Teacher: It hasn't got a roof. I didn't put a roof on for a special reason. I wanted you to have a look inside the house ... I'm going to pretend that I'm a bird. What do birds do, Jena?
[Ben flapping 'wings'].
Jena: Fly.
Teacher: They fly, don't they? If a bird flew over this house and had a look down inside, I wonder what it would see, I'm going to choose some special people who are sitting down to be birds. Andrew, would you like to be a bird and fly over the pigs' house and tell me what you can see in there? Tell me what rooms you can see.
Andrew: Everything.
Teacher: What's everything? What sort of rooms are in there?
Andrew: Bedroom, dining room, bedroom.
Teacher: Thank you. Eloise... would you like to be a bird flying over the house? ... What can you see Eloise? How many...
Eloise: Some beds.
Teacher: Some beds.
Eloise: Kitchen
Teacher: And a kitchen!

Use of adjuncts (door frames and doors; windows; people; furniture) and the teacher working together with children ensured that they continued to work in the block area, and the building continued to be related to house construction.

Plan-view orientation

At all times the children were encouraged to draw a plan. Initially, children drew the plan view only after house construction, later the children drew it prior to construction. The teacher continually modelled how to draw a plan view by helping children see this perspective and through drawing her own plan view and then constructing the house. Later, children's plan views were shown at group time, where the teacher discussed the use of space and the bird's-eye perspective in the drawings.

A design component of technology education: Outcomes of the study

Throughout the teaching sequence the children's abilities to engage in technology education were further developed. The designs are shown to illustrate this development and to highlight the challenges facing teachers as they organise technological experiences for very young children.

As illustrated in 15.7–15.9, it is evident that the children were able to define boundaries, which is a complex spatial relations concept, and to draw from a variety of perspectives, including a plan view. The complexity of the plan view developed over the two-week period for most children. This was particularly evident in Jena's sequence of two plan views drawn during and after the teaching program (see Figure 15.7 and 15.8, respectively).

In Figure 15.7, Jena has drawn a rudimentary plan view of her own house. She has provided an external boundary and drawn elements within it. Jena named each part of her drawing as she drew. Although Jena created a boundary for the house she was unable to create rooms or define objects for each of the rooms. However, two weeks later, Jena's design work has become more sophisticated (see Figure 15.8). She has created a distinct boundary and spaces within it. Although each area represented another house, Jena had clearly taken on the genre of design work being modelled to the children by the teacher. Later design work demonstrated further detail and more focused attention on the design of one house (see Fleer, 1993). A clear progression of development was visible in Jena's designs.

The development of the children's representational skills occurred throughout the data collection period. A range of representations in utilising a plan view was evident. Figures 15.9 and 15.10 show the variations noted between children in drawing from this perspective.

Design use

Although many children increased their drawing repertoire by being able to include a plan-view perspective, few children were able to actively use their designs. Many children focused their attention on drawing their designs after they had completed their construction

Figure 15.7 An emerging plan-view orientation drawn by Jena in April

Figure 15.8 Jena's design in May

work. This approach to designing, making and appraising was supported by the teacher. It was felt that children needed many opportunities in which to represent their thinking. Drawing the finished product was equally valued to drawing work prior to construction.

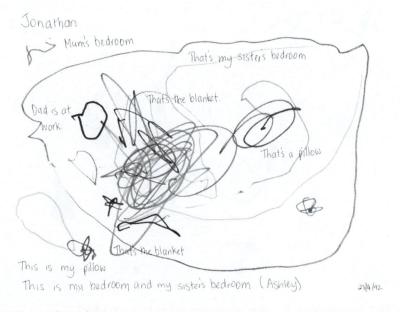

Figure 15.9 Jonathan's design

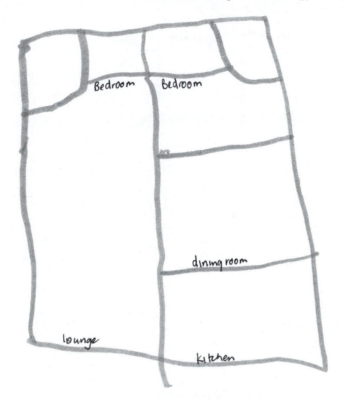

Figure 15.10 Jeremy's design

It was noted at the commencement of the teaching sequence that the children's developing representational skills did not necessarily allow them to draw to the level of sophistication required for the block-building work frequently engaged in during free play. For example, representing particular rooms, stairs, doors and windows requires an understanding of a high level of symbol use, spatial knowledge and the ability to estimate ratio or scale. A sophisticated block building would be hard for most children to detail on paper in advance of building.

Given these challenges, it was pleasing to see during the teaching sequence that some children were able to represent their ideas well on paper (e.g., Figure 15.10). A further example is Figure 15.11, in which Lucy was able to represent four areas within her plan of the child-care centre ('that area' was the open play space within the centre). Although the relative space allowed for each area is not reflected in reality, the relationship between the spaces resembles that of the child-care centre.

An analysis of the video material taken of the teaching sequence indicated that two children were able to develop a design of the child-care centre and then construct the centre using blocks (see Figure 15.12). Both children drew their designs independently, but worked collaboratively on their block building. Each child made regular references to their floor plan as they constructed, revising as they built. An interesting observation made from the video data was the different north–south orientation being followed by

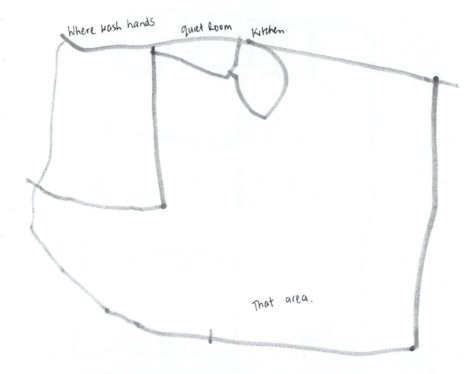

Where wash hands   Quiet Room   Kitchen

That area.

Figure 15.11 Lucy's design of her child-care centre

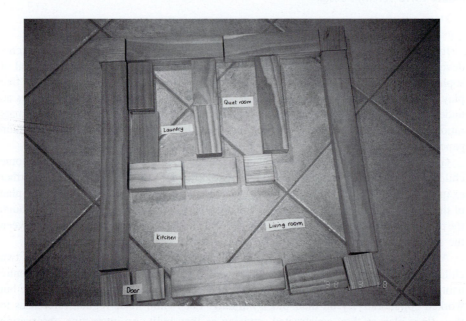

Figure 15.12 Block building of the child-care centre

each child. Neither child had discussed the orientation they were using in their block building. As a result, a great deal of negotiation and discussion followed. (One child took the leading role in the construction work and the other child co-operated by following her re-orientation).

DISCUSSION AND SUMMARY

The case study outlined in this chapter illustrates young children's developing representational skills from the commencement to the conclusion of a technological learning sequence. The teacher modelled for them the importance of designing prior to their engagement in construction work as well as drawing their completed constructions. An analysis of the children's designs revealed that their representational skills had developed rapidly over the two weeks. This was as a direct result of the children engaging in the technology education program, and expressing their ideas graphically as well as in construction with blocks.

The children in the case study had limited cultural experiences of designing, making and appraising. The ability to think visually is enhanced when children's orientations include a plan view. Some indigenous children regularly draw from a plan view on paper and in the sand, especially in storytelling practice; thus it can be argued that a plan-view perspective may be culturally determined and not innate. Introducing a plan view to very young children provides an additional medium in which children can think when engaging in technology education, and fostering visual thinking in technology education is an area that early childhood teachers need to consider.

It can no longer be assumed that a plan-view perspective occurs later in children's development in art. The cultural setting shapes children's drawing abilities and perspectives in the same way as it does other areas of children's development, so early childhood teachers need to take an active part in constructing school and preschool learning environments in ways which allow children to think visually so as to further foster their technological capabilities. Vygotsky argued that instruction stimulated development. In this chapter, it was shown how technology education fostered rapid and sophisticated development in drawing.

> Instruction is useful when it moves ahead of development. When it does, it impels or wakens a whole series of functions that are in a stage of maturation lying in the zone of proximal development. (Vygotsky cited in Newman and Holzman, 1993:60)

Planning for the development of technological capability awakens sophisticated visual processing skills in children, thus highlighting the importance of and need for the adult in shaping children's visual thinking. Further thought and research are urgently needed if we are to better understand the interface between cultural practices and visual thinking in technology education.

Acknowledgment

Special acknowledgment is made of Karen Baron who implemented (with a lot of fine tuning) the technology program detailed in the case study. Alan Nicol provided invaluable technical support through videotaping the teaching sequence. Extensive discussions with Robyn Lendon allowed for the understandings associated with cultural orientations in visual thinking to emerge.

References

Australian Education Council (1992) *National Curriculum Statement in the Arts* (Draft). Canberra: AGPS.

A National Statement on Technology for Australian Schools (1994) Carlton, Victoria: Curriculum Corporation:

Beat, K. (1991) Design it, build it, use it: Girls and construction kits. In *Science for Girls*, edited by A. Kelly. A. Milton Keynes, U.K.: Open University.

Bruner, J. (1987) The transactional self. In *Making Sense. The Child's Construction of the World*, edited by J. Bruner & H. Haste. New York: Methuen.

Fleer, M. (1993) Can we incorporate the principles of the National Statement on Technology Education into our early childhood programs? *Australian Journal of Early Childhood,* **13**(4), 19–32.

Fleer, M. (1995) Does cognition lead development or development lead cognition? In *DAPcentrism: Challenging Developmentally Appropriate Practice*, edited by M. Fleer. AECA: Canberra.

Fleer, M. (1997) 'Draw me a picture of where you live'; Data gathered in the Goldfields Region, Western Australia (unpublished).

Newman, F. & Holzman, L. (1993) *Lev Vygotsky. Revolutionary Scientist.* Routledge: London.

Technology: The National Profile (1994) Curriculum Corporation: Carlton, Victoria.

Vygotsky, L.A. (1978) *Mind in Society: The Development of Higher Psychological Processes.* Cambridge: Harvard University Press.

16

CHAPTER

EARLY CHILDHOOD ARTS ENVIRONMENTS

Functional and inspirational?

Wendy Shepherd and Jennifer Eaton

This chapter is written in the spirit of sharing with teachers and parents our practice and our thinking about early childhood environments, young children and the arts. The thoughts of Comenius, Pestalozzi, Froebel, Dewey, Greenman, Malaguzzi and Gandini have all contributed to our understanding of learning environments and their role in early childhood education. Feeney and Moravcik, Kolbe, Gardner and Forman have contributed to our understanding of the ways in which children express themselves (through the arts and arts media) and the value of these experiences for their development in all of the domains.

The information contained in this chapter is not written as a *recipe* or *plan*, rather it should be considered an opportunity for staff to take stock and to consider a particular setting in the light of the following questions: 'Is it a functional space where teachers teach children to learn,' or 'is it an environment that inspires the children and the adults to think, to imagine, to create and to collaborate', and 'is it a setting filled with the regulation furniture and objects that declare the space an institution,' or 'is it an environment that has visible traces or the zest of the people who inhabit the space?'. There is a need for *both* function and inspiration if we value and respect children's thinking and learning in all of their forms of expression.

The role of the teacher is significant in this process. We have found assurance in Froebel's view that the teacher's task is 'not the communication of knowledge ... but the calling forth of new knowledge'. Froebel also endorses the notion that it is necessary for teachers to *invest themselves in* and to *own* their environment and the things in it, to bring to the classroom elements from nature for the children to handle and observe (Froebel cited in Lawrence, 1970:250–251).

There is no short cut to creating nurturing and stimulating environments that will engage children purposefully in *arts play,* the term we use for the exploration and use of art media across all of the visual and performing arts areas through play.

Fundamental strategies in the process of creating functional and inspirational learning environments include:

- evaluating the philosophy that guides the program,
- reflecting on daily practice,
- generating in the centre a culture and climate which support collaboration,
- engendering within the learning community a sense of responsibility for both the environment and the resources.

It is important that the adults and children who work, play and create in an environment have a sense of ownership and belonging. In other words, valuing and being valued within a setting is central to a philosophy and program that promote competency, effectiveness, connectedness and belonging.

In valuing environments and the resources we bring to them, our personal sense of aesthetics comes into play. We need to think about what we place into the environment and how it is organised. In preparing an inviting, aesthetically pleasing environment, we can 'make the ordinary look extraordinary' (Kolbe, 1996). Reflecting on the debate about young children's appreciation of beauty and aesthetic responses, Feeney and Moravcik (1987: 8) suggested that children do benefit from aesthetic experiences:

> Children are fascinated by beauty. They love nature and enjoy creating, looking at and talking about art. They express their feelings and ideas through succinct and picturesque language; song, sometimes boisterous and sometimes lyrical; and expressive movements — the essence of poetry, music and dance.

Greenman (1991) also endorsed this view and recommended caring for the environment by giving thoughtful attention to light, colour, texture, sound and smell. These aspects are often overlooked in early childhood spaces which need to be functional and organised for daily routines. He reminds us that 'beauty is important because we feel better in beautiful places. We often feel ennobled, special, more at one with life' (p.13). For some practitioners the functional aspects of the environment or resources seem more important, and so aesthetic qualities are not considered. Aesthetic places where there is a sense of order and serenity — places which are both *functional* and *inspirational* — are most desirable for young children in early childhood settings. They are not difficult to organise nor are they expensive to set up or to maintain. They require only careful consideration in the selection, organisation and arrangement of furniture and equipment indoors, outdoors, and in communal spaces.

Consideration is not simply a matter of changing things around and putting a vase of flowers on the shelf. It requires thinking about the children, their learning styles and their interests. The adults who work in the setting must also consider making each play space into an enclosed arrangement so that children are afforded inviting, private spaces and adults are able to supervise without intruding. This can be done easily, using low shelving and plain wooden dividers. Children like enclosed spaces. Kirkby (1989:7) explains this characteristic of children as *'the need to see without being seen'*. Children also like stability and need to know that their home corner area, for example, will be in the same place each day. They need to know where and how to access clay, paints and musical instruments and where to work with these materials. Equipment should be arranged and stored in a way that provides children with choices and opportunities to work collaboratively with their peers in play, projects and investigations. The way in which resources are organised and displayed must be accessible, inviting and intriguing. Elements within these designated play spaces can change but the basic materials and equipment should remain the same. For example, the changes can be in the type, colour, size and shape of paper in the drawing area, the variety of props or clothing in the home corner area, or colour, type and textures in the painting and collage areas. As well as the materials providing a source of surprise and delight, containers for presentation and display of resources also require thought. Plastic ice-cream containers do little to enhance resources — they may be functional but they are not inspirational!

Environments must also support children's social construction of knowledge. The development of a collaborative climate for learning which promotes and supports productive peer collaboration is the foundation of a sound early childhood program. A collaborative climate and an inspirational environment foster children's imagination in arts play across the curriculum areas. Integration of the arts is an exciting approach, only possible when children are afforded long blocks of uninterrupted time to be involved in their work and in the development of their relationships with their peers. Children will, if given the gift of time, invest their interest, passion and desire to express themselves in meaningful ways within an aesthetic, enriched, homelike environment. As early childhood practitioners, we want to have an enduring impact on children's thinking and learning. With the support of the environment as the 'third teacher', we *can* make a lasting impression.

> Rooms and courts set up our expectations and are the cells that store our memories. To serve us well in this regard they must be carefully fashioned, shaped so that we can (and want to) remember them, sized to allow freedom of movement regardless of the activities intended, and sheltered from undesirable noises, smells and distractions — from sensory phenomena inappropriate for or destructive to the cluster of thoughts and impressions being formed (Lyndon & Moore, 1994:197).

If change *is* to be effected it must be done in collaboration with all of the people who will be working within a setting. Sharing the vision and goals for creating an inspirational learning environment ensures that all of the staff are included in the changes, both in thinking about the program and in the presentation of the environment and practice.

REFLECTING ON YOUR PHILOSOPHY FOR EARLY CHILDHOOD EDUCATION AND THE ARTS

Begin with the very core of your practice: your philosophy and your view of the child. The principles of an educational philosophy are informed by the knowledge gained in pre-service training and in your teaching experiences. Personal beliefs and values which are embedded within the principles of a philosophy also provide an insight into the teacher's image of the child, the child's family and their colleagues. If we believe that children are competent, inveterate explorers and tenacious problem solvers (who feel amazement and wonder at nature and their environment), then we should afford them opportunities to demonstrate that they are capable of making choices, expressing themselves, making discoveries, testing hypotheses, being curious, being delighted and working harmoniously with others within a program that is not bound by a rigid timetable.

Our philosophy should be dynamic, and referred to often, not a document that once written is forgotten, stored in a folder or handbook and never referred to again. A teacher's philosophy should provide the guidelines for daily practice when working with children and their families, with colleagues and the community. This philosophy should be evaluated when making decisions. Take the time to test each principle within the philosophy with 'if we believe ... then we should be doing ...'. This will start the process of reflection on current teaching practice, the program, our professional relationships and the environment. Reflective evaluation of our teaching philosophy, often tends to reveal a lack of open-ended experiences for children because as teachers we love to teach and model and to structure the day to fit in with our daily routines and timetable. It is only with experience that we begin to understand how young children learn. With experience we are more open to the interests of the child and we begin to regard our role more as a facilitator or guide, letting go of the need to *teach*. When we begin to believe children are competent and capable we can then begin to plan a program that has an emphasis on the *process* which supports children's *exploration* of arts media, and provide more diverse opportunities for dramatic play, music, movement or creative storytelling. When reflecting on our relationships with our colleagues and the children's families we should consult, discuss and share the decisions being made about the organisation of the program and the environment.

COLLABORATION WITH COLLEAGUES AND FAMILIES

If a teacher takes the brave step forward of collaborating with colleagues and families, the rewards are many, including shared knowledge and insights, clarity of thought and a deeper understanding of the different learning styles of the children within the group. Staff who work collaboratively enjoy the challenge and intellectual involvement of critically analysing their work. Through collaboration, staff are no longer working in isolation. They become aware of, and informed about, each of the children within a school, centre or group, and their respective interests and skills. Together, staff begin to think more intensely about their program and planning. This thinking is further developed with the teacher discussing with colleagues and families what they believe the children are exploring or experiencing. This is not as daunting as it may sound; it can be a very satisfying experience, as there is now an audience for the preparation and documentation of the program. Documentation is not simply a narrative description of the program, it is much more than this. Forman describes the process clearly:

> Strictly speaking, documentation is not a form of assessment of individual progress, but rather it is a form of explaining, to the constituents of the school, the depth of the children's learning and the educational rationale of curriculum activities (1996:86).

Teachers and families benefit from this collaboration as information is disseminated and shared. Children ultimately become the beneficiaries of this collective decision making.

REFLECTING ON THE ENVIRONMENT

Enhancing the centre/school climate

Reflection, evaluation and collaboration are not possible in an environment that cannot uphold this practice or ethos. The centre or school climate should project cohesion and harmony; it must facilitate the work of the staff and welcome both children and their families. This climate is influenced by environmental factors, including both physical (function) and metaphysical (ambience) elements. While the physical elements of size, shape, aspect, location and layout cannot usually be altered, the ambience may be improved by the use of soft colours, textures, lighting, furniture and soft furnishings, and by the way in which the space is organised and used. Environments should have a welcoming and comfortable ambience for both adults and children, free from clutter and visual chaos (Shepherd & Eaton, 1997).

If the processes of reflection, evaluation and collaboration have been discussed and adopted by staff, a climate of serious endeavour, provocation, valuing and respect can be cultivated. In a climate of trust and respect, a sense of ownership and pride for the environment is gradually nurtured.

It may take time to develop cohesive and supportive relationships, but once families are included and involved in discussion about the children and their programme, they will usually respond and participate. Documentation displaying the work of the children and the staff will provide families with an invitation to share their image of their child within the context of their family and culture. As a result, a two-way sharing of information is established. This form of communication between teachers, staff and families is just one aspect of the process. The environment is another, enhancing the staff's efforts to communicate a positive message to families. In our concerted efforts to ensure our settings and schools serve the purpose for which they were intended, adults often overlook the need to ensure that the environment is welcoming and comfortable so that the adults as well as the children feel they have a place within the setting.

Environmental messages to avoid

The environmental cues or messages *within* environments are powerful. Our schools and centres often send messages of an institution which can be forbidding, chaotic, dishevelled and tired looking. Foyers, hallways and classrooms are public spaces in both form and function. The appearance of these spaces and their organisation have changed little over the decades. There are often no signs of nature or beauty, only the usual hallmarks of public institutions: notice boards, signs, boxes, lost property, garbage bins and frayed carpet squares. Rows of hat hooks, lockers and signs on classroom doors as well as goods waiting to be unpacked generate messages of anonymity and disinterest of the school's population. 'Serviceable' colours and furniture do not necessarily withstand the impact of generations of children and teachers better than softer, more neutral colours and furniture. Classroom displays which include washing lines of paintings can send powerful signals of visual disorder. Functional containers of readers, writing materials, maths equipment and musical instruments often do not invite children to use them, as they are often stacked or stored on top of shelving units or pianos, or some other out-of-the-way place. This method of storage inhibits choice and promotes dependence on the teacher.

Enhancing the environment

If we begin to take pride in the presentation of the environment and take our time and care with the organisation of spaces, we can gradually peel back the layers of the 'institution' to reveal a warm and inviting learning environment. The practical aspects of creating and organising a welcoming, comfortable, attractive and inspiring environment *are* achievable. Consider the following questions in relation to your own setting.

- Is there ease of access into the setting?

  Gates, paths and entrance ways provide the first message about the centre or school climate.

- Are there places that provide a welcoming space to meet or gather?

  Verandahs and hallways should provide the visitor with a sense of being invited to enter and spend some time inside. Ensure that these spaces look welcoming by ensuring that they are furnished with comfortable chairs, a minimal number of printed messages, low tables, flowers or plants and someone to welcome visitors.

- Is the classroom light, airy and organised for ease of movement?

  Remove old blinds and curtains and replace with plain, simple coverings. Remove the displays from the windows and doors, get rid of old unnecessary cupboards and lockers. Less is best, as there is more room to organise learning centres and interest areas.

- Are the learning centres and play areas within the classroom and in the outdoor environment inviting, stimulating and cosy?

  The equipment should be clean, not outdated, aesthetically pleasing and homelike.

- Is the work of the children displayed respectfully and in a professional manner?

  A small selection of the children's work mounted or framed along with photographs of the children involved in the process is more visually pleasing and places an emphasis on the *process* rather than the *product*.

- Are the furniture, equipment, toys and materials clean, attractive and in good repair?

  Evaluate each item. Is it really necessary? Is it in need of repair? Is it possible to do without it, or can it be replaced with a more naturalistic item? Ensure that children's furniture is clean, and include children in the maintenance of their furniture.

- Are there elements of nature in pleasing displays throughout the setting?

  Children enjoy objects from nature such as shells, pods, plants, seeds, sea sponges, leaves and stones. Display them in naturalistic settings such as water, sand or earth.

- Are the materials stored in attractive containers?

  Baskets are a softer, more home-like alternative to plastic crates. Sturdy cane baskets instantly soften the look of a classroom.

- Is the piano a focus of beauty or a convenient storage unit?

  If you have a piano it should be kept polished and free of piles of books, parts of games and puzzle pieces.

- Is there a sense of serenity in the way the furniture and equipment is organised?

  The way a room is set out should afford a sense of order and stability.

- Are there places and pieces of furniture in which adults and visitors to the room can feel comfortable and welcomed?

  Adult chairs and tables should have a place in all areas of a school or centre.

- Are there examples of beautiful works of art from different cultures in the room?

    The diversity of cultures represented within the school and community should be represented in the artefacts, paintings, sculptures and soft furnishings of the classroom. Cartoon character fabric and furnishings undervalues children's sense of aesthetics.

- Is the essence of the staff and children apparent in the room?

    There should be photographs of the children, families and staff in the room, as well as other objects of interest. Children are capable of being careful with precious objects. The room should impart a sense of caring in the way in which objects are displayed.

CREATING ENVIRONMENTS THAT ARE SOURCES OF INSPIRATION, WONDER AND DELIGHT

Through reflection on your philosophy and practice and collaboration with colleagues and parents, a sense of what is appropriate for your setting is established. Creating and enhancing inspirational environments and a culture of caring and ownership, pave the way for creating environments that are both functional and inspirational. Creating places of wonder and delight is born of valuing and owning the environment and resources. The organisation of the environment, as well as being aesthetically pleasing, should also reflect and relate to children's thinking, interests and curiosity, and include elements from nature.

> Wherever I looked, I found a prodigality of pattern and colour for which I was quite unprepared. It was a revelation of the splendour and fecundity of the natural world from which I have never recovered. (Attenborough, 1979:7)

When we view a sunset, smell a fragrant flower, hear a beautiful sound, taste a delicious morsel and feel the velvety paw of a cat, we are suddenly immersed in a sensory experience that promotes within us a sense of exhilaration, happiness and awe, and often an urgent desire to express our thoughts to a significant other or others. For a child this response is heightened as they are not yet world weary or complacent about the beauty that surrounds them. Children delight in a shell, an insect, a prism of light or the sound of a musical instrument, and they are prompted to explore with their every sense. As the adults responsible for organising learning environments, it behoves us to ensure that what is presented to children, whether simple or complex, from nature or manufactured, designed, created or simply arranged, is pleasing and inspirational.

Thoughtful use of colour, textures, natural materials and lighting that enhances objects or activities, creates an environment that is not commercial or institutional. A sense of peace and harmony can be inspired by including objects in the learning environment which promote within children the desire to look, touch, feel, smell, reflect, contemplate and create.

If the teacher believes that children have the right to be surrounded by and immersed in, rooms and equipment that are themselves beautiful, whimsical, interesting and curious as well as practical, then the learning environment becomes a source of wonder, inspiration and provocation for play. This provides opportunities for children to experience, to express, to wonder and to dream, and to find around every corner a source of surprise and delight.

What are the messages in our learning environments that indicate a valuing of art, the natural environment, beauty and self expression? How can we promote within children an appreciation of and sensitivity to the things all around them? How can we promote within them a sense of aesthetic awareness? Is it really that important? Latham made the following observation:

> The years between two and seven seem to be crucial in how children deal with the mysteries. Within these years they form beliefs, biases, artistry, curiosity and a sense of self that carries them forward into adulthood. If allowed and encouraged, all children can remain active and curious philosophers and scientists throughout their lives (1997:12).

RETHINKING YOUR USE OF THE ENVIRONMENT: INDOORS AND OUTDOORS

As noted earlier, the processes of reflection and evaluation of one's working environment are crucial to our role as educators. It is very easy to become complacent about what we do, how and why we do it. Becoming a reflective practitioner means being open to change, thinking about what we do and why, seeking the perspectives of others, discussing a range of possibilities and making changes where necessary. To provide an enriched arts program for children, both the indoor and the outdoor environments should be regarded as equally important in their potential for arts-based experiences.

The indoor environment

There is perhaps nothing more important as a means to encourage children's exploration through the arts than the spaces we provide for them to do so. The importance of space in children's play environments is highlighted by Loris Malaguzzi, the founder of the Reggio Emilia early childhood centres in Northern Italy. He stated:

> We value space because of its power to organise, promote pleasant relationships between people of different ages, create a handsome environment, provide changes, promote choices and activity, and its potential for sparking all kinds of social, affective and cognitive learning. All of this contributes to a sense of well-being and security in children. We also think that the space has to be a sort of aquarium that mirrors the ideas, values, attitude and cultures of the people who live within it (Edwards, Gandini & Forman, 1993:148–149).

The spaces we have to work with in a centre or school are a 'given' and not many centres or schools have the financial capital to make structural changes. However, we can be inventive with the ways in which we work with the spaces we have. Whilst dealing with the frustration of such an issue, the staff *can* make good use of the spaces, both indoors and out. For example, hallways, verandahs and foyer spaces can offer a multitude of opportunities for arts-related experiences, such as being used as a performance space for drama play, for play with musical instruments, for movement and dance, for drawing, for book reading and storytelling. Often just the addition of a few basic resources such as a tape recorder, scarves, mirrors (children love to watch themselves at play), chairs for the audience or a few dress-up items is all that is needed to transform a space.

As Greenman suggested, 'many of us live, work, spend nearly all of our time in spaces that never become places ... Places are spaces charged with meaning' (1991:11). These are powerful sentiments. By affording children the opportunity to make their own mark on a space, to give it meaning by arranging and rearranging it from time to time to suit their needs is a valuable experience and allows children to feel a sense of ownership. Although something of a cliche now, the humble cardboard box is a perfect transportable, transformable space. It can be a prop in a dramatisation, a puppet theatre or a 'private' place for telling or reading stories; a great number of imaginative events can take place in a cardboard box.

An indoor space can also be transformed with the addition of elements such as soft lighting and sheer fabrics such as lawn, muslin or netting draped from the ceiling to create an interesting and inspiring atmosphere. A piece of fabric suspended from the ceiling can be used to create an exciting performance space. It can be a backdrop for dance, a curtain for a drama or puppetry scene, or simply a shield from the rest of the room that gives a sense of privacy to a small group of children who want to 'escape' from the buzz of a busy playroom, to think, reflect and plan. Avoid using old curtains or unhemmed pieces of fabric. Think about the impact you wish to make and spare a few minutes to purchase a length of appropriate fabric, hem it and secure it, concealing the materials used in suspending it.

The outdoor environment

The outdoor environment is often overlooked as a place in which arts experiences can occur on a daily basis, being predominantly used as a space for gross-motor play. There are a number of ways to simplify the process of establishing and maintaining an effective and manageable outdoor program which incorporates a range of arts activities.

With regard to the visual arts, a designated area set aside for painting, drawing and claywork is very important. Having these three media near to each other enables children to combine their use more easily. This is generally most manageable when organised on a verandah protected from sun, wind and rain. In order to achieve this arrangement you will need only a few basic materials and pieces of equipment. Tables and chairs that are able to remain in the same position on the verandah with a nearby storage unit such as a small cupboard or basket available to house the necessary resources enables ease of setting up and packing away. The cupboard or basket might contain such resources as a canvas cloth to cover table(s), textas, crayons, paper, clipboards, scissors, paint pots, brushes, clay tools and clay.

What is particularly important about the successful organisation of such an area is that it remain in a designated space — staff are more likely to set up such activities on a daily basis if it is 'easy' for them to do so. More detail on the value of having designated spaces is described later in the chapter. Providing other opportunities for other arts play in the outdoor environment is also simple to achieve. Creating designated spaces outdoors for children's socio-dramatic play with a range of props, for example a 'home corner' with a basket of dress ups, or a set of tables and chairs that can be transformed into an office, a hairdressing salon, a service station or a laundromat gives children the materials, space and time to engage in elaborate drama play. This list is only a small example of what is possible. These props should be introduced either in response to children's play interests or to provoke discussion and play.

A performance space for children's movement and music play outdoors is achievable with some very basic materials. At one end of the scale, the simple arrangement of chairs in a semicircle gives the visual cue that something is going to take place that requires an audience. A slightly more elaborate organisation of space and resources could involve the setting up of a platform or stage area for children's movement, music or drama play. The construction of an amphitheatre or alcove for such activities is ideal if funding permits. With the addition of resources such as a portable tape recorder, a basket of instruments and lengths of cloth, you are enabling children to choose to express themselves in an environment that clearly values and supports such endeavours.

These 'set ups' should be available to children daily, and should not be regarded as one-off or occasional special events. Through these experiences children are able to 'negotiate shared meaning and understanding which enhances their ability to collaborate with their peers across many curriculum areas' (Williams, 1992:109). In addition, an area for children's book reading and storytelling should also be a daily provision in the outdoor environment. Too often we underestimate children's capacity to care for and manage such precious items as books and musical instruments when outdoors. If a place is created for these, then children can learn to handle and use these materials with as much care as is expected when they play with them indoors. For example, cushions on rugs create an inviting play space. Make careful choices about colour and textures when selecting soft furnishings so that books, instruments and props look inviting and inspiring.

Designated spaces for children's arts play

What messages do we send to children if we constantly alter, rearrange or pack away their play environment? We have found that children's interests are sustained when they are able to revisit a play space or learning centre with the certainty that the materials they need or wish to use are available and accessible. Too often centre staff think children will become bored unless they change the room around regularly and have a different set of experiences every day. Staff are also concerned that parents will not have 'evidence' of their program by way of a different product or products going home each day with the children. Instead, when children are able to revisit a play space, repeat experiences and refine skills, they tend to progress to a more complex and elaborate form of play. Children in early childhood settings find comfort in knowing where to find materials and in knowing that they can return to them each day. Affording children the opportunity to repeat and refine their play schemas leads to more sophisticated play and more complex thinking.

It has been our experience that children are more likely to invest considerable time and effort in a project when they know that it will not necessarily have to be packed away at the end of a play session or at the end of a day. The process of returning to a play scene, renegotiating roles, making decisions about whether or not to change props or materials or music for example, is a challenge for young children, and requires considerable cognitive and social skills. Establishing designated play spaces for children as well as remaining flexible about the use of resources and space enables children to make choices and develop a sense of ownership of the learning environment.

THE TEACHER'S ROLE

Already we have highlighted a number of tasks for the teacher to undertake, including reflection and evaluation, collaboration with colleagues and families, considering the use of space and creating an inspiring environment both indoors and outdoors. We will now address the teacher's organisation of time, the importance of promoting peer collaboration and the documentation and display of children's work.

The organisation of time

The organisation of time can be a determining factor in a successful program for young children. Children need and deserve to feel unhurried throughout the day and to relish the joy of having long, uninterrupted periods of time to play and explore with their peers. Some early childhood educators schedule the daily program into fifteen- or thirty-minute intervals. Children are therefore unable to become engaged for extended periods of time. When given the opportunity, young children are capable of sustaining their interest and exploration for much longer periods of time than we usually give them credit for. If children come to understand that they will not be required to 'finish' and 'pack away' what they are doing constantly throughout the day, they will invest more effort, thought and passion into their endeavours.

There is a need to organise the environment to ensure that spaces are available for children to continue uninterrupted in their play. This requires an attitude of flexibility amongst staff and a willingness to support children's need for sustaining their interest and revisiting their experiences throughout the day and over a week if necessary. It is also important for staff to organise time in such a way that routines can be calm and enjoyable, and part of the program, not ruling the program. In this way, you are more likely to be successful in creating a rhythm of the day which is unhurried and relaxed for everyone. Children are more able to think creatively and gain a sense of satisfaction instead of being frustrated by time constraints and the constant packing away of their play environments.

Facilitating and supporting peer collaboration

Another role of the teacher is to create an environment that supports children's peer collaboration. A classroom culture that promotes peer collaboration gives children a sense of belonging. This view is reflected in the thoughts of Rodd who states:

> ... human beings are social beings and as such have a need to belong, to find a place in the group (Adler,1958). People, both adults and children, are motivated to behave in ways which help them achieve a sense of significance in the groups in which they live. When people believe they belong, they also feel connected, capable and competent, willing to contribute to meet the needs of the group (1994:21).

Of course we want children to feel they are capable and competent learners and to know they have much to contribute. In an environment that supports peer collaboration, children as young as eighteen months of age have been observed working together on a shared experience where negotiation, discussion, gesturing and organising takes place. As Shepherd and Eaton observe:

> In the organisation of the environment, we need to ensure the establishment of spaces where children can work together in collaboration. Such opportunities for children to work in pairs and shared small group experiences enhances their social construction of knowledge. Staff should assess their playrooms and surrounding areas for spaces in which children can work in uninterrupted and relaxed mode that is conducive to observation, discussion, active participation and reflection (1997:46).

Children's exploration through the arts is an interactive process. What we as teachers need to do, is to assist children in taking that step further which will challenge their thoughts and their practice. When working collaboratively on a project or investigation, children make suggestions and predictions, and develop hypotheses. Through peer collaboration, children learn to *forecast,* that is, to suggest or predict. Children are capable of responding to challenging and provocative questions which guide them to contemplate aspects of their work.

Children can be encouraged to evaluate their work in a way that moves them forward to a deeper understanding and a higher order of thinking, by asking of them questions that are not predictable or routine. Once again, this will occur best through reflection and shared discussion. Young children are not only capable of, but also deserve the opportunity to truly collaborate and reflect on what it is that interests them deeply. As Katz (1996) stated 'the disposition to go on learning is strengthened through interactive learning'.

Display and documentation of children's work

Documentation of children's work is the cornerstone of the sharing process of learning. Documentation is invaluable for many reasons. When children see their work, including the written form of their thoughts, ideas and words, displayed with care and respect, their self-esteem can soar to great heights. Documentation also enables children to revisit their work, their experiences (Vecchi, 1993), and can act as provocation for future exploration and investigation.

Documentation is also a mechanism for illustrating children's growth and development. It can highlight children's complex thinking and planning through the evolution of an idea, an interest or an in-depth study. Whilst a display of the end product of children's work is a valid outcome, the documentation of the process or 'journey taken' is often most significant.

Whilst some art forms are visual and often yield an end product that is the result of sustained effort, some art forms do not have a tangible product, for example, an impromptu musical or drama performance. Unless these events are captured on videotape, the processes involved in these often elaborate, imaginative 'productions' are 'lost' once the performance is complete. However, by taking photographs and/or notes throughout such events, the excitement and involvement of the children can later be shared with others along with the detail of what actually took place. This is also an important way of informing parents about the value of various arts experiences for children.

Documentation can be in the form of photographs, written anecdotes, videotapes, audiotape recordings and as portfolio samples of children's work and transcripts of individual and group discussions or interviews. Documentation involves staff and families in the collection of data, making relevant observations, reflecting, analysing and hypothesising. It is not a simple exercise, rather it is a challenging, time-consuming intellectual pursuit. However, it is an absolutely worthwhile investment of the teacher's time. It is like offering children a mirror, providing visible traces of their thinking, their understanding and their interpretation of their world.

SUMMARY

The notion that an environment can support learning and shapes behaviour is not new. This concept is based on the beliefs of the former and current early childhood philosophers and theorists. Over the years we as educators have lost sight of this view, for many reasons. Changes in our responsibilities and accountability have impacted on the programs we provide for young children. In an effort to 'fit it all in' our programmes have had to accommodate the requirements of teachers to cover all of the key learning areas, as well as the many policies and the need to acknowledge and embrace the cultural diversity represented within our learning communities. Quality issues have also become a focus for all teachers, coordinators, principals and managers. Time is definitely a constraint, particularly in long day care.

In our efforts to ensure that we are including everything and working towards high quality practice, we have often literally overlooked the need to *inspire* young children to engage themselves meaningfully in their work, and to promote children's exploration of, and thinking through, the arts. It could be that early childhood educators have been seduced by the glossy catalogues of commercial 'educational' equipment and resources. These products have been presented as magic keys to unlocking children's imagination and desire to learn and play. We have succumbed to the quick fix for children's learning, as at the end of a busy day the teacher has very little time or motivation to produce resources or to worry about caring for the learning environment. We have also begun to lose contact with the elements in nature and the basic open-ended experiences that were commonly provided for young children in the past.

It is time to return to sound early childhood practice, divest the environment of institutional trappings and rethink the place of commercial 'educational' toys, equipment, products and resources. Offer children simple, basic, good quality materials for open-ended activities. When children have the gifts of time, basic materials and the opportunity to practise their skills in a collaborative environment, their knowledge, understanding and creativity grows. Consider Froebel's concept of 'gifts and occupations', in which children were provided with beautiful yet simple objects and the time to explore them thoroughly so that their understanding and creativity could flourish. It should not be an educator's goal to keep children 'busy and amused'. Children need significant experiences in order to build on prior knowledge, and opportunities to collaborate with others in order to make meaning of their world. In an aesthetic environment children's learning and forms of expression are honoured, valued and respected.

References

Attenborough, D. (1979) *Life on Earth*. London: Book Club Associates.

Edwards, C., Gandini, L. & Forman, G. (eds) (1993) *The Hundred Languages of Children: The Reggio Emilia Approach to Early Childhood Education*. New Jersey: Ablex.

Feeney, S. & Moravcik, E. (1987) A thing of beauty: Aesthetic development in young children. *Young Children,* **42**(6), 7–15.

Forman, G. (1996) Design, documentation and discourse: Cornerstones of negotiated curriculum. In Proceedings, *Weaving Webs: Collaborative teaching and learning in early years curriculum*, pp. 83–109. The University of Melbourne.

Gandini, L. (1993) Educational caring spaces. In *The Hundred Languages of Children: The Reggio Emilia Approach to Early Childhood Education*, edited by C. Edwards, L. Gandini & G. Forman. New Jersey: Ablex.

Greenman, J. (1988) *Caring Spaces, Learning Places*. California: Exchange Press.

Greenman, J. (1991) Places for childhoods in the 1900's. In Proceedings, *19th National Conference of the Australian Early Childhood Association*. Adelaide: Australian Early Childhood Association.

Katz, L. (1996) Children as learners. In Proceedings, *Weaving Webs Conference: Collaborative teaching and learning in early years curriculum*. University of Melbourne.

Kirkby, M. (1989) Nature as refuge in children's environment, *Children's Environments Quarterly,* **6**(1), 7–12.

Kolbe, U. (1996) Making the ordinary seem extraordinary: Strategies in deepening visual awareness in young children. Paper presented Developing adults, developing children. 6th European Conference on the quality of early childhood education, Lisbon, September 1996.

Latham, G. (1996) Fostering and preserving wonderment, *Australian Journal of Early Childhood, Collected Titles on Early Childhood,* **21**(1), 12–15.

Lawrence, E. (1970) *The Origins and Growth of Modern Education.* London: Penguin.

Lyndon, D. and Moore, C.W. (1994) *Chambers for a Memory Palace.* Massachusetts: The MIT Press.

Malaguzzi, L. (1993) History, ideas and basic philosophy. In *The Hundred Languages of Children: The Reggio Emilia Approach to Early Childhood Education*, edited by C. Edwards, L. Gandini and G. Forman. New Jersey: Ablex.

Rodd, J. (1994) *Leadership in Early Childhood: The Pathway to Professionalism.* Sydney: Allen and Unwin.

Shepherd, W. & Eaton, J. (1997) Creating environments that intrigue and delight children and adults, *Child Care Information Exchange,* **117**, 42–47.

Vecchi, V. (1993) The role of the atelierista, In *The Hundred Languages of Children: The Reggio Emilia Approach to Early Childhood Education*, edited by C. Edwards, L. Gandini and G. Forman. New Jersey: Ablex.

Williams, G.M. (1992) Developing communication through movement and dance, *Early Childhood Development and Care,* **81**, 109–115.

17

THINKING WITH THE BODY

Dancing ideas

Wendy Schiller and John Schiller

Movement is observable; human motion is a basic form of human communication and a fundamental function of life (Meier et al., 1991). Young children's movements are carefully documented and analysed as early indicators of motor development (Wade & Davis, 1982). Yet, as parents and educators, we often overlook the potential of movement, with its functional and expressive qualities, both as an authentic means of communication and in the experiences we plan for and have with children. Movement is a language which a child utilises from birth; there are dimensions of efficiency, strength, effort and physical challenge in functional movement but there are also expressive, creative and aesthetic dimensions to the movements children make. Malaguzzi acknowledged this in including movement in the hundred languages that children use (Edwards et al., 1993). Howard Gardner (1983) included bodily–kinaesthetic intelligence as one of his proposed multiple intelligences, and, much earlier, Plato proposed a principle of mind and body harmony — gymnastics for the body and music for the soul — as an essential component of education for citizenship.

THE MIND AND BODY CONNECTION

Movement is thus not only a manifestation of physical wellbeing but, with sensory experience, forms the foundation of intellectual function (Greenman cited in Zearin, 1997). May (1975) supported this mind and body connection through movement in stating that young children have 'sensitivity of the body' but that adults have to relearn to 'think with the body' (p. 12). That is, ways of knowing which are open in childhood may, through neglect, become lost to adults because of Western cultural practices and societal processes which value the abstract and rational, and devalue physical, nonverbal and expressive language. Although little research has been conducted into movement and social development there have been positive signs. Sroufe (1978) established links between toddler's social competence and movement abilities. Schiller (1992) also established links between physical proximity and intimacy in adult–child interaction patterns and motoric competence of preschool children. Honig (1990) urged carers to maintain positive body contact and intimacy through hugs and attention to body rhythms rather than putting children into high chairs, walkers and strollers, thus isolating them from the body in the name of fostering independence. Crum (1991) proposed that from birth children should be exposed to a 'movement culture'. That is, in some societies, from an early age children are part of an ethos where families participate in song, dance, oration and physical activity as part of work and leisure, although perhaps this too is being lost by some of the sophisticated, technologically-literate societies in which we live.

CREATING A MOVEMENT CULTURE

Participation in a movement culture demands a repertoire of competencies that come from earliest memory, through informal teaching opportunities, motivation and encouragement to play and to practise the skills necessary for participation, and an understanding of the meaning and context of movement. Thus, children are given a predisposition to activity, movement and dance, and so experience fun and enjoyment in participation. Isenberg and Jalongo (1993) proposed a link between playfulness and creativity because they both rely on children's ability to use symbols as part of play and problem-solving, regardless of background, gender or race. Dyer and Schiller (1996) maintained that when movement is dissected, held at arm's length and decontextualised, confidence is quickly diminished. This applies to adults as well as to children.

So how is it that as adults and teachers of young children, our confidence, enjoyment and proficiency in using our bodies and voices in moving and singing have diminished and we feel inadequacy, insecurity and timidity instead? Do we have to relearn skills, rethink attitudes or reconstruct approaches to movement and dance? In this chapter a National Teaching Project is examined which attempted all three, to try to encourage student teachers in the final year of their preservice early childhood course to participate in movement and dance composition as a way of learning to think with the body and find enjoyment and confidence in this approach to an arts curriculum for young children.

MOVEMENT AND DANCE IN EARLY CHILDHOOD CURRICULA

Dance educators such as Boorman (1969), Gough (1993), Smith-Autard (1994), Spurgeon (1997) and Stinson (1988) advocated that teachers should build on children's natural and fundamental movement patterns to begin dance experiences or movement sequences with young children. However, Stinson was careful to clarify the relationship between movement and dance:

> Movement is not always dance. However, dance involves movement. Movement is the raw material out of which dance is made, just as music is made from sound. The more you understand the raw material, the better you will be able to turn your ideas and those of your children into meaningful dance experiences (1988:11).

Therefore, to participate in or teach dance in a meaningful way requires a working knowledge and experience of fundamental movement patterns and principles (Smith-Autard,

1994), a structured model or conceptual framework on which to 'hang ideas' in order to plan for dance (Adshead, 1981), and a philosophical approach which recognises that if children are to think with their bodies, and dance ideas, not steps, then they must have ownership of their dances (Colby, 1928).

Too often dance has been taught by the 'sink-or-swim' method (Blom & Chaplin, 1989:5). The teacher demonstrates, the class responds. Children often follow and keep up, or they give up. Unless children, particularly young children, can experience the thrill of improvising and creating their own, meaningful dances, they quickly lose interest and just go through the motions. They dance steps, automatically and without any understanding or feeling for what they have achieved. Stinson (1988) stated that this is often seen in performance by children who are dancing the teacher's dance and showing off, rather than sharing their own achievements. Such inappropriate practice contributes to dance being seen as the 'difficult' art (Blom & Chaplin, 1989).

Similarly, many teachers have concerns about the skills necessary to teach dance, expressing the view that they are not sufficiently talented, that they do not have the confidence, competence or specialist training necessary to teach dance and that there are not enough guides and resources readily accessible 'to get them started' (SETS, 1994–96; Macquarie University, Continuing Education Program Evaluations, 1996). Teacher education students state that they are not skilful, knowledgeable or expressive movers (Gallahue, 1990), and so are fearful of exposing their awkwardness with children. They also identify a mystique surrounding choreographing or composing movement sequences or dances for classroom settings, and are unsure of how to proceed when there are few resources available. Their problems are often increased because of geographic isolation and the necessity to study movement and dance via distance education mode, especially in a subject area which traditionally depends on workshop interaction and rapport between teachers and students.

The challenge in this Australian National Teaching Development Project was to develop guidelines and materials which fulfilled the same purpose as workshop sessions in building student teachers' confidence and competence, and to translate a teaching approach to dance with young children into appropriate distance education strategies which teacher education students would find accessible, and feel comfortable using in child care centres, preschools and school classrooms throughout Australia.

Pedagogical principles utilised in this project

'Learning through movement', a third year curriculum elective unit in the Bachelor of Early Childhood Education at Macquarie University in Sydney, had proved popular with early childhood and primary teacher education students as well as with experienced teachers because of '... its relevance to classroom practice and to the curriculum', and, because '... it fills a gap in available knowledge and teaching skills in an essential area of children's learning'. At a personal level, however, students and teachers consistently reported a '... lack confidence, knowledge and skills in movement education', saw movement as '...essential but too difficult to tackle', and felt '...overcome by the mystique and necessary creativity required' (Student Evaluations of Teaching and Subject (SETS), 1994). Therefore, the underlying philosophy or rationale for the project was 'learning by doing' — even if at a distance! Students were requested to work with a group of 6 to 8 children (aged between 3 and 8 years) throughout the semester-length project.

PURPOSE OF THE PROJECT

Initially the project related to distance teacher education students, but resources were made available to those students studying by on-campus or distance mode. The project goals were as follows:

- Through access to examples of teaching which illustrated different teaching approaches and styles, distance students will develop confidence in using specialised teaching techniques for movement and dance composition focusing on 3- to 8-year-old children.
- Student teachers will see both male and female dance teachers working with young children in classroom settings.
- Distance students will expand their knowledge and skills as teachers in movement and dance, and develop positive attitudes to the movement and dance component of the new Creative Arts K-6 Syllabus (NSW Board of Studies, 1998).
- Student teachers will view, analyse and use multi-dimensional approaches to teaching dance.
- Student teachers will be able to select and develop their own resources for teaching movement and dance.

The following practical outcomes were planned.

- A teaching and learning resource package containing a videotape, an audiotape and a learning guide.
- Learning approaches, technologies and teaching strategies enabling student teachers, especially distance education students, to engage with the materials in a practical way to facilitate the teaching of movement and dance in their own communities.

PREPARATION OF INSTRUCTIONAL RESOURCES FOR MOVEMENT AND DANCE CONCEPTS, SEQUENCES AND TECHNIQUES

Producing videotape sequences

The major outcome of this project was the production of videotape sequences illustrating how to introduce movement composition to adults who have had very little or no experience in movement and dance, but who are expected to teach dance as part of early childhood and primary cirricula. The majority of the teaching techniques were demonstrated by a male and a female lecturer working with a regular class of internal student teachers and then working with these same student teachers paired with 3- and- 4-year-old children from a day-care centre which is part of the Institute of Early Childhood. Additional teaching techniques to provide greater variety of approach became possible after the project commenced, with a third university lecturer offering to demonstrate techniques in Tai Chi and circle dancing, and the opportunity for one of the lecturers to demonstrate the techniques with two classes of 5- to 7-year-old children in an inner city school in Sydney.

Stimuli for some of the teaching sequences included the use of classroom objects as props, such as chairs, and inexpensive resources, such as lengths of elastic material, soft woollen balls, ribbons, children's shoes and lengths of material. Integration across the curriculum, using maths, language, art, music, science and drama was highlighted in the videotaped lessons in order to make the content of movement and dance accessible to all teachers. Movement for relaxation using Tai Chi techniques was also included in the videotaped lessons with adults and children to enhance perception of different philosophies and cultural diversity in movement styles.

A common videotaping format was used for all teaching sessions. Two video cameras recorded the entire lesson, with the cameras videotaping continuously. One camera remained mostly stationary to give an overview of the class and teacher, with some panning to ensure that the teacher remained in view all the time. The other, hand-held camera was moved around the room with the teacher as the central focus and attention being paid to interesting movement sequences created by the children. This gave two perspectives of the lesson: that of both teacher and learner. This technique enabled videotaping of complete lessons with only minor breaks, as videotapes were exchanged in each of the cameras at the end of either twenty or thirty minute sequences. All sessions were videotaped under normal lighting conditions in a movement studio at the university and an old assembly hall in the inner city school.

Previous experiences with videotaping teaching sequences had demonstrated that the recording of sound in a classroom setting would be an important issue (Schiller, 1992). Therefore, a remote-controlled transmitter microphone, clipped to the lecturer's clothing was used to ensure quality sound and allow for flexible movement around the room. In addition to this primary sound source, a second microphone on each of the cameras recorded the general sounds from the room on a second channel on each of the videotapes so that sound sources could be mixed in the final editing. However, despite considerable care in preparing for audio recording, problems occurred in the first recording sessions due to the inability of the transmitter packs attached to the remote microphone to cope with any intense movement by the lecturer, such as hops, leaps and jumps. Furthermore, slight movement of batteries in the pack meant that clicking noises and occasional short periods of silence occurred in the recording. Also, at one of the key recording sessions, microphones were inadvertently turned off, necessitating the complex dubbing of sound during the editing phase. A more sensitive remote microphone system used in later recording sessions, and closer, critical attention to sound recording by technicians overcame these problems.

The aim of the project was to make dance accessible so settings and materials were kept simple and realistic. All children in the classes participated, including those with disabilities.

The rationale for videotaping entire lessons was that, during the editing process, specific sequences could be isolated to show interactions between individuals, pairs and small groups. The intention was that the flow of sequences could be stopped at appropriate times so that the viewer (the distance education student) could reflect on the concept before trialling it with a small group of children. The facility to stop and start the videotape and to repeat more complex sequences until the concept became clear was seen as the major strength of using videotape to demonstrate movement and dance concepts. However, it was acknowledged that the linear nature of this form of access to movement sequences would not fully meet the needs of the student, so future plans are being made to place these sequences on CD-ROM or the Internet, where non-linear access is possible.

Producing a self-instructional learning guide

The other major emphasis in the first stage of the project was on developing self-instructional materials in printed form to accompany the videotape. This self-instructional guide would supplement the video by: (a) detailing concepts and sequences, (b) providing an educational rationale for each component, (c) suggesting ways of working with adults and children, (d) proposing ideas on how to organise and approach the teaching of movement and dance, and (e) encouraging the development of concepts for local contexts and specific communities. The guide was divided into the above five major topics. Each topic contained an overview of issues involved, background material, suggested teaching strategies, a list of the accompanying video sequences, required readings and references, and self-test questions.

Original music for movement and dance

In addition to the above resources, the original project proposal detailed the production of an audiotape of original music to accompany movement and dance sequences. As the selection of appropriate music is a time-consuming and difficult task for the uninitiated teacher of movement and dance, an audio tape of original music and rhythms, using a piano and electronic instruments, was planned to illustrate the use of music and rhythms in movement and dance composition. Two musicians familiar with accompanying dance using percussion, piano, drums, and electronic music were engaged to record this music. Each completed a pilot tape which was used in movement classes in the first stages of the project, and, following feedback from lecturers and student teachers, additional sections were added, new compositions sought, and adjustments were made prior to final recording in a sound studio and mixing for the master compact disc. The CD and audio cassette tape were then trialled in on-campus movement and dance sessions with internal students and at teacher in-service workshops prior to their release for use by students and teachers in centres and classrooms.

Trialling of materials

During the first semester of the first stage of this project, printed materials and video extracts were trialled in draft form by thirty-five distance education student teachers. Based on their feedback, the printed materials were restructured and expanded, and further editing of the video material was undertaken to provide a wider range of examples, which were then cross-referenced with the printed material.

In the following semester, largely as a result of student recommendation, one hundred and twenty early childhood student teachers enrolled in the dance and movement unit. Sixty students completed the subject by distance education and sixty enrolled as on-campus students. Both groups trialled the materials and approaches developed in the unit. In a modified on-campus approach lectures were replaced by readings and the self-instructional package, but weekly on-campus tutorial sessions were held. The distance education group had their own copy of videotaped lessons and workshops in lieu of the weekly tutorial and attended one full-day session on campus. However, not all students were able to attend the on-campus session due to the expense of travel and their geographical distance from the university.

Monitoring and evaluation

Monitoring and evaluation of this project included analysis of previous student teachers' written expectations and perceptions of teaching movement to young children (Schiller, 1992). Anonymous written evaluation was sought from distance education students on two occasions during the semester. Information was sought about students' perceptions of the usefulness of the videotapes and ways in which the videotapes and printed materials had been used to prepare for the unit assignments. For distance education students, a focus group discussion was conducted midway through the semester at the on-campus, one-day workshop and verbal feedback was sought regarding the first set of videotapes and the techniques used during these workshop sessions.

Following the conclusion of the first semester of the project, structured interviews were conducted by a research assistant, using Cohen and Schiller's (1988) interviewing techniques, via telephone, with twenty distance education students selected randomly from the unit enrolment of thirty-five. These telephone interviews sought confidential responses from the students regarding their confidence in teaching the dance component of the unit, how they perceived their classroom practices changing as a result of completing the unit, their perception of the most useful components of the unit, and suggestions for improving the materials. Specific questions were asked regarding the length, appropriateness, clarity and usefulness of the video sequences and the printed self-instructional materials. Following the presentation of this unit in the following semester, twenty percent of the sixty distance education students enrolled were selected randomly for a telephone interview and asked the same questions. All telephone interviews were recorded on audio tape and transcribed.

Contribution of a project reference group

A project reference group of key people in dance in NSW was also involved in the development and monitoring processes of this project. They evaluated: (a) the practicality, applicability and accessibility of techniques for teachers and distance education students, (b) the identification of student outcomes in relation to project objectives, (c) whether the project fulfilled student teacher needs and expectations in relation to movement composition, and (d) the packaging and marketability of the resources developed to be used independently or in combination — namely, a videotape, an audiotape and a self-instructional learning guide.

Outcomes of the National Teaching Development Project

Through integrated use of video sequences and self-instructional printed material, distance education student teachers were able to use different teaching approaches and styles in order to develop confidence in using specialised teaching techniques for movement and dance composition with and for 3- to 8-year-old children. The teaching techniques demonstrated by a male and a female lecturer working with a class of internal, adult student teachers and then working with these same student teachers paired with 3- and 4-year-old children from a day-care centre, were also found to be effective. Techniques in working with classes of 5- to 7-year-old children in an inner city school were also found to be valuable and applicable for distance education students.

ISSUES IN THE PROJECT

Working with young children involving movement sequences and dance composition requires camera operators to capture short segments or bursts of activity which the young child offers and which cannot be pre-planned. Hence the camera operators were required both to scan the group of children to record group responses and simultaneously to focus on individuals who were engrossed in their explorations. Often the mere awareness of a camera lens nearby stopped the young child's movement altogether and caused them to lose concentration. Hence the task was quite daunting for the teachers and camera operators. So much can happen in a movement class which cannot be captured on tape as the operator is facing the wrong way or the view of a particular child is blocked by another person.

The first group of early childhood student teachers enrolled as distance education students in the unit had been mailed rough edits of videotapes of entire lessons in which internal student teachers were seen working with young children and an instructor. Initially, student teachers were enthusiastic about this resource and reported that they had participated in the video classes in front of the television set (often with their own class). However, as pressure of assignments increased and time became a precious commodity, students requested shorter, selected excerpts from the videotaped classes, so that they could gauge the direction and focus of the concept, and develop their own extensions from the stimulus, without viewing the entire classes and watching the evolution of ideas.

Distance students, who had tried to shortcut the process and had therefore not understood the teaching approaches illustrated, or who had not used the Laban Analysis of Movement framework simply attempted to replicate the work illustrated on the video. As a result, these attempts were disappointing for the children, the teacher and for the lecturer who was to assess the work. Teaching dance cannot be developed by rote learning of movement patterns or through repetition of ideas without meaning; this method trivialises the experience.

Where students watched the videos in conjunction with the readings and the suggested ideas for working with a small group of children, the teaching approach and the concepts developed were more meaningful (as reported in interviews by the students). Short-circuiting the process shortchanged the student teacher in terms of meaningful learning. They did learn that teaching dance is a process that cannot be done by rote and routine and many admitted this in their evaluation of the unit. What appears straightforward on videotape in the hands of an experienced teacher can be a recipe for disaster unless it is made meaningful for a student teacher.

Feedback through interviews

Every distance education student interviewed reported increased confidence in teaching dance composition, with one-third stating the increase quite emphatically. Some felt that their attitude to teaching dance had changed, resulting in more successful lessons. Some registered surprise that the use of a problem-solving methodology to create dance and movement sequences from children's experiences could be so successful. Others believed that because they used a more egalitarian, problem-solving approach with the children, they and the children benefitted directly from this joint input, and children felt greater ownership of the dances and movement sequences constructed in class.

Eighty percent of distance education students interviewed felt that the written material was well organised, comprehensive, interesting, easy to understand, and accessible in format. Some felt overwhelmed by the amount of reading and viewing required. The majority of students relied mainly on the written material, seeing the videotapes as an additional resource, rather than as part of an integrated way of learning, whereas the designers of the material saw the video footage as leading in to the written material and then deepening meaning and understanding of concepts. Approximately half of the student teachers interviewed suggested that the video was a critical element in giving them the confidence to try the techniques and processes suggested. Response to the more tightly edited video sequences was more positive than that regarding the trial materials, demonstrating that care in editing is essential.

One-third of the students who gave feedback on the unit through telephone interviews stated that they had effectively changed their teaching style to a more collaborative approach, exploring meaning in movement with children, rather than imposing set dances and choreography for performance *upon* children. Comments included:

> It's a revelation that young children will make a dance out of any activity — going shopping, cleaning, breakfast — anything.

> After trying the ideas I became aware of how much more children could learn through these techniques.

> Now I have many more ideas and different approaches to dance to try with children (Davids, 1997).

As lecturers and curriculum developers, we were disappointed that some of the videos of dance concepts developed with young children by the distance education students still showed too much evidence of teacher intervention and structuring in the children's performance. Perhaps more consideration should be given to the word 'performance', because student teachers are still interpreting this as involving rehearsal, costumes and as an endpoint in dance composition, rather than as part of a process concerned with communicating a concept to an audience and eliciting feedback.

Although the students showed in their scope and sequence plan how the ideas for the dance evolved from the children's ideas, offerings and interests, with the notion of performance came the concept of closure and the urge to tie the ends together into a neat, complete package for the children and their audience. So the quest for developing meaning in dance composition requires us to go back to the basics and reconsider transmission versus *valuing* in young children's dance composition.

All student teachers interviewed commented that, as a result of using the printed and videotaped materials they had developed more confidence in teaching movement and dance composition, and that they understood the teaching techniques and the process of eliciting ideas from children which they would use and build upon for dance composition. The following comments from the telephone interviews were typical and demonstrate that this approach has been successful:

> The assignments were most appropriate, practical, useful. I've kept all my folders to use them in teaching. I didn't feel I was doing anything just for the sake of getting a degree. I felt like I was doing it because I have to teach. There is a huge difference between enjoying the unit and really getting into it, and treating it as just another unit.

> I thought that this unit was great because it gave you all the background information but it also gave you all the tools to actually go out there and teach it.

> Watching the videos of how they did the lessons ... showed you individual responses — because the video was a little bit of lecture and actual workshop — so it gave you both.

It was useful because it was practical. I was using it as I was being taught. It wasn't something that I had to finish the unit and then implement it. I was learning with the children — finding what worked and what didn't and what I felt comfortable with doing and just making my own adjustments as I went along.

I wasn't confident in teaching movement before ... now I will be incorporating movement into the curriculum. I think it's just my attitude — I am just confident, that's probably what's changed (Davids, 1997).

Finally, the assignments of the distance education students showed that the comments made at interview were accurate; namely, that children were composing their own dances; that they felt owndership of their performances for their group; and that they were capable of problem solving, composition, recogition of their peers' input and achievements and evaluation of dance (see Figures 17.1 and 17.2).

FUTURE PLANS

Having demonstrated successfully that videotaped and printed materials can be appropriate substitutes for interactive workshops in the teaching of creative movement and dance techniques and processes to early childhood student teachers, the next stage of the project will focus on using these materials in more innovative ways. For example, rather than using complete videotaped lessons, edited sequences will be combined to focus on particular techniques or concepts, additional video footage will be prepared to explain and or reinforce, and further links (including the use of graphics), between the printed material and the video sequences will be developed.

However, the major problem with this approach (and this is also a problem in face-to-face workshops) is that the needs of the individual student teacher differ so markedly. For the resources to provide appropriate assistance the movement sequences need to be quickly accessible in a variety of ways, at different levels of complexity, and at different

Figure 17.1 The sequence for a 'Rocket' dance composed and drawn by Nicola (7 yrs) as part of a class science project.

Holly

I thought the dance was very good. And I liked when we ran around the stage. And I thought rosie was great, and it was a bit hard at first

Figure 17.2 Holly's evaluation shows her feelings as a dance-maker and performer in a group 'Solar System' dance, presented in class

times. The linear nature of videotape, in which all sequences can only be accessed sequentially, even with the rapid forward and reverse functions of the VCR, appears to be a significant constraint. Some student teachers wanted access to the entire lesson first, others merely wanted to see some sections of the lesson before they attempted it with their children. Some wanted more teaching examples at a similar level of difficulty to illustrate the concept while others wanted more challenging illustrations early in their viewing. Some wanted examples grouped around topics, while others would have liked to view examples from a variety of concepts. Further, if the cost of duplication and postage of videotaped and printed materials is considered, extensive use of this approach could be prohibitive. Therefore, an extension of this project will be to use this approach in the development of an interactive, multimedia package. At the current levels of technology, use of CD-ROM and the Internet could provide a multi-level scaffold to adult learning that is personalised, explorative and non-linear in its approach. This package would have considerable potential to personalise the approaches used and to improve student teachers' competence and confidence in formulating their own approach to movement and dance composition with children.

Finally, as mentioned previously, the videos and self-instructional package were used with a group of sixty internal early childhood student teachers in the final stages of the project. Results from informal discussion and from SETS (Student Evaluation of Teaching and Subject) survey forms indicated a preference for lectures rather than the use of readings and videotaped examples. Therefore, further investigation of the different learning needs and preferences in learning style between on-campus and distance education students is needed.

CONCLUSION

As a result of their participation in this project, all students interviewed felt that the mystique of dance composition had been resolved, and that dance was accessible for teachers regardless of facilities and social or geographical isolation. It had grown from being a 'curriculum frill' to a right for all children. Hence, a movement culture may have been born, where children are free to dance their ideas, rather than the teachers' steps.

Acknowledgement

The authors would like to thank Jenny Fyfe, the teachers, parents and the students of Figtree Primary School, especially Nicole and Holly for sharing their dances with us.

References

Adshead, J. (1981) *The Study of Dance.* London: Dance Books.
Blom, L. & Chaplin, L. (1989) *The Intimate Act of Choreography.* London: Dance Books.
Boorman, J. (1969) *Creative Dance in the First Three Grades.* Canada: Longman.
Centre for Higher Education and Professional Development (1994) *Student Evaluation of Teaching and Subject (SETS).* Sydney: Macquarie University.
Cohen, D. & Schiller, W. (1988) Curriculum in Early Childhood Centres. *Curriculum Perspectives,* **8**(1),31–38.
Colby, C. (1928) *Natural Rhythms and Dances.* New York: A.S. Barnes.

Crum, B. (1991) Conventional thought and practice in physical education: Problems of the professional - prospects for change. *ISEP/NAHEPE Conference Proceedings*, Atlanta, Georgia.

Davids, J. (1997) Transcripts of telephone interviews. Committee of Advancement of University of Teaching (CAUT) Report, Institute of Early Childhood, Macquarie University.

Dyer, S & Schiller, W. (1996) Not wilting flowers again! Problem finding and problem solving in movement and performance. In *Issues in Expressive Arts Curriculum for Early Childhood*, edited by W. Schiller, pp. 47–54. Amsterdam: Gordon and Breach Publishers.

Edwards, C., Gandini, L. & Forman, G. (1993) *The Hundred Languages of Children*. Norwood, NJ: Ablex.

Elkind, D. (ed.) (1991) *Perspectives in Early Childhood Education: Growing with Young Children towards the 21st Century*. Washington, DC: NAEYC.

Gallahue, D. (1990) Moving and learning: Linkages that last. In *Moving and Learning for the Young Child*, edited by W. Stinson. Reston, VA: AAHPERD.

Gardner, H. (1983) *Frames of the Mind*. New York: Basic Books.

Gough, M. (1993) *In Touch with Dance*. London: Whitehorn.

Greenman, J. (1988) *Caring Spaces, Learning Places: Children's Environments That Work*. Redmond, WA: Exchange Press.

Honig, A. (1990) Baby moves: In relation to learning. In *Moving and Learning for the Young Child*, edited by W.J. Stinson. Reston, VI: AAHPERD.

Isenberg, J. & Jalongo, M. (1993) *Creative Expression and Play in the Early Childhood Curriculum*. Englewood Cliffs, NJ: Merrill.

May, R. (1975) *The Courage to Create*. New York: Bantam Books.

Meier, J., Hanson, M. & Olson, L. (1991) Physical education and health education in early childhood. In *Perspectives in Early Childhood Education: Growing with Young Children toward the 21st Century*, edited by D. Elkind. Washington, DC: National Association for the Education of Young Children.

NSW Board of Studies (1998) *Draft Creative Arts K–6 Syllabus*. Sydney: NSW Board of Studies.

Plato (n.d.) *The Republic* (B. Jowett, Trans.) New York: The Modern Library.

Schiller, W. (1992) Patterns of adult/child interaction in a preschool gross motor program. PhD thesis, Macquarie University, Australia.

Schiller, W. (ed.) (1996) *Issues in Expressive Arts Curriculum for Early Childhood*. Amsterdam: Gordon and Breach Publishers.

Smith-Autard, J. (1994) *The Art of Dance in Education*. London: A.&C. Black.

Spurgeon, D. (1997) The men's movement. *Conference Proceedings for the Seventh Dance and the Child International Conference*. Kuopio, Finland: daCi, 28 July –3 Aug.

Spurgeon, D. (1992) *Dance Moves*. Sydney: Harcourt, Brace Jovanovitch.

Sroufe, L. (1978) Attachment and the roots of competence. *Human Nature*, **1**, Oct.

Stinson, W. (ed.) (1990) *Moving and Learning for the Young Child*. Reston, VA: AAHPERD.

Stinson, S. (1988) *Dance for Young Children : Finding the Magic in Movement*. Reston: VA. American Alliance for Health, Physical Education, Recreation and Dance.

Wade, M. & Davis, W. (1982) Motor skill development in young children: Current views in assessment and programming. In *Current Topics in Early Childhood Education* , vol. 4, edited by L.G. Katz, pp. 55–70. Champaign, Ill: ERIC.

Zearin, C. (1997) Toddlers at play: Environments at work. *Young Children*, **52**(3),72–77.

18

CHILD-INITIATED CURRICULUM AND IMAGES OF CHILDREN

Sue Dockett

INTRODUCTION

The term curriculum means many things to many people. In this chapter, curriculum refers to the content to be covered in a particular area — the 'intended curriculum' (Arthur et al., 1996) — as well as what actually happens throughout the day — the 'emergent curriculum' (Jones & Nimmo, 1994), which includes all elements of school life, rather than only what is taught. In this chapter questions will be raised about how we conceptualise the curriculum and how approaches to curricula are linked to beliefs about children. Discussions with young children reveal differences between what adults regard as being important to include in a curriculum and what interests or intrigues children. For example, Harriet's (2 yrs 10 mths) reactions to the death of Diana, Princess of Wales, raised some specific issues for her.

Harriet:	Why are they putting flowers on the fence?
Mother:	Because Diana died.
Harriet:	Why did she die?
Mother:	Well, she was in a car accident. The car was going too fast and the driver had been drinking and the car crashed.
Harriet:	Where is Diana now?
Mother:	She's not anywhere. Her body is in the hospital.
Harriet:	So when is she coming home?
Mother:	She won't be coming home. Her body is in the hospital and some people think her spirit is in heaven.
Harriet:	What's a spirit?
Mother:	Well, it's part of a person that some people think leaves the body and goes to heaven when people die.
Harriet:	Where is it?
Mother:	Some people say its up in the sky.
Harriet:	Look Mum, we can see Diana! [As the news broadcast showed pictures of Diana.] She's still there!

Mother:	Yes, we can see pictures of her and we can see her body, but she's not alive any more. She's not breathing and she can't talk and she can't move. We can see her, but she can't see us. She can't see anyone, because she's dead.
Harriet:	She not see anybody?
Mother:	No, she can't see anybody.
Harriet:	Can she see flowers?
Mother:	No, she can't see flowers.
Harriet:	Why do people put all those flowers there? Diana won't see them.

Harriet's fascination with Diana and with explanations of death and dying continued for some time. A few weeks later she asked, 'Can Diana have another turn? If you die before you finish?' It was not a transitory interest, but an issue that she was grappling with, trying to understand and make sense of.

Similarly, eight-year-old Sarah voiced her concern on a particularly hot summer day when she stated: 'The problem for the trees is that they can't be in the shade, because they *are* the shade'. Sarah then asked questions about the weather patterns and influences. She was interested in meteorological information and explanations of the impact of very high temperatures on the environment.

In neither case was the interest expressed by these children incorporated into the curriculum of the relevant early childhood setting. In Harriet's case, there was little thought given to the idea that it could be appropriate to discuss issues such as death and dying with such young children. In Sarah's case, other curriculum priorities had already been decided, and there was no room to add anything extra.

How do we acknowledge the issues that are important to children? In a crowded curriculum, how can educators respond to such issues? Are we locked into approaches which concentrate on covering prescribed content, regardless of input from children? Do we adapt the curriculum to make it relevant for children, or ensure that all children cover the same content? What underlying images of children influence curriculum planning?

CHILD-INITIATED CURRICULUM

For many years, child-centred curriculum has been promoted as an essential feature of early childhood education (Arthur et al., 1996), distinguishing this from other phases of education. A child-centred approach acknowledges the needs, strengths and interests of children and responds to these through curriculum decisions and approaches. Tinworth has noted that a child-centred curriculum is 'based on an estimation of children's needs and interests' (1997:25). That is, educators make decisions about what children need, the strengths they have in some areas, and the interests they display, and develop the planned curriculum in a way that responds to these. This contrasts with a child-initiated curriculum, in which 'the child has an active role in the initiation of interests, questions and hypotheses and remains a collaborator in the process and form of subsequent inquiry, exploration and creative expression' (Tinworth, 1997:25). The differences between child-centred and child-initiated curricula essentially involve power and control: in a child-centred curriculum, adults make decisions about what is relevant for children; in a child-initiated curriculum, children make some decisions and work collaboratively with adults to explore and investigate issues that are relevant and meaningful to them. A child-initiated curriculum does not mean that adults have no role. Rather, adults have a critical, yet subtle, role to play in creating an environment which stimulates questions and exploration, provides opportunities for children to express their ideas, and challenges their understandings. The environment that is created must be safe, in both the physical and the psychological sense. Children who feel safe are more likely to take risks, more likely to ask questions to which they do not know the answer, more likely to persist in their search for answers, and more likely to share this with others including the educator.

The value of a child-initiated curriculum is two-fold. Firstly, children become engaged in content that is of interest and relevance to them. The focus is on content that children consider 'worth knowing', and because of this, intrinsic motivation and commitment to the experiences are likely to be high. Secondly, it is empowering for children to have adults take them, and their interests, seriously. When teachers listen and respond to children's interests or concerns they are conveying the message that what children have to say is worth listening to. The process of responding to children's interests, as well as the content of those interests, conveys to children the importance of their own voices.

BALANCING 'CHILD-CENTRED' AND 'CHILD-INITIATED' CURRICULUM

A balance between a child-centred and a child-initiated curriculum is both achievable and desirable. The educational context is such that coverage of certain aspects of knowledge, skills, understandings and values is mandatory. Often, ideas are provided to give educators suggestions as to how such coverage may be attained. In following such curriculum guidelines and directions children may not have substantive input nor generate their own questions through a child-initiated approach. Some may argue that this is appropriate: adults know more about the world and what is important and educators have been trained to develop and implement curricula. Educators are also accountable for what children learn and do not learn. How can educators be sure that they will cover the mandatory curriculum if they are not in control of what is taught? These questions assume that there is a direct relationship between learning and teaching, where what is taught is learnt by the students. Yet we have all had experiences in which this is not the case. The questions also assume a particular view of children as recipients, rather than as collaborators or co-constructors, of knowledge. This view is reflective of widely held views about children and about what characterises the period of childhood.

VIEWS OF CURRICULA AND VIEWS OF CHILDREN

In the example of Harriet and her questions about Princess Diana, the responsiveness of her mother is an essential part of a shared dialogue in which the agenda is open and in which the adult facilitates the asking of questions and the seeking of understanding. Harriet's mother demonstrates her belief that it is important to pursue an agenda set by the child. She clearly regards this agenda as a legitimate form and topic of inquiry. A less responsive adult might have ignored Harriet's concerns, responded with a non-answer such as 'just because', or changed the topic of conversation.

Quite often adults will be confronted by children asking about issues that they have never considered, do not regard as important or consider not developmentally appropriate for children. How adults respond and whether or not they regard children's agendas as a legitimate basis for curriculum relates very much to the images they have of children and childhood.

VIEWS OF CHILDHOOD

Adults often describe their childhood with nostalgia. This nostalgic view suggests that childhood is a period of innocence during which children ought to be protected from the harshness of the world around them. It assumes that children, unlike adults, have little power or resources with which to protect themselves. This perceived lack of power is evident in the ways in which adults decide who is a child and who is not (Cannella, 1997) as well as in the political and legal arenas (Rayner, 1991). In an early childhood context, children's lack of power is reflected in the ways adults determine what children need to know and how it should be learned.

Views of childhood innocence are linked to beliefs about children's lack of (or limited) knowledge (Silin, 1995), and this link is reflected in curriculum decisions. Planning a curriculum involves making decisions about what young children need to know, as well as about what they do not need to know. Examples of these areas include sex education, an extended vocabulary of swear words, and the intricacies of Einstein's theory of relativity. In this planning, there is an implicit assumption that not sharing knowledge about these things will mean that children will not come to know about them (and that children do not already know them). Further, there is the assumption that children are not competent to make such decisions themselves (Cannella, 1997). In conversations with children, one of the things that becomes clear is that children learn how to disguise some knowledge and to hide this from adults. For example, many children are quite familiar with a range of swear words as well as the settings in which they can use them with impunity.

To assist in curriculum decisions, educators may turn to child development theory. Typically, child development theory is based on the description of patterns, stages and rules of development. These are applied generally, so that all children are expected to move in a biologically determined pattern along the path to becoming an adult. According to Mason and Steadman (1997:33) 'these general rules have the effect of objectifying and decontextualising understanding of children', with the result that we focus on how children compare with the standard descriptions of developmental progression, rather than how children respond to the context in which they exist and function. The role of educators then becomes one of ensuring that children move through the designated stages, displaying appropriate actions and understandings in order to become mature and functional adults. The emphasis is on children becoming adults and on their progressing along a predetermined path to this outcome.

As a result of reference to developmental theory, educators build up expectations regarding what children should be like, what they should be doing and when certain stages of development should occur. While this approach provides a framework for planning learning experiences, it also means that any child who does not fit the standard pattern is labelled as being 'abnormal' or in need of extra assistance to reach the goals expected of them (Cannella, 1997). This framework rarely takes into account social or cultural variables.

Across the world, the universal applicability of traditional theories of child development is being questioned. Woodhead (1996) argues that such theories are culture-bound and

Katz questions reliance on a body of knowledge derived from the 'relatively limited sample of human experience' of North American and European children (1996:140).

Educators' beliefs about children have several consequences. One is that adults make decisions for children on the assumption that children are not capable of identifying what they need, or what they need to know. These include curriculum decisions about which issues should be covered, and when and how they should be covered. The basis for these decisions is often child development theory, with its universal descriptions of how children learn and develop.

A further consequence is that the diversity of children, and of childhoods, is neither recognised nor appreciated. Rather, what is valued is the progression children make to becoming more adult-like. Only then are they allowed some responsibilities for choosing areas to pursue or explore.

There are many ways in which children are undeniably less mature than adults. It is not so much this difference in maturity that is being questioned — rather it is the essential negativity often associated with being less mature. Childhood is something we all experience on the road to becoming adults; we need to ensure that the period of childhood is valued, not just the steps children take towards becoming an adult (Mason & Steadman, 1997).

AN ALTERNATIVE VIEW

Many social and cultural groups see children as being competent and capable of making valuable contributions to their society, and their educational approaches reflect an image of children as strong and powerful learners capable of controlling their own learning. For example, educators in Reggio Emilia centres hold an image that focuses 'not so much on the limits and weaknesses of children, but rather their surprising and extraordinary strengths and capabilities, linked with an inexhaustible need for expression and realisation' (Malaguzzi, 1993:72).

A view of children that considers the social and cultural contexts in which they exist leads to different view of childhood, based on the premise that childhood is a social and cultural construct, meaning different things in different contexts (Dencik, 1989). According to Mason and Steadman (1997:35) this view

> gives priority to the 'personhood' of children, to their 'lived experience' (James & Prout, 1995:92) and to perceiving children as 'human beings' rather than as 'human becomings' (Waksler, 1991). This paradigm views children as acting on, as well as being acted upon, the social world. It posits that they are 'possessed of individual agency, as competent social actors and interpreters of the world...' (James & Prout, 1995:90–95).

Of particular importance in this view is the positioning of children as actors in the social world, where they exert influence over the contexts in which they live (such as the family or school) as well as being influenced by those same contexts. This view emphasises the ability of children to influence what goes on around them as well as to be influenced. It suggests that curriculum decisions that are meaningful and relevant for a particular group of children will incorporate the voices of those children.

IMPLICATIONS OF A CHILD-INITIATED CURRICULUM

One of the ways in which educators can respond to issues that are important, relevant and meaningful for young children is to implement a child-initiated curriculum. This involves a commitment to including children's voices in curriculum decisions, and challenging our views and expectations of children. This is likely to be achieved when the following occur.

- The curriculum reflects issues that are important, relevant and meaningful for the children.

  Children are interested in much of what happens around them. Often they are trying to understand issues that are complex and multifaceted. Curriculum decisions should recognise this and aim to treat children's concerns seriously, rather than 'sanitising' the curriculum by glossing over any injustice, unfairness, anger or trauma associated with certain issues. While it is realistic for educators to want to avoid the full horror of some situations, it cannot be assumed that all children are unaware of these, or uninterested in exploring and trying to understand these issues.

     At times, educators simplify the curriculum on the assumption that children are unable to understand complex issues. In many situations this may be a valid assumption, however some children will be fascinated by questions or problems that educators have never considered or do not feel confident in pursuing. Educators who respond to such challenges demonstrate that they are prepared to take children's concerns seriously.

- Curriculum content is worth knowing, and curriculum experiences are worth doing.

  The basis of an appropriate curriculum for children is derived not only from a critical knowledge of child development, curriculum content and syllabus documents, but also from acknowledgment that certain issues are important to children, and therefore worth knowing. Adopting aspects of a child-initiated curriculum can ensure that issues of importance to children are explored. A child-initiated curriculum can be a part of a child-centred approach, but it is essential that some decisions about what is to be learnt and what is worth knowing are influenced by the children concerned, rather than solely by adults deciding what they need to know.

- The early childhood curriculum is considered for both short- and long-term consequences.

  The curriculum in the early childhood years has at least two functions: responding to what is important, relevant and meaningful for children at the present time, and establishing the foundations for future development. Early childhood education has both short- and long-term effects (Bredekamp & Rosegrant, 1992) and each of these is important to consider in curriculum planning; The purpose of early childhood education is not solely to prepare children for future education.

- A balance is achieved between child-initiated and mandatory curriculum content.

  A curriculum can reflect a balance between children's interests and prescribed content. It is important for children to be given opportunities to influence curriculum decisions and that educators respond to these opportunities appropriately. There will be times when educators promote specific knowledge to which children may not have access without such assistance. There will also be times when children will be motivated and interested to explore in great detail issues and situations that educators do not regard as essential, or with which they do not feel comfortable. A focus on a child-initiated curriculum indicates that educators take children seriously and that they are prepared to support this approach with the commitment of their time, resources and interest.

• The curriculum promotes connections between home and school.

Hearing children's voices requires recognition of the knowledge and understandings they bring to educational settings and of the interplay between home and the educational setting. The experiences children have at home or outside the early childhood setting contribute to their knowledge and understanding of various issues, and it is essential that educators recognise the importance of these experiences. At times this situation has the potential to produce conflict when different expectations are featured in different contexts, or when adults in different contexts do not agree about what is important. Ideally, recognising what happens at home can lead to a sense of partnership between parents, educators and children, and the establishment of shared educational goals.

• Children are the focus of the curriculum.

Educators need to be wary of accepting stage-like descriptions of learning and development and applying these without regard to the social and cultural contexts in which learning and development occurs. Regardless of the developmental sequence outlined, there will always be children who do not fit the pattern. Before these children are labelled as 'abnormal', educators need to question the template being used and take into account the contexts in which the children are operating. A focus on the children and the manipulation of the curriculum to fit them — rather than of the children to fit the curriculum — establishes a basis for being responsive to issues and questions that are relevant for those children.

• The curriculum extends beyond the individual.

Understanding individual children is an integral element of curriculum planning and implementation. It is important to respond to individual children's needs, interests and concerns. However we also need to consider the social and cultural contexts (of children and of ourselves) in which we respond. In particular, MacNaughton questions the focus on individuals and 'the view that knowledge of the individual child is and should be the sole knowledge for curriculum planning' (1996:16). She exhorts educators to focus on social justice and social goals. Such a focus is in keeping with the suggestion from Silin that 'as children talk about their worlds, we must also create opportunities for them to respond actively to the discomforting as well as the familiar' (1995:9).

A focus on social justice in the curriculum recognises that the decisions and interactions within early childhood environments have an impact on broader social issues.

• Assumptions about learning and knowing are challenged.

In any curriculum implementation there is a need to consider beliefs about learning and teaching as well as beliefs about knowledge and what is important to know. In particular, educators should question not only what children are expected to know, but also how this knowledge is to be constructed, as well as its relationship with the children's experiences and interests.

• The role of adults in promoting children's learning is reconsidered.

Adopting a child-initiated curriculum requires a reconsideration of the role of the educator in promoting children's learning. In such an approach, the educator is not regarded as the source of all knowledge, or even the source of all questions. Rather, educators create an environment rich in 'questions, ideas and provocative experiences' (Tinworth, 1997:25) which promotes children's investigations.

CONCLUSION

Acknowledging that children are grappling with difficult issues and that these issues have a place in the curriculum does not imply that educators should simply place children in difficult situations in order to help them develop the ability to manage. While this chapter questions the image of the child as vulnerable, it does not suggest that children are invulnerable. It does aim to promote recognition of the idea that what is relevant, important or of concern in children's lives can be different from what adults expect. Often adults' expectations of children are intertwined with beliefs and understandings of developmental theory, as well as with perceptions of childhood as a time of innocence and protection. In order to plan a curriculum which reflects issues of concern for children and which achieves a balance between these issues and knowledge that is perceived as being socially and culturally relevant, we need to listen to the voices of children and to question our expectations of, and assumptions about children.

Acknowledgment

An extended version of this chapter was presented at the Seventh Australia and New Zealand Conference on the First Years of School, 'New approaches to old puzzles–Reconceptualising the early years of school', held at the Australian National University in Canberra from 13–16 January, 1998.

References

Arthur, L., Beecher, B., Dockett, S., Farmer, S. & Death, E. (1996) *Programming and Planning in Early Childhood Services* (2nd edn). Sydney: Harcourt Brace.

Bredekamp, S. & Rosegrant, T. (1992) *Reaching Potentials: Appropriate Curriculum and Assessment for Young Children*. Washington, DC: NAEYC.

Cannella, G. S. (1997) *Deconstructing Early Childhood Education*. New York: Peter Lang.

Dencik, L. (1989) Growing up in the postmodern age: On the child's situation in the modern family, and on the position of the family in the modern welfare state. *Acta Sociologic*, **32**(2).

Jones, E. & Nimmo, J. (1994) *Emergent Curriculum*. Washington DC: NAEYC.

Katz, L. G. (1996) Child development knowledge and teacher preparation: Confronting assumptions. *Early Childhood Research Quarterly*, **11**(2), 135–146.

MacNaughton, G. (1996) Curriculum for curriculum change in post-modern times: Some ethical considerations. Keynote address at the Weaving Webs Conference, University of Melbourne, July.

Malaguzzi, L. (1993) History, ideas and basic philosophy. In *The Hundred Languages of Children: The Reggio Emilia Approach to Early Childhood Education*, edited by C. Edwards, L. Gandini and G. Forman. Norwood, NJ: Ablex.

Mason, J. & Steadman, B. (1997) The significance of the conceptualisation of childhood for child protection policy. *Family Matters*, **46**, 31–36.

Rayner, M. (1991) Taking seriously the child's right to be heard. In *The UN Children's Convention and Australia*, edited by P. Alston and G. Brennan. Sydney: The Human Rights and Equal Opportunity Commission.

Silin, J. (1995) Toward a more socially relevant curriculum. *Every Child*, **1**(6), 8–9.

Tinworth, S. (1997) Whose good idea was it? Child initiated curriculum. *Australian Journal of Early Childhood*, **22**(3), 24–29.

Woodhead, M. (1996) *In Search of the Rainbow: Pathways to Quality in Large-scale Programs for Young Disadvantaged Children*. The Hague: Bernard van Leer Foundation.

19

FINDING THE BALANCE

Enhancing piano lessons as learning experiences for young children

Emily Ap

INTRODUCTION

A seven-year-old piano student came to lessons one day and sat down to perform a Mozart 'Rondo'. He played with confidence and feeling. At the end of a most convincing performance he turned to me and said with a hint of despair, 'That was all wrong, wasn't it?' The reason for his comment was that he had improvised most of the left-hand chords. His improvisation harmonised pleasingly with the right-hand melody but he had not played it according to the written score. This incident led me to consider young children, who often begin lessons with enthusiasm, soon lose interest and the music lessons become a source of frustration, possibly due to the lack of opportunity to explore and play. Music lessons may be one of the earliest situations where children are made to feel that they are doing something wrong.

Traditionally, piano pedagogy has been concerned with playing, recreating and interpreting piano repertoire. There is usually little room for improvisation or diverging from the set notation. It is a paradox that learning an instrument 'celebrates and uses the creative expressions of others, while effectively muffling the creative potential of its student participants' (Graham, 1998:24). The implication for the young child is that much of the lesson will be involved with correcting inaccuracies in pitch and rhythm. The situation is of concern especially when children feel that they need to apologise every time a note or a passage is played incorrectly. For many children, constant correction may create a dependency upon the teacher as an instructor rather than facilitator (Hatch & Freeman, 1988). Imposition of adult standards has been the accepted way to teach piano repertoire where the teacher who 'knows' must somehow impart knowledge to piano students who are 'not in the know'.

Such an approach is difficult to reconcile with the idea of learning music as a creative process where every child's unique way of expression can find acceptance. For creativity to occur, the child needs to feel safe to take a chance with something new where activity will not be labelled a 'mistake'(Saltz & Johnson, 1977). This is not to say that interpretation should be 'thrown to the wind' and the child allowed to play with disregard for stylistic differences. Children are capable of playing with feeling if it stems from their own experience.

In piano tuition, assessment tends to emphasise product as a measure of achievement and although assessment has a valid place, care needs to be taken to counterbalance the learning experience with meeting psychological and developmental interests of young children to prevent a 'loss of happiness' (Ross, 1986:viii). It has been shown that where achievement and performance-oriented pedagogy is a focus, children have less confidence and a lower self-esteem than children where performance was not stressed (Stipek, 1993), and that poor self-concept in musical ability is related to negative music experiences in early childhood (McLendon, 1982).

A child's progression through grade levels or repertoire can also become a source of stress and obsession for parents who want to make sure that their child is 'keeping up' with other children. It is not only parents who enforce this expectation but also teachers and a success-oriented, achievement-based society. Often it is a race to get to the eighth grade which is seen by some as the 'finishing line' for piano lessons. However, proficiency is not achieved in a matter of months or even years, but through a culmination of rich, integrated musical experiences (Sloboda, 1990). Musical experience is a process; there is no absolute point of arrival.

DIDACTIC TEACHING APPROACHES

There have been repeated assertions that didactic teaching methods affect children's intrinsic motivation to learn (Katz, 1988) by undermining their attempts at mastery, the way they perceive their own competence (Kamii, 1985), and their ability to think creatively (Cropley, 1992). Studies have also found that didactic teaching methods in preschools have produced less creative children who have more negative attitudes towards their activities (Hyson, Van Trieste & Rauch, 1989, cited in Burts et al., 1993:24). The assumption can be made that a highly didactic piano pedagogy combined with a lack of creative opportunities could partly contribute to high levels of boredom and a lack of interest amongst young piano students. For these reasons, didactic approaches are believed by many researchers to be developmentally inappropriate for young children.

Conversely, there have been researchers who have asserted that whilst much of the research favours child-centred approaches, some skills are best taught using didactic methods and it is therefore important to identify the specific learning goals and to match them with the appropriate instructional approach (Stipek et al., 1995). Fowell and Lawton (1992) described a program where both developmental and instructional theory were successfully incorporated. Overall, the debate for and against didactic approaches indicates that a balance is needed in particular learning situations, especially those which involve acquiring a set of skills as in learning the piano.

IS AN EARLY START IN PIANO LESSONS NECESSARY?

Given that piano pedagogy is primarily based on a didactic approach and is seen as best avoided in early childhood, it could be argued that piano lessons should not be commenced at an early age. This view, however, assumes that there is only one way to teach piano, that is through a highly structured methodology based on technical accomplishment. There are justifications for concerns that young children are being 'hothoused' and 'hurried' as child prodigies or to give them a competitive edge (Elkind,1981:xii; Sigel, 1987:212). However it would be 'throwing the baby out with the bathwater' if recommendations were made to defer piano lessons based on this rationale. It is not simply a question of wanting to 'hurry' the child into adulthood. Studies show that cultivating the skills needed to play the piano requires time and that high levels of performance can be facilitated by early starting ages (Ericsson et al., 1990).

Early exposure to music experiences finds support in the body of literature examining the educational benefits of music education which can be divided into two categories: those relating to music and the arts, and those relating to extramusical benefits (Draper & Gayle, 1987). Of great significance for early childhood piano teachers are recent studies which have found strong links between music and spatial reasoning skills (Rauscher et al., 1994, 1997). With respect to extramusical benefits of early music education, these studies are particularly important as they establish causal links in an area where previous literature had been dominated by correlational research methodology. These current findings also strongly support the notion that young children should be encouraged to have piano lessons and lead to consideration beyond whether young children should learn piano and how they should learn.

Contemporary early childhood educators advocate approaches based on ideas by Rousseau, Pestalozzi and Froebel which place development and the interests of children as central to education. Researchers in arts and music education have stressed the importance of providing opportunities for appropriate music experiences for all children, the basis of which is to foster creativity, self-expression and personal competence (Peery & Peery, 1987). In an investigation of talented individuals, Sosniak (1990) found that the early years were spent in exploratory, playful music experiences with little emphasis on precision. Furthermore, they appeared to have acquired musical skill through these early experiences which set the stage for a positive attitude to enable them to continue the development of technique (Sosniak, 1990:155). Other researchers stress that optimum learning appears to take place when early childhood programs are made developmentally appropriate (Bredekamp & Copple, 1997) and when teaching emphasises a process approach and child-centred experiences (Dunn & Kontos, 1997). The combined research areas of musical achievement and child development indicate an early start in music lessons provided that the focus in those early years does not result in the neglect of 'imagination and creativity' (Schiller & Veale, 1996:8). There may be opportunities to enhance the process of learning piano for young children by combining acquisition of skills with exploratory, playful musical experiences.

DEVELOPMENTALLY APPROPRIATE PRACTICE

Research about developmentally appropriate practice may provide guidelines towards finding an approach to take in early childhood piano pedagogy. The model for developmentally appropriate practice is grounded in the learning and developmental theories of Piaget, Vygotsky and Erikson (Bredekamp & Rosegrant, 1992) which propose that children's growth results from their actions on the environment, social interactions and intrinsically motivating experiences.

Developmentally appropriate practice has been widely debated in the field of early childhood on issues such as cultural diversity, class, and multiple ways of teaching and knowing (Walsh, 1991; Lubeck, 1994). Kessler (1991:137) argues that context is not given due consideration in the child development discourse and that there are some occasions where adult instruction is useful. Other researchers have responded that there has been a misunderstanding of what developmentally appropriate practice is aiming to represent (Kostelnik, 1992; Burts et al., 1993).

Bredekamp stresses that in piano pedagogy, disciplined skill achievement and play activities need not be viewed as two ends of a continuum (personal communication, April, 1998) and that thinking should move away from an 'either/or' to a 'both and' perception (Bredekamp & Copple, 1997:23). Her four-stage cyclical learning model incorporates concepts of creativity and artistry in two of the stages described as exploration and inquiry (Bredekamp & Rosegrant, 1992:33). Conceptualising artistry and creativity in such a model reconciles the polarity in perception of these areas. Wright (1991) also asserts that skill versus creativity is a perceived dichotomy which can be lessened when teaching is based on knowledge of child development and principles of early childhood education.

In the United States, the National Association for the Education of Young Children (NAEYC) has developed guidelines for developmentally appropriate programs. Areas requiring attention are awareness of child development, individualising of programs, parental involvement, creating a supportive learning community and implementing appropriate programs (Bredekamp & Copple, 1997). The following sections briefly explore the theoretical applicability of these concepts in relation to piano lessons.

Awareness of child development and the importance of play

In the past, failure to include knowledge about development in early childhood programs has led to inappropriate adult expectations (Bredekamp, 1991). By the same token, if piano pedagogy fails to understand the developmental needs of a young child, a similar situation may occur. Anecdotal accounts have described piano lessons where teachers have rapped their young students on the knuckles or unrealistically expected that a child should sit still for a long period.

Within the existing piano pedagogy the practical, aural and theoretical components are frequently taught separately and often by different teachers. But adult-prescribed boundaries are not necessarily the way young children understand and see the world. Instead, children 'roam across disciplinary structures' (Comte, 1993:158) and 'see learning as a seamless cloth' (Schiller & Veale, 1996:11). Research findings indicate that learning can be enhanced when teachers incorporate principles of play (Smith, 1995), and it is well documented that play is not a trivial activity but the way children learn and know about the world (Piaget, 1962; Vygotsky, 1976). Studies have shown that aspects of skill acquisition can be taught through games (Hoffman, 1996) and integration of the arts (Ap, 1997). The importance of a playful approach to music lessons is best summed up by Sloboda and Davidson (1996:187):

> It has been a source of some surprise and sadness that several young musicians we interviewed …are so focused on achievement, competition, and being the 'best' that they almost look down ...to music for pleasure as 'a waste of time'...we suspect that those individuals for whom music is 'all work and no play' will never achieve the highest levels of expressive performance.

As play has also been shown to be linked to creativity (Jalongo, 1995), it would be desirable to integrate creative processes together with a sense of playfulness into early childhood piano lessons. Furthermore, the divergent nature of creative activities provides opportunities for children to explore sounds in contexts where there is no right or wrong way to play the piano. Researchers have asserted that creativity needs to be fostered not through performance alone but also through listening, responding critically and emotionally, and through encouragement to improvise and compose (Levi, 1991; Gordon, 1997).

Considering the importance which studies have placed on nurturing creativity, it is surprising that it has been a neglected area in young children's piano tuition. Learning experiences are enhanced when programs are designed with the belief that children develop at varying rates, that 'no two children are exactly alike' (Kostelnik et al., 1993:41), and that children should be treated as individuals.

Individualising programs

Wright (1991:3) stresses that teachers have a responsibility 'to recognise and value individual differences' when planning programs. As piano lessons usually take place on a one-to-one basis they are particularly well suited to individualised learning.

Going beyond individualisation is the possibility of personalising the learning based on the child's existing knowledge, experience and interests, so that it is meaningful to the individual child. This enables the learning process to be 'owned by the learner' (Horn, 1993:71). Studies indicate that there are positive effects on intrinsic motivation when learning is personalised and contextualised (Cordova & Lepper, 1996). Gardner (1995:208) emphasises that personalisation is the heart of multiple intelligences theory where 'human differences' should be taken seriously, and each child given the best opportunity to master learning.

Teachers need to be aware of the interplay of factors which would help them produce programs 'tailor-made' for the individual child and family. Vygotskian theory stresses the importance of social and cultural influences on development and points out that optimum learning at the zone of proximal development occurs when a teacher can encourage interest by challenging the child to discover new and fascinating material (Berk, 1994:30). In music lessons, a teacher may:

> facilitate the exercise of imagination that are being controlled and owned by the student... we can contribute to the development of creative imaginations in our students by encouraging their improvisatory skills. Improvisation is a skill largely lost to 'classically trained' musicians and educators, and yet it is a fundamental tool for channeling creative energy and releasing fear of performance and composition (Horn, 1993:3).

Gaining a holistic understanding of the child's individual needs can be fostered through being familiar with the child's home environment and with the significant people in the child's life. This leads to the next key area identified in developmentally appropriate programs which is parental and familial involvement.

Parental involvement

Studies conducted over a thirty-year period (Bronfenbrenner, 1979) show that there is a strong relationship between parental involvement and success in children's educational outcomes (Berger, 1995; Mapp, 1997). Studies have also reported that when adults (parents) become 'play partners' (Sylva, 1984:80) their child's learning experiences are dramatically enriched. In a study which investigated talented individuals, Sosniak (1990:154) found that interest and experience came 'as a natural consequence of membership in a family which valued the activity'.

Problems associated with early childhood piano lessons, such as motivating children to practise, could relate to a lack of opportunity for parental involvement. In the majority of cases, children are 'dropped off ' at lessons or take lessons at school where the parents and teacher rarely have the opportunity to meet. A recent study of parental influences in music achievement found that high parental involvement and interest in lessons and practice greatly increased the development of their child's musical ability (Davidson et al., 1996). Ericsson et al. (1990:119) found that 'systematic practice is not inherently motivating' and must be initially maintained and encouraged 'through the active support of teachers and parents'. It is further reported that the quality of parental involvement and family style can be correlated with motivational and academic outcomes (Ginsburg & Bronstein, 1993), thus emphasising the need to look at the level and quality of parental involvement in music lessons. The closest exemplar of a music instrumental program which encourages parental involvement is the 'Suzuki method' based on the philosophy of Dr. Shinichi Suzuki. The method recognises that parental presence at lessons and assistance at home practice are crucial for developing the child's ability to learn a musical instrument (Suzuki,1986; Warby, 1997). Parents and teachers are scaffolding the child's learning. Parent involvement extends into the social support of a 'caring community of learners' (Bredekamp & Copple, 1997:16) and this represents the fourth key area which requires attention in considering an appropriate program.

Creating a supportive learning community

Research shows that support through group activity has positive benefits for learning (Kotloff, 1993). The community helps maintain support of a student's interests and involvement by placing social value on the music activity and performance as part of a process (Sosniak, 1990). Group support is an area which needs particular attention in piano pedagogy as learning piano often occurs in isolation. By comparison, children learning other musical instruments have more opportunities for peer and community interaction through playing in bands, orchestras or other ensembles.

Implementing an appropriate program

A program was implemented which specifically aimed for children to participate in activities encouraging creative responses to and personalisation of a set piano piece from a series titled Piano Fun by Australian composer, Roderick MacFarlane. The implementation reflected the emphasis within the New South Wales K-6 Draft Creative

Arts Syllabus (1998) upon incorporating creative activities involving performance, listening and composition (organising sound) into children's music experiences. The creative activities were:

1. Art response

   The children were asked to create a poem, story, painting, drawing, collage or construction as a response to the MacFarlane piece which they were learning.

2. 'Sound effects' story

   The children were asked to create sound effects on the piano to 'match' a story to be read by a parent at home. The children's pieces had descriptive titles such as 'Mr. Plod' and 'Jungle Jog' which were incorporated into the story.

3. 'Meet the Composer' concert

   This activity comprised a concert and an 'Art response' exhibition where children could view peer responses to piano pieces using mixed media, meet the composer, and perform their chosen pieces. It was anticipated that the children's attendance at and participation in a live performance would be an invaluable learning experience (Suthers, 1996). The concert experience could also provide role models by enabling young children to see other children and adults engaged in the activity of piano playing. It has been suggested that children need to be shown art and artists in action where 'the use of models for learning can also include practising artists' (Stewart, 1993:170).

4. Improvisation/personal interpretation

   The children explored ways to interpret in the MacFarlane piece by improvising to produce a different feeling and/or meaning in the piece. For example, children were given choices to explore changes in tempo, dynamics, tone, style, melody or create their own changes.

5. Composition

   Children were given a choice of one or more activities to try which involved composing to a given title or their own idea.

THE RESEARCH STUDY

A research study was undertaken with the aim of, firstly implementing a program 'that put[s] children, and not the art form, first' (Comte, 1993:162), where young children can learn to play piano repertoire through a more varied, enjoyable and appropriate approach, and secondly to examine the effects this may have on the piano learning experience. This research was developed to investigate the question: Does an enriched developmentally appropriate teaching approach enhance piano lessons for young children? The following subsidiary questions emerged from this question:

• Was the creative piano program interesting and enjoyable for the children?

- Did the creative piano program enhance mastery of piano playing?
- Were imagination and creativity evident from children's responses?
- Was an element of play present during program implementation?
- Were the lessons individualised for the children and their families?
- How were parents and community involved in lessons?
- What happens when parents are involved in lessons?
- Are there any outcomes affected by age, gender, cultural factors or length of time learning the piano?

CHOOSING A METHODOLOGY

As the researcher is also a teacher, it was considered pertinent to use a form of research which could concurrently improve practice. Action research was chosen as a suitable methodology because it allowed for the improvement of practice through the perspectives of current constructivist theories which could possibly provide solutions to some of the problems which I was experiencing in piano teaching.

Doing teacher research is particularly pertinent, even necessary in instrumental teaching as private studio music teachers are frequently isolated from each other. There is no opportunity to enter a 'staff room' where ideas and problems can be informally discussed or access to curriculum advisers to help bridge the gap between theory and practice. The quality of teaching rests heavily on the ability of individual teachers to reflect, inquire and take action.

Moreover, the nature of action research allows the teacher and researcher to inform his/her own practice not only through examining existing research, but to engage in research which will be directly relevant to each unique situation.

PARTICIPANTS

The piano studio comprised 37 students between the ages of 3 and 18 years. The whole studio participated in the creative activities and performed in the concert. However, the study sample comprised only the children in the piano studio between the ages of 5 and 10, a total of 22 students. (Permission to participate in the study was given by the parents). Of the 22 students, 14 had their mothers present at lessons; three had attending fathers; two had alternating mother and father presence; one had a mother who attended occasionally and one had a mother who refused to be present. Most were of middle to upper socioeconomic status according to occupation and education (levels I or II on the Hollingshead Two Factor Index of Social Position, 1991). Eighteen of the fathers and 16 of the mothers had tertiary qualifications. Nineteen children came from families where both parents live in the same household, and one child came from a divorced family and lived with his mother. Twenty of the children had one sibling and two children were the only child in the family. All of the families live in the Northern suburbs which are considered to be the more affluent areas of Sydney. Thirteen of the 22 children come from families where both parents were from an Asian background, six of the participants were Caucasian, and three were from families where one parent was from an Asian background.

Case studies

As well as observing the 22 participants, this study examined seven individual cases of children of varying ages. The case studies were selected on the basis of varying cultural backgrounds, music experience, age range and parental support. Described as instrumental case studies, they illuminate the important issues of the study and provide a 'supportive role' to aid understanding (Stake, 1994:237). Parameters for the case studies were 1) during piano lesson time, 2) the concert situation and 3) observations by the parent of each case study child over a 12-week period. Pseudonyms are used to maintain anonymity of all the participants.

PROCEDURE AND INSTRUMENTATION

Six weeks prior to the implementation of the creative activities, the teacher played a selection of three or four suitable pieces from the series Piano Fun, by the composer, Roderick MacFarlane, and the children chose a piece which appealed to them. They were also asked to listen to tape recordings of the pieces. The children and parents were informed that a concert would take place where the piece would be performed and that the composer would be attending. The children spent about five minutes working on the piece at each lesson and were given a section to practise at home. Parents were informed that an arts activities program would be implemented as an integral part of the teacher's research. Parents were asked to assist in the research by attending every lesson and helping their child with the designated tasks during home practices.

At the beginning of each lesson, the children were asked, 'What would you like to do first?', that is, which creative activity or a piano piece. Their preferences were noted in the teacher's journal. Notes of observations and anecdotes were maintained in a teacher's journal during the implementation period. The creative activities were incorporated into the usual piano lessons over a period of 12 weeks.

The following methods of recording were used: teacher's journal entries, audio recordings of lessons, structured interviews, visual and document data of creative activities and a parent questionnaire. These methods were chosen based on the ease and relative unobtrusiveness with which they could be incorporated into lessons. Triangulation was possible when data could be examined from a variety of sources. Further triangulation was sought through comparing the researcher's conclusions to those of an external analyst who was 'blind' to the aims and the results of the study.

A pilot questionnaire was devised and given for comment to a colleague who has conducted educational research using survey methodology. Based on their recommendations, several changes were made to the questionnaire to increase the clarity of its wording and format. The questionnaire was also trialed by two parents of non-English speaking background with older children in the piano studio who are not involved in the research study but who participated in the creative activities.

After all the creative activities had been implemented, parents were asked to complete the questionnaire consisting of 14 closed questions with opportunities for comment. The questions sought parental responses regarding their perceptions of their child's enjoyment of the creative activities program. Parents were asked to complete the questionnaire during the lesson as this would ensure a high return. With the teacher and researcher present during completion, the questionnaire could also be spot-checked for questions omitted and ambiguities immediately clarified.

An analysis was also made of recordings of the children's compositions by a composer who is a graduate of the State Conservatorium of Music, Sydney, with over 40 years of experience teaching composition and music theory.

RESULTS

'Meet the Composer' concert and 'Art Response' exhibition

The 'Meet the Composer' concert took place on a sunny afternoon in June. There was spontaneous and informal interaction between the composer, MacFarlane and the students which was facilitated by the children's teacher who also compered the concert. After each child was announced, the composer was asked questions about the background to his pieces. The teacher also discussed the various art responses and the children were asked questions about their art responses. At the end of many of the performances MacFarlane volunteered positive comments about the performances and his impressions of the art responses. When I commented that Andrew thought the 'Jelly Bean Jig' sounded like a steam train engine and whistle, MacFarlane, enthusiastically agreed. At other times, such as after a performance of 'Lemon Rind Rag', MacFarlane exclaimed, 'that was great, that's exactly how I wanted it to sound!' or 'You really captured the spirit of the piece and made it come to life'.

The presence of family, as well as the composer and his wife, enabled the concert to be an opportunity to 'create a caring community of learners' (Bredekamp, 1997:1). MacFarlane commented, 'You've got a really great feeling going here. Everyone is so enthusiastic and there isn't that coldness, that tense feeling that you sometimes get at concerts.' MacFarlane and his wife, who also teaches piano, reported later that they tried the art responses with their own students with success.

At the concert, the children were most interested in the art responses of the older children rather than those of similar aged children. There was greatest interest in a construction by a 12-year-old boy for the piece 'Sydney Stomp' which he had said sounded 'like a construction yard with the hammers banging'. The younger children were most interested in his use of a Lego bulldozer which was building a wall with drink cans. Children made comments such as 'I want to make one like that' and 'I wish I could do that'. The works of the older children sparked more enthusiasm in the younger children. For example, David commented, 'I want to make something more interesting next time.' Seeing others' works was a source of inspiration and interest for the younger children. This experience mirrors the comments by Schiller and Veale:

> By exposure to other children's art, by seeing artists at work and discussing various performances, exhibitions and media presentations, children begin to appreciate their own and others work, as well as developing an empathy with other creators and with various forms of expression (Schiller & Veale, 1996:10).

The concert was shown to be an important part of the functioning of the piano studio which engendered community support and assisted in making piano lessons less of an isolating experience. 'He really enjoyed seeing what the others had done in their art responses', commented one mother of a seven-year-old child; 'she wants to learn some of the other pieces after hearing them played by the others', said another mother.

Individual activities

On the basis of their interest, participation and responses towards the creative activities, the 22 children in the study were categorised into three overlapping groups.

The results of the three groupings of children are summarised in Tables 19.1 and 19.2.

Group I

There were four children in Group I and three in the overlapping Group I/II.

An analysis of the data relating to the art responses showed that these children closely followed the teacher's suggestion to write a poem or draw a picture. Five children in Group I and Group I/II did drawings for their art responses using coloured pencils, felt markers or computer images as in Figure 19.1.

Most of the art responses had been done on their own without parental assistance, illustrating the titles of their pieces rather than capturing the mood of the music. The parents of children in these groups tended to assist in the learning of repertoire rather than engaging in the creative activities.

In the creative activity 'Sound effects' story, Group I children showed a greater amount of reserve and appeared to lack confidence. They needed more encouragement than children in Groups II and III. Almost all of the children looked to me for instruction and appeared reluctant to try until I showed them what they could do. Initially, I thought that they were not interested in the activity, but after I demonstrated with fists, elbows and palms, puzzled faces broke out into smiles and some of them attempted the activity with more confidence. However, they did not utilise the whole keyboard as did the children of Group III, but made sounds using a small section of the keyboard. One mother wrote of her daughter, 'she was a little timid at first but got more confident later on'. This finding is supported by Collins (1990:111) who states that many children 'do not know where to start, are afraid to take risks and experiment [they] do not trust their ability to discover a voice within themselves'.

Of the three groups, these children exhibited the most docile behaviour at lessons. They were not opinionated and were reluctant to answer interview questions. When asked 'What shall we do first today?' they showed a range of preferences. They were also very obedient, followed practice instructions and completed the improvisation checklists dutifully. Two children did not attempt the composition activity. The other two completed the checklist but could not recall the composition. Two of the children, brother and a sister, in the overlapping group had composed tunes for the nursery rhymes 'To market, to market to buy a fat pig' and 'This little pig went to market'. In the analysis of all the children's compositions by the teacher as well as an external analyst, these compositions were seen to be the least divergent in terms of musical style. The compositions were improvisations of nursery rhyme tunes and did not incorporate harmony as was evident in compositions of children in Groups II and III.

All the children in Group I had learnt the MacFarlane piece very quickly and mastered it to performance standard within a few weeks. They all attended the concert and one mother identified that her child had felt nervous prior to the concert. All of the children

Table 19.1 Characteristics of the three groups of children participating in creative activities piano program.

Group	Participation in activites					
	learning piece	art response	'sound effects' story	concert	improvisation	composition
I	quickly mastered pieces	low parental involvement, least imaginative	shy attempts, inhibited, used small section of keyboard	1 was nervous before performance	2 not attempted 2 completed checklists	2 completed checklist, 2 not attempted
Between groups		art responses related to title of pieces, did not reflect the mood of the piece				1 completed checklist, 2 composed simple melodies
II	quickly mastered pieces	high parental involvement, pieces reflected mood of piece	needed some encouragement at first, then became enthusiatic	confident performances	completed checklists, enjoyed activity, imaginative ideas	3 completed checklist 3 composed a piece using harmony; 1 composed 9 pieces using harmony
Between groups	slower mastery of pieces					
III	1 learnt right-hand only; 2 did not learn piece	high parental involvement, pieces reflected mood of piece highly imaginative	uninhibited, used full keyboard, wanted to spend more time on activity	1 was nervous before performance 1 did not attend, 1 discountinued lessons prior to concert	highly imaginative enthusiatic attempts during lesson, did not completed checklist during home practice	3 not attempted 1 composed using harmony

Table 19.2 Cultural background and observed behaviour of children participating in creative activities piano program

Group	Cultural background of parent involved in lessons	Behaviour in lessons in lessons
I	Hong Kong Chinese – 4	docile, more inhibited, least opinionated
Between groups	Hong Kong Chinese – 3	
II	Hong Kong Chinese – 3 Other Asian – 3 Other Australians – 2	enthusiastic, interested participation confident, self-motivated, able to think independently
Between groups	Hong Kong Chinese – 1 Other Australians – 2	
III	Malaysian Chinese – 1 Other Australians – 3	exuberant, least inhibited, talkative, opinionated, less able to concentrate

FLAT CHAT

I like dogs because I like to see them run. I like fish because I like to see them swim. I also like horses because they are beautiful.

Figure 19.1 Art response for 'Flat Chat'

in Group I and the overlapping Group I/II had parents from Hong Kong, two of which were siblings from a family where the mother is from Hong Kong and the father is Caucasian.

Case study 1

One of the children in Group I, John (8 yrs), is the eldest of two children and has been learning the piano for three years. He has progressed well in mastery of technique and is very quietly spoken during lessons. He rarely makes any comment and only speaks when he is spoken to. He appears to be very mature for his age and rarely expresses his emotions. On one occasion, he continued to play the piano whilst I was speaking and immediately his mother reprimanded him and said to him in Cantonese, 'Listen and obey your teacher'. Upon being asked to do an art response, John replied that he did not like drawing or painting. For several weeks, he had not given the art response much thought and it was finally suggested that he might do an acrostic poem, which he produced the following week illustrated by computer graphics. He was willing to try the 'Sound effects' story, and alternately smiled or grimaced apologetically as he attempted it. In the improvisation activity, he dutifully completed all the teacher suggestions on the checklist but did not wish to create his own improvisation. He did not attempt the composition. John was the fastest student to learn the MacFarlane piece, mastering it within four weeks.

Group II

Observational data shows that the seven children in this group could be described as enthusiastic, self-motivated and interested in the creative activities. The cultural background of children in this group were three Hong Kong Chinese, three of other Asian background, and two European/Anglo-Australians.

In choosing the MacFarlane piece, many of the children said that they liked 'this kind of music'. Richard's (7 yrs) mother noted in the questionnaire that he particularly enjoyed learning the new piece because 'we listen to a lot of jazz music at home, so he was very keen on the MacFarlane pieces'. When asked, 'What shall we do first today?', five of the children consistently chose to play the MacFarlane piece first. (This continued to occur up to four weeks after the concert.) Many of MacFarlane's compositions are in a jazz and popular music idiom which is the music that most children are exposed to in contemporary Sydney society. Questionnaire and observational data showed that the children preferred the popular style of music and enjoyed responding to it. Other studies support this finding and suggest that learning preferred music increases the time that children will spend on the musical learning tasks, as well as develop more positive attitudes towards music classes (LeBlanc & Cote, 1983; Murphy & Brown, 1986). This group of children were also highly cooperative, confident and showed an ability to think and follow their own ideas independently from teacher suggestion. Parents of children in this group were enthusiastic and involved through providing support at lessons, home practice and contributing ideas towards the art responses and other activities. In the 'Sound effects' story, one mother described that it was 'like making mud-pies with sounds' which was an insightful description and showed that when parents are included in lessons they can support the teacher's objectives, which may otherwise be unnoticed or even discouraged. Julia's and Mandy's mother said that her two daughters enjoyed the 'Sound effects' story and 'always started that first before practising'.

Figure 19.2 Art response for 'Dance of the Red Socks'

Upon analysis of the art responses by the children in Group II, it was obvious that there had been a high level of parental involvement. Parents were involved by helping to make the object (e.g. sewing on buttons for eyes), providing, finding or purchasing materials, providing creative ideas and spending time with their child.

Case study 2

The creative activities assisted the learning of repertoire for Brent (8 yrs) who was learning 'Dance of the Red Socks'. For the art response, Brent and his mother made a puppet with red socks (see Figure 19.2).

During the improvisation activity, Brent's mother said, 'that sounds like the Death of the Red Socks' when Brent played the piece very slowly. Brent then became very enthusiastic and came up with several other names, 'this is the red socks funeral, now they are going hopping, the red socks fall off a cliff'. The following week, he played the piece very quickly with an expressive sudden ending saying: 'The red socks ran so quickly that they just dropped dead'. Brent's mother commented that home practices had become more enjoyable. It was observed that when music lessons are approached playfully with parents in attendance, the children's attitudes towards practice became more positive. It did not take Brent long to learn this piece, which was slightly more difficult than his other pieces. Four of the seven children who composed music came from Group II. An analysis of the compositions by the researcher as well as the external assessor showed that there was more originality, imagination, as well as an understanding of music harmony concepts evident in these compositions compared to the other three compositions by children in the other groups. An interesting outcome is that age and experience at piano playing did not hinder the ability to compose.

Case study 3

The youngest child to compose was Byron (5 yrs). His mother had previously told me that he enjoys exploring sounds at the piano and picking out known tunes. 'One night we went out and there were a lot of pretty lights in the trees. The next day he played this', said his mother as Byron played his composition. The quality of his composition, 'Forests', was luminous and impressionistic, and was remarkable in its ability to capture the sparkling fairy lights in the trees. The children's composition experiences appear to reject the popular belief that improvisation and composition takes place after technical skills have been acquired which is supported by McMillan's observation that even children without formal music lessons are capable of improvising and composing (1993:119).

Case study 4

Prior to the implementation of the creative activities program, David (8), had composed at home but was reluctant to play his compositions at the lesson. I had not insisted that he perform on those occasions and I was uncertain how he would respond to the composition activity this time. In the following week after being assigned the composition activity, David had attempted to write down one of his compositions, 'The Toddle Woddle'. He said that there were other pieces 'in my head, but it's too hard to write them all down'. I asked him to play them for me and I transcribed some of them for him. I asked him to record them on tape and suggested to his mother that we encourage him to keep a portfolio of taped composition. In the weeks following the composition activity, David started to compose more music.

He soon presented me with a tape and told me that he was composing songs for his two-year-old cousin who always badgers him to tell her stories. They include titles such as 'The Moon', 'The Beachball' and are strikingly similar to MacFarlane's syncopated style. One piece which he titled 'Lauren's Magic' is a piece written for his sister and strongly reflects one of the titles of MacFarlane's pieces, 'Melissa's Magical Melody'. Meeting the composer and listening to him play appears to have made a strong impact on David's work. During the period of data collection, David composed ten pieces which utilised a variety of harmonic accompaniment and melody.

Another exciting outcome is that David has been asked to play the piano at a school concert and he will be preparing a number of his compositions, grouped into a suite, which he has named 'Mr. Magic's Suite', for that occasion. David's case illustrates what is described by Hendrick (1992:51) as a democratic concept of education where children are given 'the power to choose, the power to try and the power to do'. His mother wrote in the questionnaire, 'He can compose, he just needed a bit of encouragement. He reckons he's so good at it (not boasting — just pleased with himself).' Encouragement to compose and assigning it as an activity gave David the confidence to pursue his interest. It was pleasing that many of the children in this group had tried the composition activity, as '... musical composition possesses such a mystique that many aspiring musicians feel very unwilling to have a go' (Hargreaves, 1986:146). This activity was viewed as a step towards building confidence to express themselves musically. It was found that developing creativity in the children was not just about getting them to create new ideas but also 'fostering the desire and develop the courage to do so' (Cropley, 1992:7).

Case study 5

One mother was always supportive and eager to assist in making piano lessons fun for her son, Andrew (9 yrs). Much of his interest and enjoyment in learning the piano can be attributed to her enthusiasm. Andrew chose to play 'Jelly Bean Jig' and his mother bought him some colourful jelly bean stickers to illustrate his music. This visually brought his music to life and created a happy atmosphere whenever he opened up the page. He and his mother made an art response based on Andrew's comment that the piece contained sections which sounded 'like a train whistle' (see Figure 19.3).

Andrew's mother was enthusiastic about the concert and asked, 'Is it OK if he dresses up a bit at the concert? I bought him a shiny vest with sequins on it — seeing it is a 'jazzy' concert, I thought he could wear something jazzy.' We decided that as Andrew also learns

Figure 19.3 Art response for 'Jelly Bean Jig'

the saxophone, he could play 'Jelly Bean Jig' on the piano, and then play it a second time on the saxophone. At the performance, he donned a sparkly silver hat, sunglasses and vest. To top it off, his saxophone rendition was enhanced by an improvised accompaniment by the composer, much to the delight of the audience.

Observational data indicated that the concert experience was a real highlight for Andrew. Present at the concert were his parents, maternal grandmother, paternal grandparents and two aunts. Andrew's maternal grandmother, gave him three 'wishing stones' which were shiny, smooth, blue-coloured glass stones to put in his pocket 'for luck. I told him that they would help him to play better'. Parents and other significant adults were an invaluable resource and provided immense support to creating a playful learning environment, once they realised that it was an acceptable part of the teaching approach.

Group III

The cultural background of the children in this group consisted of three European/Anglo-Australians and one Malaysian Chinese. The children in Group III were very enthusiastic about the 'Sound effects' story, art response and improvisation activities and all indicated creative activities as their first preference when asked, 'What shall we do first today?' In the 'Sound effects' story this group of children did not show any inhibitions and plunged into the activity with enthusiasm, relishing producing loud sounds. They did not hesitate to utilise the whole piano keyboard and used elbows and palms to create descending glissandos. The children in this group were more exuberant and outspoken in their behaviour at lessons than the Group I and some of the Group II children.

Figure 19.4 Art response for 'Sinister Blues'

Questionnaire data indicated that there had been very little parental involvement in both the creative activities and the practising of the piece. The improvisation was also tried with much interest even though the MacFarlane piece had not been completely mastered. Children in this group showed much less mastery of their chosen piece. Two of the children had learnt the right-hand part only, one child had not mastered either hand and one of the ten-year-old children discontinued lessons after completing the art response and 'Sound effects' story. Her progress in learning repertoire had been very slow. The mother said, 'she doesn't have any time to practise' as the child was involved in many extra-curricular activities. However, she was one of the first students to complete the art response for her piece titled 'Sinister Blues' in which she made a blue snake (see Figure 19.4).

Case study 6

Jeff (8 yrs) can be described as a 'difficult' student to teach in the sense that he does very little practice at home and does not concentrate or sit still for long. Fortunately, the duration of his lesson is flexible and usually lasts between 5 to 10 minutes. Other children of his age have twenty to thirty minute lessons. The length of his lessons could be described as child guided. Once I tried to extend his lesson time even though he was showing signs of restlessness and he placed his hands over his ears and shouted loudly as if to block out what I was saying. 'Sometimes I think he has ADD', his mother once said with resignation. 'His teacher at school says he has low concentration but his school work is quite good, actually...but he has trouble making friends'. His mother mentioned recently that she was considering sending him to boarding school when he reaches high school. 'He needs a bit of discipline,' she said. Jeff is the only child in this study who did not have a parent attend his lessons. His mother prefers to wait in the car 'and catch up with some sleep'. Recently, she asked if he could have more lessons during the week, 'at least he gets to practise when he comes to you'. When I mentioned to his mother that I was researching the younger students in the studio, she said, 'Yeah, sure, do what you like with him here, but don't ask me to do anything with him at home!'

Jeff's behaviour at lessons is unusual. He says what he thinks, does not follow instructions and seems to be undisciplined. Many adults would describe the behaviour as 'naughty'. However, with respect to the 'Sound effects' story, Jeff's response produced a most unexpected outcome. He was the only child in the study who came up with the idea to incorporate two sound effects simultaneously. 'This is the rain and this is the clown walking and jumping', he announced making staccato sounds with his right-hand whilst the left-hand fingers 'walked' up and down the keys. He did not hesitate to use his fists and palms to make loud noises and utilised the whole keyboard with enthusiasm. The other children had also not considered using the frame of the piano to produce sounds, but Jeff thought of tapping on the wood to make the 'pitter patter' of the rain. Jeff's 'Sound effects' story can be described as exuberant, enthusiastic and creative. 'I want to do it again', he demanded when it was over. At that lesson, Jeff performed the 'Sound effects' story three times. It was the longest lesson we have had and lasted 15 minutes. He refused to play anything else after that. 'Do you have another one? I want to do another one next time'. I suggested that he should try the story again at home and maybe think of some new things to do. The following week, when I asked him if he had tried the activity at home, he answered, '...but mum told me not to do it and get on with the practice'.

Schiller and Veale (1996:11) suggest ways to extend appreciation of children's paintings beyond a 'put it on the fridge door' phenomenon'. Unfortunately, the products of exploration and composition in piano music often do not even make it to the fridge door, so to speak. Exploration can be unintentionally discouraged by adults. Furthermore, learning can be dampened when the teacher's aims are not adequately conveyed to the parents or if parents fail to show interest in the child's activity. Jeff tried another story but this time, he seemed to get bored and was back to his old restless self. He did not show any interest in learning the MacFarlane piece or any of the other activities in the program and did not attend the concert.

Case study 7

Katy (7 yrs) can be described as being slower than other children in achieving piano technical skill and progressing through repertoire, however, she showed enthusiasm at the idea of writing a poem to accompany her piece. Her poem, with the same title as her piece, showed a depth of understanding for the feeling in the music which was particularly insightful:

Late Evening at South West Rocks

The sun started to climb down, as it slowly became sunset.
Everything looked orange when the sun saw it.
And the shadows of the people looked blue.
It was beautiful and relaxing.
Some people went outside to relax.
Others stayed inside just to see it set.
And some went to sleep with the sun on them.
Some people had dinner with the sun on the table.
It was really nice.
Kids played tip.

At the concert, MacFarlane said, 'I was on holidays up near Kempsey, and feeling very relaxed when I wrote the music. I just wanted it to describe that sense of peace and calmness'. Katy had captured that essence in her poem. For weeks after the concert, this piece remained Katy's favourite which she insisted on playing first at every lesson.

DISCUSSION

The results provide insights into two areas for discussion in relation to children's experiences at piano lessons 1) finding a balance in teaching approaches and 2) the influence of cultural background on parenting styles.

The results supported the literature which states that a developmentally appropriate approach to music programming enhances children's interest and enjoyment of piano lessons. This study found that children who would have been identified by adults in a traditional approach to piano lessons, as 'naughty', 'uninterested' or even 'unmusical' because they were talkative, interruptive, questioning convention or not willing to follow instruction, were the same children who were very creative, willing to try the activities without hesitation and participated with enthusiasm in a more open program. Research shows that teachers in a variety of cultures prefer children who are courteous, considerate, punctual, industrious, well-rounded, receptive and obedient. Characteristics such as 'willingness to take risks, or be innovative, bold, flexible, and original' (Cropley, 1992:19), many of the characteristics of creative behaviour, were not identified as a preference. An important outcome of encouraging creativity activities is that it enabled the more exuberant children, such as Jeff, to be valued and nurtured. When programs are developmentally appropriate, children such as these 'perceive themselves as successful learners for the first time' (Kostelnik et al., 1993:33).

Moreover, the results of this study appear to indicate that children's interest and attitudes towards piano lessons improve when the teaching approach views the child more holistically. This was made possible through rapport between teacher and parents which occurred as a result of parental involvement. Not only did piano lessons appear to be enhanced for children and parents but there was also evidence of support for the teacher's individualised aims. Similarly, an important finding in relation to the 'art responses' related to teacher reflection. The art responses opened up discussion about other aspects of the child's life as parents sensed that the teacher was interested in the whole child and his or her other abilities. The teacher could appreciate the child in different ways, not just through his/her ability to play the piano. Families were able to inform the teacher about the children's progress in other activities. For example, in this study, Dana proudly showed the teacher trophies from and photographs of her ice skating activities. The teacher's own perceptions of the child's capabilities were enhanced and the teacher's expectations of Dana's piano lessons were seen in a more realistic and balanced light. In the case of David, creative activities enabled him to 'discover a distinctive creative voice within'(Collins, 1990:113) which increased his motivation and interest to learn piano because confidence and belief in himself had been enhanced. As a result of engaging in creative activities, his ability to compose has been allowed to unfold. This would probably have remained unrecognised if the teaching approach had been weighted towards attaining piano performance skills alone. This case poignantly illustrates Gardner's (1990:23) comment that 'if children think they're smart that's a very important point in their favour. But not everybody can be smart when there is a single ruler, a single calibration system. We have to try to help all students discover areas where they have some strengths'. Whilst it is important to underscore the need to incorporate creative, child-guided approaches into teaching, care also needs to be taken not to tip the balance too much towards using these methods alone as this may also result in a lack of development in piano technique.

A further evaluation of the results shows that antecedents to the implementation of the creative activities program, that is, parents' cultural background and their approach to learning the piano, may be contributing factors influencing how the child progresses at the piano. While the outcome of these factors is not known, the results indicate a link between cultural factors influencing parenting style and children's behaviour. In this study, the possibility that the children may have a reciprocal influence on parental behaviour was not examined but this would make an interesting topic for further investigation.

The parents of children in Group I were interested in their children's lessons but placed emphasis on the acquisition of technique and mastery of repertoire over participation in creative activities. They also appeared to be more controlling and emphasised discipline in their approaches to practice and achievement in lessons. Parents of children in Group

II encouraged their children to participate in the creative activities as well as continuing to supervise and place importance in the learning of repertoire. They also enthusiastically contributed to making learning the piano into playful experiences. Many of the children in Group III showed much enthusiasm and displayed originality in their work, sometimes almost in spite of their parents. Parents of these children appeared to hold beliefs that it was better if the child worked independently without their assistance. It was observed that children whose family style could be described as permissive (Baumrind, 1993), also had lower achievement in mastery of repertoire. The more authoritarian (Baumrind, 1993) parents had children who excelled in mastery of piano repertoire and the more permissive parents had children who showed creativity and imagination. This finding may reflect the idea that children respond to playing the piano in ways that are consistent with their parent's values and that the outcomes of a perceived parenting style may vary under different cultural conditions (Mekertichian & Bowes, 1996). There are similarities between these findings and those reported in studies which have found positive associations between Chinese 'authoritarian' parenting style and high academic achievement (Chao, 1994:1111). Figure 19.5 illustrates the relationship between cultural background of the parents, parenting style and the children's outcomes at piano lessons in this study.

Of special concern, from a constructivist viewpoint, are the children in Group I whose parents' approach to learning stressed discipline, skill acquisition, competition and did not perceive the creative activities as an important priority. It is possible that these children would be less likely to develop music creativity in the early years of piano lessons. This assumption is supported by Sloboda (1990:171), who stresses that 'anything which disrupts the ability of children to make emotional responses to music is likely to endanger the growth of skill in a way that no amount of subsequent practice can overcome'.

Figure 19.5 Cultural background, parenting approaches and children's outcomes

Cultural background	Hong Kong Chinese	Hong Kong Chinese, Other Asians European-Australians	Other Asians European-Australians
Parenting approaches	didactic, adult guided, emphasised skills	authoriative, placed importance in both process and product, balanced approach	more permissive child-guided emphasised enjoyment
Children's outcomes	Group I (1) less imagination and less creativity than in Groups II & III	Group II (1) more imagination and creativity takes place as in Group III	Group III (1) more imagination and creativity takes as in Group II.
place	(2) mastery of skills and repertoire takes place quickly as in Group II	(2) mastery of skills and repertoire takes place quickly as in Group I	(2) less mastery of skills and repertoire than in Groups I & II

What emerges from the study are issues related to differences in learning style between children from Asian and Western cultures. In families where parents came from Kong Kong more emphasis tended to be placed on achievement and obedience and the children appeared to be more creatively inhibited. This may be attributable to the high importance placed on academic achievement in traditional Chinese culture (Ho, 1986). These findings are similar to those reported by Huntsinger et al. (1997:371) who found that Chinese parents emphasised academic activities using more formal, instructional approaches. The finding that Hong Kong families did not place creative activities as a priority may be related to Chinese values of family interdependence over the fostering of individuality (Lin & Fu, 1990). Children were also notably more obedient and reprimanded at lessons if they showed lack of respect or did not pay attention. The Chinese word for teacher is 'one who is born before you' and implies respect and obedience. These concepts of respect and importance of familial harmony are grounded in Confucian principles of filial piety where all elders are respected and obeyed unquestioningly (Kelley & Tseng, 1992). These findings also support the notion that parental beliefs about formal instruction and academic achievement affects their child's divergent thinking abilities (Dunn & Kontos, 1997) and that the home environments created by authoritarian mothers are less likely to nurture creativity (Tennent & Berthelsen, 1997).

The benefits of parental presence were at the highest level with parents of Group II children where communication occurred as a two-way process. Not only was the teacher able to report progress to the parent, but the parents reported to the teacher incidents that affected the daily life of the child. As the teacher saw parents on a regular basis, the quality of teaching appeared to be enhanced to become more individualised to suit the changing interests of the child. Other researchers have identified that communication is an important component of parental involvement (Berger, 1996) and is described as a 'reciprocal relationship' (Bredekamp & Copple, 1997:22) between families and teacher.

The current study found that parents' assistance with creative activities, which do not require previous musical knowledge, enhanced the self-efficacy with regards to parental involvement in piano lessons. These findings provide support for the results obtained by Davidson et al. (1996) that successful learners have high levels of parental support. For example, Kevin's mother purchased six sets of piano albums with accompanying compact discs for him to listen to and learn. (He was particularly interested in the Burgmuller 'Studies' which he had started to practise himself and had learnt two pieces by his next lesson.) Consequently, parental involvement in lessons enriched Kevin's interest by providing him with new stimuli and new repertoire to discover and explore independently of his teacher.

Andrew's case also shows that the involvement of the mother is an important factor in the enjoyment of lessons and contributes to a high level of mastery and creativity. Evidence of the development of creativity in Andrew and other children in Group II can be linked to the playfulness of their mothers. Interestingly, the findings indicate that maternal employment and educational level did not affect the mothers' ability to participate enthusiastically in their child's piano lessons. Maternal involvement and self-efficacy was important however, and was seen to be related to the quantity and quality of interaction between the mother and the teacher. It is also possible that these findings could be culturally based as many of the Anglo-Australian mothers became involved in creative activities whilst, as previously discussed, many of the mothers from an Asian background were more reserved and less inclined to be playful. It was also observed that the art responses which were divergent to teacher suggestion were mainly from children in Groups II and III who had European/Anglo-Australian mothers. This is consistent with findings that Anglo-Australian mothers valued 'creative [rather] than conforming personality characteristics' in their children (Tennent & Berthelsen, 1997:101).

Self-efficacy of parents could also be an important determining factor as to the extent of the children's involvement. In this study, parental self-efficacy may have been raised as a result of the music learning being placed into interesting, familiar contexts for the parent as well as the child. Previously, some parents had not felt comfortable helping their child at home with the technical aspects of the music as they did not have any formal musical training themselves. A study by Swick (1987b), which showed that parental efficacy increases with parental involvement, offers support for this view. Parents who had previously said that they felt they could not help their child showed increased participation with home practice through the creative activities. Assistance with non-musical aspects of lessons developed their confidence to participate with the musical aspects of lessons as well.

Many of the Group I and III children were initially interested in the activities, but without the parent's enthusiasm and encouragement their participation in the activities seemed limited. Of greatest concern are the children in Group III , whose parents were uninvolved and who did not acquire adequate skill in piano performance, as these children would be the most likely to lose interest in piano lessons and drop-out. Children in this group would be unlikely to respond well to piano programs which prioritise skill acquisition and do not incorporate creative activities. Parents of children in Group III had a more carefree attitude towards lessons and practice which may have resulted in the slower mastery of repertoire. ('I don't really want to force her to practise', said Anna's mother, 'Just as long as she enjoys lessons, that's the main thing.') These parents appreciated the creative activities and one parent stated, 'piano has become fun'. However, unlike the Group II parents, they had not reached a level of understanding and involvement which allowed them to value and use playful methods to encourage enjoyable practices.

The overall results expose the myth that a high level of performance achievement is the essential factor in musical growth. The findings appear to indicate that: 'enjoyment is every bit as important as labour. Indeed, the latter without the former might produce some kind of technician, but is likely to kill the very thing that often makes musicians so highly valued' (Sloboda, 1990:176). Thus, the results show that a balance needs to be struck between performance achievement and enjoyment. The children in Group II and their parents appear to have found that balance as indicated by positive outcomes in both mastery of piano performance skills and evidence of children's enjoyment, creativity and imagination.

CONCLUSIONS

Significance of research

This research is particularly important as it connects key issues in the distinct areas of piano pedagogy and early childhood education which have not been linked either theoretically or empirically thus far. From the viewpoint of piano pedagogy, this research documents a program to teach piano to young children based on theoretical knowledge as well as practical implementation.

Limitations

The main weakness of implementation was that the activities were somewhat constrained due to time limits on research. Insufficient time had been allocated, particularly for the 'Sound effects' story and improvisation activities.

Interestingly, in this research, many of the methodological strengths of action research also proved to be its weaknesses, in particular to issues of generalisability in its specificity of situation and unrepresentative, restrictive sampling. The fact that the researcher was also the teacher presents tendency for subjectivity in analysis, however as Carr and Kemmis (1986:192) argue, the study of praxis 'must embody values and interests' which is an important part of the understanding of the practice that is being critically examined.

The questionnaire was completed during the lesson which meant that there was some distraction as parents sometimes stopped to observe the ongoing lesson. It is difficult to assess whether this affected the quality of the answers. Replication of this research may consider providing parents with a separate area where they can think without disruption.

The number of interview questions and responses were restricted as they were asked during lesson times. More issues may have emerged had there been additional time to probe and develop the comments.

There also existed a conflict in role of researcher and teacher in allocating time for exploring and gaining more data through interviews. The teacher found it difficult to take detailed notes and quotes in the journal whilst trying to teach. The research lacked a collaborative aspect, which is a recommended component of action research. It would have been difficult to get other piano teachers or colleagues to attend many lessons over the lengthy period of implementation. The teacher and researcher felt that it would not be appropriate to involve parents in data collection in this particular study as they were already asked to assist with the creative activities at home.

Implications

The pattern of findings from this study shows that teaching young children the piano can be effectively addressed within the framework of early childhood constructivist models of development. This study should be viewed as a first step towards finding the balance which reconciles a developmentally appropriate approach to young children's piano lessons with the systematic acquisition of piano techniques.

The research results have practical implications for piano and other instrumental teachers; parents of young children learning piano; pedagogy; program implementation; and future research directions. It is highly relevant to instrumental music pedagogy as it provides the basis for development of a more comprehensive curriculum, as well as provides future reference for much needed changes in assessment planning (Ross, 1986). Although the cases in this research refer to piano students, findings can be generalised to instrumental pedagogy in general.

The need exists for teachers to inform parents that piano lessons are a long-term commitment (Sosniak, 1990), and assessing the progress of a child through technical ability alone may discourage an attitude of persistence. However, expecting a young child to understand the idea of 'long term' is not realistic. Therefore, the activity needs to be interesting here and now. The findings recommend that a child-oriented teaching approach promotes a sense of enjoyment and interest for the child, parent and teacher. Moreover, this approach does not compromise the acquisition of skill and aids the learning and understanding of repertoire.

The problem of maintaining quality home practice can be enhanced by actively encouraging parental presence at lessons, which mean that parents gain a clearer understanding of teacher expectations. Additionally, it is important for parents to consider attending lessons and developing a rapport with the teacher so that learning objectives can be supported and reinforced at home. Teachers may need to reorganise their studios so that parental involvement can occur. The majority of parents appear interested and willing to participate in their child's music lessons, however, teachers need to let them know how they can get involved. In Australian studios, piano repertoire has been predominantly selected from 17th to 20th century European classical traditions and selected on the basis of aesthetic appreciation and technical development. However, the functions of music are more widespread than learning to play an instrument and include ritual, work, social, ceremonial, entertainment as well as the aesthetic. Piano teachers perhaps need to bear in mind that interest and enjoyment occur when the repertoire is familiar to the child. The pieces which children often want to learn are those which they have heard before in 'ads' or folk tunes, nursery rhymes, children's songs and popular songs. Piano pedagogy needs to consider incorporating more repertoire which is culturally meaningful to child. This would include jazz and popular styles used in films and television. Familiarity is an important component for motivation to learn a piece. Therefore, listening to repertoire is important as it familiarises repertoire which would be otherwise unknown.

Concert attendance also sparks enthusiasm to learn a new piece after they have heard another child playing it. Teachers need to be open to enriching opportunities to help students enjoy the process of learning the piano by organising studio concerts and group 'excursions' to listen to professional musicians.

Piano teachers are in a unique situation where individualisation of lessons is highly achievable as most lessons occur on a one-to-one basis. Opportunity for parents to be present at lessons is equally achievable. Professional music education organisations may help by engendering a culture which values parental involvement in music lessons, as this will help overcome resistance from teachers who may see this as a major change to their teaching practices. Professional organisations can take on the important role of developing teacher training programs, as in Suzuki methodology, which encourages the practice of involving parents.

Creative activities can allow for less competitive and stressful assessment in learning the piano with the development of individual process portfolios (Gronlund, 1998). Evaluation could be taken in the form of analysis of musical content of compositions and the understanding of style and feeling in music through art and literary responses.

Longitudinal case studies into children's piano lessons would be highly informative as they would document the journey of children and their families through the process of music lessons. Past research covering a longer time-span has been essentially retrospective research. A longitudinal action research study would adapt very well to the music teacher/researcher who is involved with the students and families over a long period, unlike the classroom school teacher whose personal teaching relationship is usually of a shorter duration. The unique situation of the instrumental music teacher has great potential to reach depths of understanding unprecedented in longitudinal educational research.

An American study has shown that low-income and parents from some minority groups view skill-based approaches as appropriate contexts for learning (Holloway et al., 1995). The present study shows that didactic learning approaches continue to be favoured amongst high-income families from Hong Kong. Therefore, future research needs to explore parental attitudes towards piano lessons and ascertain if there are any special strategies that need to be employed when working within particular socioeconomic and cultural groups.

In this study, developmentally appropriate approaches appear to have produced positive outcomes for the majority of the children, which was expected. That is, the results indicated a high success rate with Group III children whose cultural background was essentially white, middle class. It also appeared to be successful with Group II children whose background was Kong Kong Chinese, other Asians and Australians. However, the outcome with regards to Group I children, who had parents from Hong Kong, and a lower response to the creative activities, was unanticipated. This outcome brings forth three important issues or questions which need further investigation. Firstly, should this group, who showed achievement in performance skills, be seen to be of greater concern because they did not appear to demonstrate a depth of feeling to the music and showed less evidence of imagination and creativity? Or conversely, do the outcomes relate to the problem of taking an European/American constructivist approach and trying to make it fit into a different culture that has fundamentally different values? This leads to a third issue regarding the need for the meaning of 'creativity' to be examined in different cultural contexts.

Long-term methods to enhance piano lessons can be encouraged through developing programs which take into account recent knowledge of child development, reciprocal parental and community support and practices which are considered to be appropriate, child-guided and enjoyable. At the same time, the acquisition of skill is an intrinsic aspect of learning to master piano playing and the adult's role is to facilitate, provide an environment of exploration and playfulness, as well as implementing the structures which a child requires for learning to take place.

This study has been about finding that balance. Finding the balance was also about reducing the distance between polarised views and approaches to piano teaching, and bringing together perceived dichotomies. The experience of being a teacher and researcher has also been about finding the balance. Polarisation between theoretical knowledge and implementation of theory into practice has been reduced by this study. The experience of action research has been both enlightening and empowering as it contributed towards the:

> Improvement of actual educational practices, the improvement of the understandings of those involved in the educational process and the improvement of the situations in which those practices are carried out (Carr & Kemmis, 1986:174).

REFERENCES

Ap, E.A.M. (1997) Let's 'play' piano: Enhancing piano lessons and home practice through play and an integrated arts approach. Master of Early Childhood research paper, Macquarie University.

Baumrind, D. (1993) The average expectable environment is not good enough: A response to Scarr. *Child Development*, **64**, 1299–1317.

Berger, E.H. (1995) Reaching for the stars: Families and schools working together. *Early Childhood Educational Journal* **23** (2), 119–123.

Berger, E.H. (1996) Communication: the key to parent involvement. *Early Childhood Educational Journal* **23**, (3), 179–189.

Berk, L.E. (1994) Vygotsky's theory: The importance of make believe play. *Young Children*, 50 (1), 30–39.

Bredekamp, S. (1991) Redeveloping early childhood education: A response to Kessler. *Early Childhood Research Quarterly*, **6**, 199–209.

Bredekamp, S. (1997) Guidelines for developmentally appropriate practices. [WWW document}. URL http://www.naeyc.org/eyly/eyly9805.htm

Bredekamp, S. & Copple, C. (Eds.) (1997) *Developmentally appropriate practice in early childhood programs*. Washington DC: National Association for the Education of Young Children (NAEYC)

Bredekamp, S. & Rosegrant, T. (Eds.) (1992) *Reaching potentials: Appropriate curriculum and assessment for young children* (Vol.1) Washington DC: National Association for the Education of Young Children (NAEYC)

Bronfenbrenner, U. (1979) *The Ecology of Human Development*. Cambridge, MA: Harvard University Press.

Burts, D.C., Hart, C.H., Charlesworth, R., DeWolf, D.M., Ray, J. Manuel, K. & Fleege, P.O. (1993) Developmental appropriateness of kindergarten programs and academic outcomes in first grade. *Journal of Research in Childhood Education*, **8**, 23–31.

Carr,W. & Kemmis, S. (1986) *Becoming Critical: Knowing Through Action Research*.Burwood, Victoria: Deakin University Press.

Chao, R. (1994) Beyond parental control and authoritarian parenting style: Understanding Chinese parenting through the cultural notion of training. *Child Development*, **65**, 1111–1119.

Collins, C. (1990) *Confronting the Future: Creativity and the Human Spirit*. New York: Teachers College Press.

Comte, M. (1993) Multi-arts: Issues and implications for schools and teacher education. In *Arts Education: Beliefs, Practices and Possibilities*, edited by E.P.Errington, pp.157–163. Geelong, Victoria: Deakin University Press.

Cordova, D.I. & Lepper, M.R. (1996) Intrinsic motivation and the process of learning: Beneficial effects of contextualization, personalization, and choice. *Journal of Educational Psychology*, **88**(4), 715–730.

Cropley, A.J. (1992) *More Ways Than One: Fostering Creativity*. Norwood, N.J.: Ablex.

Davidson, J.W., Howe, M.J.A., Moore, D.G. & Sloboda, J.A.(1996) The role of parental influences in the development of musical performances. *British Journal of Developmental Psychology*, **14**, 399–412.

Draper, T.W.,& Gayle, C. (1987) An analysis of historical reasons for teaching music to young children: Is it the same old song? In *Music and Child Development*, edited by J.C. Peery, I.W. Peery and T.W. Draper, pp. 194–205. NY: Springer Verlag.

Dunn, L. & Kontos, S. (1997) What have we learned about developmentally appropriate practice? *Young Children*, **52**(5), 4–13.

Elkind, D. (1981) *The hurried child: Growing up too fast too soon*. Reading, MA: Addison-Wesley.

Ericsson, A., Tesch-Romer, C. & Krampe, R. (1990) The role of practice and motivation in the acquisition of expert-level performance in real life. In *Encouraging the Development of Exceptional Skills and Talents*, edited by M.J.A. Howe, pp.109–130. Leicester, UK: The British Psychological Society.

Fowell, N. & Lawton, J. (1992) An alternative view of developmentally appropriate practice in early childhood education. *Early Childhood Research Quarterly*, **7**, 53–73.

Gardner, H. (1990) Multiple intelligences: implications for art and creativity. In *Artistic Intelligences: Implications for Education*, edited by W.J. Moody, pp.11–27. New York: Teachers College Press.

Gardner, H. (1995) Reflections on multiple intelligences: Myths and messages. *Phi Delta Kappan*, **77**(3), 200–209.

Ginsburg, G.S. & Bronstein, P. (1993) Family factors related to children's intrinsic/extrinsic motivational orientation and academic performance. *Child Development*, **64**, 1461–1474.

Gordon, E. (1997) Preparing young children to improvise at a later time. *Early Childhood Connections*, **3**(4), 6–12.

Graham, D. (1998) Teaching for creativity in musical performance. *Music Educators Journal*, **84** (5), 24–28.

Gronlund, G. (1998) Portfolios as an assessment tool: Is collection of work enough? *Young Children*, **53**(3), 4–10.

Hargreaves, D.J. (1986) *The Developmental Psychology of Music*. Cambridge: Cambridge University Press.

Hatch, J.A. & Freeman, E.B. (1988) Who's pushing whom? Stress and kindergarten. *Phi Delta Kappan*, **70**, 145–147.

Hendrick, J. (1992) Where does it all begin? Teaching the principles of democracy in the early years. *Young Children*, **47**, 51–53.

Ho, D.Y.F. (1986) Chinese pattern of socialization: A critical review. In *The Psychology of the Chinese People*, edited by M.H. Bond, pp.1–37. New York: Oxford University Press.

Hoffman. B.C. (1996) The thrill of drill. *Teaching Music*, **4**, 33–34.

Hollingshead, A.B. (1991) Two Factor Index of Social Position. In *Handbook of Research Design and Social Measurement* (5th edn), edited by D.C. Miller, pp.351–359. Newbury Park, CA: Sage.

Holloway, S.D., Rambaud, M.F., Fuller, B. & Eggers-Pierola, C. (1995) What is 'appropriate practice' at home and in child care? Low income mothers' views on preparing their children for school. *Early Childhood Research Quarterly*, **10**, 451–73.

Horn, K. (1993) Tradition, habit and being alive. In *Arts Education: Beliefs, Practices and Possibilities*, edited by E.P. Errington, pp. 69–75. Geelong, Victoria: Deakin University Press.

Huntsinger, C.S., Jose, P.E., Liaw, F.R. & Ching, W.D. (1997) Cultural differences in early mathematics learning: A comparison of Euro-American, Chinese American, and Taiwan-Chinese families. *International Journal of Behavioural Development*, **21**(2), 371–388.

Jalongo, M.R. (1995) Awaken to the artistry within young children. ERIC Document reproduction service No.EJ 512454, Abstract.

Kamii, C. (1985) Leading primary education toward excellence: Beyond worksheets and drill. *Young Children*, **40**, 3–9.

Katz, L. (1988) Engaging children's minds: The implications of research for early childhood education. In *A Resource Guide to Public School Early Childhood Programs*, edited by C. Warger, pp.32–52. Alexandria, VA: Association for Supervision and Curriculum Development.

Kelley, M.L. & Tseng, H.M. (1992) Cultural differences in child rearing: A comparison of immigrant Chinese and Caucasian American mothers. *Journal of Cross-Cultural Psychology*, **23**(4), 444–455.

Kessler, S.A. (1991) Early childhood education as development: Critique of the metaphor. *Early Education and Development*, **2**, 137–152.

Kostelnik, M.J. (1992) Myths associated with developmentally appropriate practice programs. *Young Children*, **47**(4), 17–23.

Kostelnik, M., Soderman, A. & Whiren, A. (1993) *Developmentally Appropriate Programs in Early Childhood Education*, pp. 31–68. New York: Merrill.

Kotloff, L.J. (1993) Fostering cooperative group spirit and individuality: Examples from a Japanese preschool. *Young Children*, **43**(3), 17–23.

LeBlanc, A. & Cote, R.(1983) Effects of tempo and performing medium on children's music preference. *Journal of Research in Music Education*, **31**, 57–66.

Levi, R. (1991) Investigating the creativity process: The role of regular musical composition experiences for the elementary child. *The Journal of Creative Behaviour*, **25**(2), 123– 136.

Lin, C.C. & Fu, V.R. (1990) A comparison of child-rearing practices among Chinese, immigrant Chinese, and Caucasian-American parents. *Child Development*, **61**, 429–433.

Lubeck, S. (1994) The politics of developmentally appropriate practice: exploring issues of culture, class and curriculum. In *Diversity and developmentally appropriate practices: Challenges for early childhood education,* edited by B. Mallory and R. New. New York: Teachers College Press.

Mapp, K. (1997) Making the connection between families and schools. *Harvard Educational Letter,* **13**(5), 1–17.

McLendon, G.H. (1982) When the class sang, I played the drum. *Music Educators Journal,* **68**(6), 36–37.

McMillan, R.(1993) A song of our own: Creative processes in the classroom. In *Arts Education: Beliefs, Practices and Possibilities,* edited by E.P. Errington, pp.115–12. Geelong, Victoria: Deakin University Press.

Mekertichian, L.K. & Bowes, J.M. (1996) Does parenting matter? The challenge of the behavioural geneticists. *Journal of Family Studies,* **2**(2), 131–145.

Murphy, M. & Brown, T. (1986) A comparison of preferences for instructional objectives between teachers and students. *Journal of Research in Music Education,* **34**, 134–139.

New South Wales Board of Studies (1998) *K-6 Draft Creative Arts Syllabus.* Sydney: NSW Board of Studies.

Peery, C. & Peery, I.W. (1987) The role of music in child development. In *Music and Child Development,* edited by J.C. Peery, I.W. Peery & T.W. Draper, pp.3–31. New York: Springer Verlag.

Piaget, J. (1962) *Play, Dreams, and Imitation in Childhood.* London: Routledge.

Rauscher, F.H., Shaw, G., Levine, L.J., Ky, K.N. & Wright, E.L. (1994) Early music training and spatial task performance- a causal relationship. Paper presented at the American Psychological Association, 102nd Annual Convention, Los Angeles, CA. [WWW document}. URL http://gopher.tmn.com:70/0/Artswire/AMC/MUSBRAIN/rasucher.81594

Rauscher, F.H., Shaw, G.L., Levine, L.J., Wright, E., Dennis, W., Newcomb, R. (1997) Music training causes long-term enhancement of preschool children's spatial- temporal reasoning. *Neurological Research,* **19**, 2–8.

Ross, M. (ed.) (1986) *Assessment in Arts Education.* Oxford: Pergamon.

Saltz, E. & Johnson, J. (1974) Training for thematic-fantasy play in culturally disadvantaged children: Preliminary results. *Journal of Educational Psychology,* **66**, 623–630.

Schiller, W. & Veale, A. (1996) The arts: The real business of education. In *Issues in Expressive Arts: Curriculum for Early Childhood,* edited by W. Schilller, pp.14. Amsterdam: Gordon and Breach Publishers.

Sigel, I. (1987) Does hothousing rob children of their childhood? *Early Childhood Research Quarterly,* **2**, 211–225.

Sloboda, J.A.(1990) Musical excellence- how does it develop? In *Encouraging the Development of Exceptional Skills and Talents,* edited by M.J.A. Howe, pp.165–178. Leicester, UK: The British Psychological Society.

Sloboda, J.A. & Davidson, J. (1996) The young performing musician. In *Musical Beginnings: Origins and Development of Musical Competence,* edited by I. Deliege & J. Sloboda. Oxford: Oxford University Press.

Smith, D. (1995) How play influences children's development at home and school. *The Journal of Physical Education, Recreation & Dance,* **66**(8), 19–23.

Sosniak, L.A. (1990) The tortoise, the hare, and the development of talent. In *Encouraging the development of exceptional skills and talents* edited by M.J.A. Howe, pp.149–164 Leicester, UK: The British Psychological Society.

Stake, R. (1994) Case studies. In *Handbook of Qualitative Research,* edited by N.K. Denzin and Y.S. Lincoln, pp.236–247. Thousand Oaks, CA: Sage.

Stewart, R. (1993) Learning processes in the visual arts: a contemporary neonarrative. In *Arts education: Beliefs, practices and possibilities,* edited by E.P.Errington, pp.165–174. Geelong, Victoria: Deakin University Press.

Stipek, D. (1993) *Motivation to learn: From theory to practice* (2nd ed.) Needhan Heights, MA: Allyn & Bacon.

Stipek, D., Feiler, R., Daniels, D. & Milburn, S. (1995) Effects of different instructional approaches on young children's achievement and motivation. *Child Development*, 66, 209–223.

Suthers, L. (1996) Introducing children to live orchestral performance. In *Issues in expressive arts: Curriculum for early childhood*, edited by W. Schiller, pp. 55–64. Amsterdam: Gordon andeach Publishers.

Suzuki, S. (1986) *Talent Education for Young Children* (Trans. K. Selden). New Albany, IN: World-Wide Press.

Swick, K.J. (1987b) Teacher reports on parental efficacy/involvement relationships. *Instructional Psychology*, **14**, 125–132.

Sylva, K. (1984) A hard-headed look at the fruits of play. *Early Child Development and Care*, 15, 171–184.

Tennent, L. & Berthelsen, D. (1997) Creativity: What does it mean in the family context? *Journal of Australian Research in Early Childhood Education*, 91–104.

Vygotsky, L.S. (1976) Play and its role in the mental development of the child. In *Play: Its Role in Development and Evolution*, edited by J.S. Bruner, A. Jolly and K. Sylva, pp.537–544. New York: Basic Books.

Walsh, D.J. (1991) Extending the discourse on developmental appropriateness: A developmental perspective. *Early Education and Development*, **2**, 109–119.

Warby, S. (1997) *With Love in my Heart and a Twinkle in my Ear: A Parents Guide to Suzuki Education*. Sydney, STEAA (NSW) Inc.

Wilson, F. R.,& Roehmann, F.L. (1987) Music and child development. Proceedings of the 1987 Biology of Music Making Denver Conference.

Wright, S. (ed.) (1991) *The Arts in Early Childhood*. Sydney: Prentice Hall.

INDEX

Aboriginal art, 8-14
    drawings, 166,167
action research, 219
adult interaction, 14, 28-29, 48-49, 97-101, 103
adult's thinking, 26, 39, 44-45, 59
aesthetic
    appreciation, 2, 30, 32, 39-41, 49, 51, 178
    experiences, 178
    literacy, 32
aggression, 97, 102
art and science, 39-41, 107
art form, 4, 50, 93
artists, 5, 16, 28-29, 30-31, 32, 33
arts
    adventures, 11
    and caregivers routines, 98, 99, 101-105
    and culture, 2, 5, 8, 32, 108
    and curriculum, 3, 27, 16-17, 25-26, 93-95
    and life, 2, 5, 7, 28-29, 32, 108
    assessment, 42, 45, 102-104
    defined, 2
    engagement, 2, 28-32, 94, 97-98, 103, 108
    environments, 28, 30, 32, 97-99
    experiences, 3, 5, 7, 25, 94, 95, 97-100, 102-
        104
    implications, 25-27, 104-106
Asia-Pacific contexts, 3, 4, 50
assessment, 2, 3, 94-95
ateliers, 34
audience, 36

baby program, 22
balance,1,2, 41, 51
basic technology, 5
block building, 98, l03
Bodenwieser, Gertrude, 38
boys and dance, 62
brain research, 132
Brown, Roger, 33
building an arts environment, 5

child development theory, 207
childhood experiences, 5, 105
child-initiated
    choice 3
    curriculum, 5, 204-211
    dance, 24
children as audience, 92, 93
children's
    conversations, 4, 11, 12, 97, 109
    literature,
    theatre, 69
    thinking, 26, 28-32, 48-49, 51, 59, 103
Choolburra, Sean, 9, 10, 15, 16
clay, 13, 14, 49, 56
    drawing, 13, 14, 57
co-construction, 4, 16
cognition,1, 2
cognitive narrative, 158-159
collaboration, 180
collaborative drawing, 56-58, 160
collage, 30, 33, 101
communication, 2, 3 38, 49, 95
    technologies, 5, 108
community, 5
computers, 107, 108
confidence, 105
constructivist approaches, 42, 132, 233
contexts, 95, 104
co-player, 35-36
creative
    dance, 38, 39
    drama, 118
    impulse, 2
    movement, 200
    process, 69, 77
creativity, 2 ,3, 40, 108, 156
cultural
    context, 3, 48
    educators, 10
    perceptions, 5

culture, 2, 8
curriculum, 3, 4, 5
  transforming 3, 45
cyberspace, 108

dance 9, 191-202
  and gender, 61
  approaches, 5, 40
  as doing, 43, 45
  composition, 42, 199
  creative, 38, 192
  experiences, 5, 38
  forms, 39
  ideas, 5, 40,41, 64
  improvisation, 63
  interpretive, 40, 44-45
  process, 38, 39, 41-42, 45-46
  vocabulary, 42
decision making, 5, 48
Delsarte, Francois, 39-40
demystifying arts, 4, 5, 43
developmentally appropriate practice, 214
Dewey, John, 132
didactic approach, 214, 233
display of children's work, 188
distance teacher education, 194
documentation, 35, 49-52, 56, 180-181, 188
documenting projects, 3, 59
drama, 79
  as social process, 125
  performances, 5, 63
dramatic signifiers, 70
drawing, 4, 5, 13, 28, 30-32 , 51, 52, 57-58
drugs, 84
dynamics, 2, 95, 107

environments for children, 177, 189
  arts, evaluating, 5, 31-32, 45-46
Exiner, Johanna, 38, 40, 41, 42-46, 66
expectations, 5
expression, 38, 40, 42, 45

flexibility, 104
Froebel, Friedrich, 33-34
frontview perspective, 5
fun, 92, 101

galleries, 5, 15-17
gallery programs, 10, 17
Gardner, Howard, 1, 39, 41, 43, 131, 191, 216
gender in arts, 5, 103

gender issues, 4, 61, 64, 105
Gilliam, Sam, 32
graphic works, 4, 49-50, 58, 59
graphics as communication , 4, 48-49, 58

H'Doubler, Margaret, 40, 44
harmonics
harmonious development, 3
Hayes, Nancy, 32
Heysen,
    Hans, 30
    Nora, 30-31
Hinkley, Coralie, 38-40, 42-46
humanities, 2

images, 31, 77, 107
imagination, 5, 44, 92, 104-105, 107-108
imaginative
    experiences, 126
    thought, 126
imaging, 5, 40, 107, 126
improvisation, 41-43, 118
indigenous art and culture, 3, 5, 7-14
inexpensive materials, 194
informances, 5, 151
inspirational environments, 177
integrated
    arts, 5, 19-27, 43, 65, 141, 152
    lessons, 135-157
interactive thinking, 123

kinaesthetic, 41, 49
Kuschner, Robert, 32

Laban, Rudolph, 38, 39, 41-42, 198
language, 45, 57, 88, 108, 120
    through rhythm, 144
learning
    styles, 234
    through movement, 40, 43, 193
literacy skills, 89
location, 104

making meaning, 4, 5, 28, 30, 40-42,49, 51-53, 59
Malaguzzi, Loris, 34, 154, 184, 191, 208
males in dance, 61
map making
mark making, 52-53, 59
media, 48, 49, 50, 58, 107-108
mind and body, 1, 31, 39, 41, 42, 44
    connection, 191

Morgan, Sally, 28, 33
motor development, 191
movement
    composition, 194
    culture, 192, 202
    patterns, 39, 42, 192
    quality, 41, 44, 52
    sequences, 150, 197,
multimedia
    artists, 112
    production, 111
    technologies, 108
multiple intelligences,1, 2, 131, 133
museum visits, 14–17
museums, 8, 14, 32
music, 19-27, 212–241

narrative, 49, 56, 57
naturalistic investigations, 4
nature of arts, 3
Noonuccal, Oodgeroo, 2, 120
nursery rhymes, 5, 82–91

observation, 49, 55
order, 52, 56, 59
outdoor environment, 185

Palcroze, Emilie, 44
parent's cultural background, 231
parental involvement, 28–29, 30, 33, 35, 217, 234
parenting approaches, 233
peer
    collaboration, 187
    interaction
    teaching, 161
performance, 5, 16, 41, 213
    in dance, 135–151, 199
    space, 185
performing arts programs, 19–24, 26, 93
personal involvement, 2, 5, 14–16, 19, 28–30, 45–46
perspective, 164–166
piano lessons, 5, 212–238
pictorial realism, 50–51
plan-view perspective, 5, 13, 163
Plato,1, 191
play, 1, 29, 33, 34, 39, 96–102, 107
poetry, 2, 89, 90, 108, 118, 124, 131, 135, 145, 151, 155, 178
popular culture, 5, 49
post modern 107, 127

preschool programs, 24, 34, 103, 104
principles of motion, 38–40, 46, 92
problem solving, 5, ,38, 44–45, 98, 105, 108, 118, 133, 179, 200
process drama, 5, 118–128
project reference group, 197
puppet
    games, 97, 101, 106
    performance, 92–93, 100–101
    stages, 100-101
    walk, 102
puppetry, 92–106
    curriculum project, 93–97, 102–103,
    utilization, 93, 97–99, 100–101

rap, 20, 23, 24, 25
reconciliation, 7, 17
reflective practitioner, 184
reflective process, 127
Reggio Emilia, 16, 34, 36, 49, 50, 154, 209
representational skills, 171, 175
research methodology, 71, 93–95, 220
rhymes, 20, 22, 24, 82-91
rhythm, 40, 131
rock art, 2
role
    of adult in integrated arts, 25–27, 43–44
    of researcher, 236
    of the adult in visual arts, 16–17, 35
    play, 118

Savage, Augusta Christine, 29
scaffolding, 35, 202, 127, 169, 217
scope and sequence plans, 199
scribbles, 51–52
sculpture, 29
selection, 105
self-instructional learning guides, 195
sexism in dance, 64
shared meanings, 158
signifiers, 68
social contexts, 49
socio-dramatic play, 120
songs, 20, 22, 24
spoken communication, 156
stereotypes, 8
stimulus for dance, 194
structured interviews, 197
teacher
    collaboration, 5
    diary entries, 21, 24

interaction 'in role', 5
intervention, 156, 159–161, 199
modelling, 170, 175
teachers
and artists, 5, 29
and arts, 3, 4, 16, 31,
as researchers, 3, 5, 34, 48, 59
teacher's role
in dance, 45–46
in drama, 78-80, 119, 121
in galleries, 14-17
in integrated arts, 25-27
in visual arts, 16, 17, 159–161
teaching dance, 5, 38, 192, 198
as a process, 198
teaching kits, 15
technology
and arts, 5
and culture, 5
education, 24, 164, 169
television, 93
puppetry, 93
theatre for children, 69
theatrical elements, 68, 77, 79

theoretical perspectives, 35, 40
thinking through
drama, 5
the arts, 1, 36, 38–40, 45–46
time organisation, 187
toddler programs, 20, 22, 24, 48, 52, 102
tradition, 2, 3, 9,10, 28-30

videotape in dance education, 194
videotaping dance lessons, 195
visible thinking
visual
arts, 156
representation, 48, 50, 77, 107, 157
thinking, 4, 5, 48–49, 54, 56, 59, 157, 164
Vygotsky, 35, 108, 118, 127, 169, 215–216

ways of knowing, 107, 108, 191
Wright, Frank Lloyd, 33

Yiribana Gallery, 8–17

zone of proximal development, 35, 115, 127, 175